SEX AND BUILDINGS

SEX AND BUILDINGS

Modern Architecture and the Sexual Revolution

Richard J. Williams

REAKTION BOOKS

Published by
Reaktion Books Ltd
33 Great Sutton Street
London EC1V 0DX, UK
www.reaktionbooks.co.uk

First published 2013

Printed and bound in Great Britain
by TJ International, Padstow, Cornwall

British Library Cataloguing in Publication Data
Williams, Richard J., 1967–
   Sex and buildings: modern architecture and the sexual revolution.
   1. Architecture and society – History – 20th century.
   2. Architecture, Modern – 20th century – Case studies.
   3. Sexual ethics – History – 20th century.
   I. Title
   720.1'03'0904-dc23

ISBN 9 781 78023 104 4

Contents

Morningside, Edinburgh. Middle-class tenement housing built *c.* 1878, photographed in 2012.

Introduction

FOR THEIR AUTHORS, most books are in some way therapeutic. This one is no exception. Its origins lie in the middle of what was in retrospect probably a textbook mid-life crisis, during which I started to dislike everything and everybody around me. Family became a monstrous set of rules and regulations, most of which were apparent only after they had been transgressed. The city in which I was living, Edinburgh, came to resemble a prison. Walking out into the street in my neighbourhood, Morningside, a Victorian suburb on the south side of the city, felt like nothing so much as a walk around the jail yard, and I felt as if its grand nineteenth-century villas had been purposely designed to express authority and keep watch on their inhabitants. Twenty-first-century Morningside was every bit as repressive as Freud's Vienna. I felt angry and frustrated a lot of the time, and spent a lot of time trying – with some success – to make other people feel the same way.

Like generations of middle-class men before me, I quickly decided the problem was sex. With two small children, a full-time career and a wife with another full-time career, life was largely a matter of psychological survival from day to day. There was an acute shortage of time for anything other than meeting the most basic needs of food, shelter and sleep. (As the psychotherapist Esther Perel wrote in *Mating in Captivity*, which quickly became a favourite, sex loves to waste time.[1]) I did the usual things middle-class people do in these circumstances. I tried various kinds of psychotherapy, and mood-altering medications; I read a lot of sexually libertarian theory – R. D. Laing, Wilhelm Reich and Herbert Marcuse – and would bore people with it at any opportunity. I became a little too easily convinced of Freud's theory of repression, and its underpinning hydraulic theory of sex – and, worryingly, I started to think if I didn't have more sex

I might, literally, explode. I fantasized about the existence of a libidinal paradise elsewhere, far from Morningside (there wasn't one, of course). In the end, both I and my family just survived, shrugged and moved on.

The episode did however produce a sustained reading around a problem that seemed to have been little explored. My temporary loathing of my surroundings was driven in part by a belief that what they policed was sex. Morningside's very architecture seemed to be repression written in stone. Each apartment and each house was designed for one family; each had carefully determined public and private faces, and a carefully determined outward image of propriety. The repression I thought I saw in the everyday architecture of the city was only underlined further by the density of churches in the area, not abandoned as they would be in any sensibly secular city but thronged every Sunday, each one offering its own unique proscription of the libido. 'Holy Corner', a big neighbourhood intersection, had no less than five churches, all with big congregations. Edinburgh seemed sometimes the very model of the nineteenth-century bourgeois city, brought uncannily to life. In Morningside, there was no sex. Sex, the joke went, were what you carried coal in.[2] These borderline psychotic thoughts about Morningside were probably brought on by reading too much Laing, a Scot with a similar loathing of his surroundings. But they led reasonably to some broader, and I still believe sensible, speculations about sex and architecture. If Morningside was the model of the sexually repressed city, what would the sexually liberal city be like? What would its buildings look like? How would its inhabitants behave? What was the role of architecture in conditioning sexual behaviour? Had such a sexually liberal place ever existed? I was prepared to accept that my starting point was actually wrong, or to put it another way, Morningside evidently *did* have a libido, just a rather closeted one. But it was clear that a more sexually open city would have started from a different architectural model.

But what did I mean by sex? Initially this seemed straightforward: some kind of act involving the genitals leading to orgasm, most likely involving another person, in my case most likely of the opposite sex. That was certainly the working idea of sex, an idea that was also, in my state of mind at the time, driving me crazy. As an intellectual project, sex needed to mean something broader. As you will see, I use the word 'erotic' and its derivatives more frequently here, referring to 'erotic' spaces, 'erotically charged' buildings, 'eroticism' in certain designers' work and so on. The 'erotic' is a strange word but it is a useful one. In its archaic (pre-twentieth-century) use it meant simply a category of taste designed to produce sexual arousal in the observer. The observer (or reader, or other consumer) was invariably an upper-class, European male, so the erotic in that sense is indelibly associated with a taste in female nudes. The erotic becomes a more interesting category in Freud, who used it to refer to any thing, or practice, that was productive of sexual pleasure, regardless of both what it was and on whom it acted. In other words, the erotic was liberated from being a category of taste to become a pathology, shifting from a cultural to a (quasi-)medical category. Its clearest example is perhaps Freud's account of the development of a child's sexuality, in which he describes the progress from an oral to anal and finally genital pleasure.[3] Simply put, in Freud's theory the child obtains bodily pleasure through sucking at a breast or thumb, then through the expulsion or withholding of faeces, then by touching the genitals. Freud famously extended eroticism to cover a whole range of other possibilities he described as perversions. Whatever we think now of his theory as a psychological tool, it remains a useful cultural one – broadly, following his example, we all can imagine the erotic in terms of bodily pleasure rather than simply as genital acts. So in practice, any place that places a premium on bodily pleasure might reasonably be described as erotic, even if its primary purpose is not sex. Saunas are generally erotic in the popular imagination; petrol stations and bicycle sheds are not. (Of course an individual bicycle shed could certainly acquire erotic character through appropriation, and no doubt many have, but bicycle sheds are not generally erotic by design.) To Freud we could probably add maverick thinkers such as Georges Bataille and Marcuse, both of whom in different ways thought of the erotic as a radical force – and then we could think of all the much later poststructuralist and feminist critiques of the erotic, which have made it into the genuinely polymorphous category we have in use now. Reading any of these people is a task really only academics have the patience for – but their ideas, through popular culture (music and films especially) have undoubtedly informed a general sense of the erotic. A much-mediated version of this academic sense of the erotic filters down further into the realm of popular psychology and sex advice, and you find the following. Look at *any* sex counselling column, anywhere in the Western world, and you will find an understanding of the erotic as (a) polymorphous, (b) potentially highly disruptive, (c) strongly informed by vision and

(d) essentially ludic, that is, a form of play. All this derives ultimately from Freud and his early twentieth-century followers, and for better or worse it has produced a generally accepted popular theory of the erotic, one that is flexible and liberal enough to normalize first female sexual desire, and then homosexual desire. That is the concept I am working with here. So when I describe a space as 'erotic' or 'erotically charged', I mean it sublimates bodily pleasure. That pleasure might always lead to sex, but it is not the genital act that principally concerns me, rather bodies, pleasure and desire.

My questions about the possibility of sexual liberation were unfashionable, but I thought they were worth asking again. I had thought for some time that contemporary regeneration projects had little place for the libido. Meeting places, yes, but of a highly prescriptive and controlled kind. Anything more than meeting was going to take place somewhere else. That was one of the themes of my previous book *The Anxious City* (2004), which as much as it celebrated the changes brought about by new capital investments in cities, was also sceptical about the behavioural imagination that underpinned them.[4] They seemed – and in fact continue to seem – no less controlling than my Morningside. Did we want to really want to recreate the bourgeois city of the nineteenth century? That certainly seemed to be where we were heading, and in this ambition architects were nothing if not complicit. I struggled to find anything in the architectural press on the topic, despite the fact that in common-sense terms, architecture frames and houses our sexual lives, and provides images of how they should be carried out. Yet there was rarely any open discussion of these things; you have to work by inference to make any headway. My first journey was therefore a journey in ideas. If architects didn't talk about sex and buildings, then who did? The first answer was in all the books by sexual radicals on my bookshelves: Freud, Jung, Kinsey, Laing, Marcuse, Reich, through to liberal therapists with interests in the same issue – Susie Orbach, Esther Perel, Adam Phillips. All were fascinated by the space of sex: how the way we imagine the spaces we live in conditions the way we think about sex.

I also knew this literature was complicated. As much as I was drawn to the sexual radicals and their understanding – following Freud – of sex as an unruly, revolutionary force, I had enough respect for (say) Michel Foucault to know that the notion of sex as liberation to which I was so drawn was really no more than a myth.[5] And from

Foucault of course there was the additional idea that sex could also be understood equally well as a social product; in other words, what one did in the bedroom, and with whom, was much more to do with one's social conditioning than the primitive workings of one's hormones. Foucault's rejection of the so-called 'repressive hypothesis' put him in the same camp as some unlikely figures: a radical feminist, Judith Butler, an uncategorizable dissident, Camille Paglia, and a fully paid-up, fox-hunting social conservative, Roger Scruton.[6] All in different ways held sex to be a product of circumstances – and indeed that it could only work in creative tension with those circumstances. Liberation held great appeal, but as a belief system, it was hard to hold on to indefinitely.

Nearly all the historical literature on sex was informed by the belief that the built environment conditioned behaviour. The six volumes of Havelock Ellis's groundbreaking *Studies in the Psychology of Sex* consistently locate sexual morality in relation to the surrounding environment.[7] Volume six, *Sex in Relation to Society* (1910), makes this plain. We need to examine 'the relationship of the sexual impulse to third persons and to the community at large', wrote Ellis, 'with all of its anciently established traditions'.[8] Ellis then systematically examined every institution and corresponding environment he could think of in terms of its conditioning effect on sex. Motherhood and early education were initial topics; then city life ('Are Town Children More Precocious Sexually Than Country Children?'), the medical profession, sexual education and nudity, the Church ('The Modern Conception of Chastity as a Virtue'), sexual abstinence, sexual hygiene, prostitution (with particular attention to its location, such as the brothel), the institution of marriage. The same argument could be made in relation to Ellis's slightly later study, *The Task of Social Hygiene* (1912), a book shot through with anxieties about the effect of urban living on the conduct of sexual lives, especially in relation to sexual health.[9] Published slightly earlier, the Swiss physician Auguste Forel's *The Sexual Question* (1905) shows a similar preoccupation with the environment of sexual behaviour; chapters Ten and Eleven covered such anxieties as money and property in relation to sex, town versus country life, 'Vagabondage', 'Americanism' (Forel meant the relative liberation of American women from manual labour), 'Saloons and Alcohol' and 'Boarding Schools'.[10] As in Havelock Ellis, the text is underpinned by a persistent anxiety that modern urban life has produced a degeneration of sexual morality.[11]

No data was supplied to support this assertion, apart from in the case of prostitution the observation that cities were by and large where prostitutes conducted their business. This anxiety is balanced by the relative liberalism of all the early sex researchers, Forel and Havelock Ellis being no exception. Their nineteenth-century anxieties notwithstanding, a critical point for the present argument is the simple connection between built environment and sex, the one clearly thought to condition the other. Whatever they wrote about sex, they imagined it located in space, and formed accordingly.

Freud's case studies described in intimate detail a bourgeois landscape in which sexual behaviour frequently became a cause of neurosis because of the way it was corralled by the city of Vienna, its public expression highly circumscribed, with dreadful social penalties for transgression. At the same time, the writer Stefan Zweig pictured a city of outward propriety, privately terrorized by the fear of sexually transmitted diseases. Almost every building, he wrote, quietly advertised a STD specialist, while on the street itself, prostitution was ubiquitous and astonishingly cheap – the price of a packet of cigarettes could secure a woman for half an hour.[12] What both Freud and Zweig observed were the psychological results of a city that outwardly despised sex, but inwardly desired it. This dreadful contradiction is powerfully inscribed in the external form of the city, defining public and private, acceptable and unacceptable, legitimate and illegitimate. In Vienna, a street such as the newly built Ringstrasse carried inescapable messages of social order. The city, like Paris, had been remade on an epic scale, with vast new spaces for both the military to deport itself and for the bourgeoisie to show itself off; these new spaces had an exaggeratedly public quality that sought to put citizens under surveillance. If the street had conventionally been an erotic space for men, these new spaces were anything but: as the Viennese architect Camillo Sitte argued, they were productive of a new kind of fear, agoraphobia.[13] In these accounts, there is always a hidden, but powerful, mechanism connecting the libido and the built environment. How it works is never exactly specified, but the principle is never in doubt: for these writers, sex was always conditioned by the built environment. Sex happened in space, they thought. How it happened, when it happened, to whom, and what they felt about it afterwards was so much a function of space.

So much for the Viennese. American sex researchers after the Second World War thought likewise, invariably writing of sex *in relation* to its surroundings. The anthropologist Margaret Mead, for example, was familiar with a worldwide range of sexual behaviours and modes of family organization. But her study *Male and Female* (1949) devoted the last of four parts to the consideration of the contemporary American situation, an analysis circumscribed throughout by the consciousness of the correct place for sex. The opening chapter of this section, 'Our Complex American Culture', describes a vast, polymorphous sexual culture, with different behaviours represented by different geographical locales. From the sidewalks of New York's Fifth Avenue to 'lonely shacks on the plains' to the micro-environment of the suburban bathroom, material space was understood to frame behaviour. In Mead's imagination, the single-family American home implies sex as a private activity between a man and woman married to each other and largely, if not exclusively, for the purposes of procreation. The title of one of the most important chapters was beguilingly simple, but telling: 'Each Family in a Home of its Own'.[14]

Mead was socially conservative, but her location of debates about sex in terms of existing institutions and institutional spaces points up the importance of location in sexual discourse. Sex is no abstraction: a social act as well as a biological one, it has to take place some*where*. Mead described the sudden evolution of the nuclear family, and its continued attractiveness in spite of the fact that almost all of the life functions that once necessarily took place in the home could now happen outside it. 'For sex satisfaction', she wrote, 'it is no longer necessary to choose between marriage and prostitution; for most of those without religious scruples sex is available on a friendly and amateur basis and without responsibility.'[15]

Mead was a contemporary of Alfred Kinsey, an entomologist at Indiana University with a decent reputation based on his research on the life cycle of the gall wasp. His academic rigour, combined with an insatiable desire to collect data, was applied in the 1940s to the study of human sexual behaviour, funded by the Rockefeller Foundation. An early product of the research was *Sexual Behavior in the Human Male* (1948), commonly known as the Kinsey Report, and one of those sporadic academic books that also is a best-seller.[16] The Report's findings were sensational. Almost everything that American society regarded as taboo turned out to be normal. Homosexuality was common, extramarital sex routine and masturbation universal. In his thorough, myopic way, Kinsey garnered a huge amount of data, recorded countless sexual acts and even extended his own researches to include sex with colleagues, all under controlled conditions.[17]

For this, Kinsey and his collaborators, Wardell Pomeroy and Clyde Martin, did an immense amount of fieldwork, modelled on Kinsey's previous work as an entomologist. Kinsey's approach to the question of sex involved the collection of a huge amount of data on habitat: that is to say, where human sexual relations took place. As became well known on the publication of *Sexual Behavior in the Human Male*, the field research included an impressively wide range of bars, clubs, restaurants and diners where people of different sexual persuasions might seek each other out. The environmental conditioning of sex is a constant throughout the Report's 804 pages. In an early part, Kinsey's researchers quizzed interviewees for non-sexual sources of childhood erotic response, producing a highly suggestive list. 'Chiefly physical' sources included 'sitting in class', 'sitting in church', 'fast elevator rides', 'taking a shower', 'motion of a car or bus', 'a skidding car', 'carnival rides' and 'a Ferris wheel'. 'Chiefly emotional' stimuli were equally spatial: 'fear of a house intruder', 'asked to go in front of class', 'being alone at night', 'looking over edge of building', 'falling from garage etc.', 'running away from home', 'entering an empty house' and 'long flight of stairs'. Some of these responses do not fit – for example 'national anthem' – but the great majority do, confirming again the relationship between built space and the imagination of sex. A later section of the Report, on prostitution, makes a related point when discussing the economics of the practice. Prostitutes cost money, the Report argues, but for many users they are cheap given the costs involved in dating – for often uncertain results. They wrote that the cost of dating 'may mount considerably through the weeks and months and even years that it may take to arrive at the first intercourse'.

> There are flowers, candy, 'coke dates', dinner engagements, parties, evening entertainments, moving pictures, theatres, night clubs, dances, picnics, week-end house parties, car rides, longer trips and all sorts of other expensive entertainment to be paid for, and gifts to be made to the girl on her birthday, at Christmas, and on innumerable other special occasions. Finally after all this the girl may break off the whole affair as soon as she realizes that the male is interested in intercourse.[18]

Here virtually the whole of the contemporary urban environment is annexed to the uncertain task of foreplay. This and countless other asides in the Kinsey Report do, however, make clear that their entire imagination of sex is circumscribed by space. The institutions of marriage, of prostitution, of childhood and adolescence are all physical spaces as well as social ones, as Kinsey's team well understood. Their field research was exceptionally extensive, and they found sexual behaviour in an extraordinary variety of built spaces, a point elaborated well by Bill Condon's biopic *Kinsey* (2004). In the movie, Kinsey's delving into 1940s Chicago's gay scene is a descent to both a figurative and literal underworld. The movie's range of cinematic spaces in which people both have sex and talk about it is emblematic of Kinsey's own polymorphous sexuality. Kinsey's most controversial conclusion, that all sexuality is polymorphous, is to a large extent represented by the variety of architectural space. The posthumous biographical material has also made clear how Kinsey developed a uniquely liberal space at his Institute for Sex Research in which not only could sexual matters be freely discussed, but also sex itself would occur between Institute members in the name of research. Whatever the ethical questions here, it is clear Kinsey worked hard to create a space in which – under controlled conditions – almost anything was possible.

This theoretical linking of sexuality and space is powerfully exhibited in Foucault's *History of Sexuality*, an unfinished project in several volumes.[19] Here Foucault invoked architecture in order to refute what he termed the 'repressive hypothesis'. For Foucault, the sexual repression of which Freud was so fond of speaking was a comforting myth. Previous societies were no more or less repressed than present-day societies; they simply represented their sexuality in different ways. The business of representation was in large part architectural. On a detailed level, Foucault thought the Victorian obsession with veiling, including the legs of inanimate pieces of furniture, spoke not of the repression of sex but a belief in sexual power. At a macro level, Foucault wrote of the ways sexual power might be inscribed in buildings, especially institutional ones. So in relation to the Victorian home, he wrote,

> sexuality was carefully confined; it moved into the home . . .
> a single locus of sexuality was acknowledged in social space as
> well as at the heart of every household, but it was a utilitarian
> and fertile one: the parents' bedroom.[20]

He went on to describe the 'preoccupation' with sex in eighteenth-century school architecture: 'the space for classes, the shape of the tables, the planning of the recreation lessons, the distribution of the dormitories (with or without partitions, with or without curtains), the rules for monitoring bedtime and sleep periods – all of this referred in the most prolix manner to the sexuality of children.'[21] All institutions, and their buildings – schools, prisons, homes, hospitals, factories – were, Foucault implied, sexed, and this, in his somewhat paranoid view of the world, meant that they were also representations of power.

Away from high theory, there was always J. G. Ballard. His dystopian fiction always represented the spaces of the modern world in erotic terms. The central reservation between two motorway carriageways could frame an experiment in erotically liberated living (*Concrete Island*, 1974); the car itself could be not only the site of sex, but also an anthropomorphic object with which one might engage directly in sexual activity (*Crash*, 1973); the high-rise modernist tower might exceed its rationalist origins to become the frame for ceaseless bacchanalia (*High Rise*, 1975). All of Ballard's work locates sex in space, and that space is invariably specifically modern. Ballard was a huge literary influence on many of my generation in Britain. Better than anyone he seemed to understand what had happened to the legacy of modernism in that country and how the spaces it had created, far from being neutral, rational containers for ordinary lives, were charged with violence and sex. I saw the creation, and later destruction, of Manchester's Hulme council estate where all this seemed to be played out on a grand scale in real life. (Tony Wilson, the music impresario and TV presenter, liked to claim the importance of Hulme parties during its period of frank decline. Without them, he would argue, no music scene.)

My second journey was in architectural space. Read the leading twentieth-century architectural journals (*L'Architecture d'Aujourd'hui*, *Architectural Review*, *Progressive Architecture* and so on) and there is an occasional, select interest in sex, with Le Corbusier being the inescapable reference point. More than his middle European contemporaries at the Bauhaus, he envisaged architecture as a practice in which a consciousness of the body was integral to building. *Towards a New Architecture* (1923) sublimated the bathroom, remaking it as a sensual space to show off the body.[22] The Modulor went further, imaginatively rethinking architecture as an expression of the human body.[23] In Le Corbusier's built work, bodily activities are celebrated. Washing, bathing and sunbathing are clearly inscribed in iconic structures, from the early Villa Schwob in La Chaux-de-Fonds to the Villa Savoye in Paris to the Unité d'Habitation in Marseilles. The latter was a multi-storey slab topped with a bathing complex, a literal celebration of the body, while other works invoked the human body in their outward form.²⁴ Le Corbusier himself cultivated a public presence as a sensuous individual. As often as there are photographs of him as a stern professional, there are pictures of him enjoying life, especially bathing. Contemporary with Le Corbusier, but unrelated to him, were eccentrics such as Wells Coates, whose Isokon flats in Hampstead, London, suggested a form of communal living beyond the family – a project with erotic potential, certainly, and much written about for that reason.

However, the experts in erotically charged modernism were the Brazilians. Part of the country's creation myth was as a sexually liberal polity, in contrast with 'cold' or 'repressed' northern nations. In architectural terms, the sexually liberal Brazil was promulgated by Oscar Niemeyer and his circle, and most enthusiastically received by Europeans. But that's indeed not much more than myth. A more accurate view of Brazil can be obtained by looking at recent Rio de Janeiro politics, where a mayor had led a concerted clean-up campaign directed not only at prostitution but at the whole image of the city as a sexual paradise: among other measures she banned the sale of post-cards with sexually provocative imagery. The outraged public reaction in 2004 to the proposed Cidade de Sexo, a sex museum in the form of a giant phallus, suggested a country more like everywhere else than it liked to think. In fact, public discourse around sex can be coy and old-fashioned by U.S. and European standards, and you struggle to find examples of buildings whose sexuality is anything more than implied. Niemeyer's accounts of youthful visits to brothels and his love for Brazilian women don't translate into anything substantial in behavioural terms.²⁵

Between them, Le Corbusier and the Brazilians cornered the market for erotic modernism, at least as far as the journals were concerned. However, one fascinating outlier, much discussed, is Ricardo Bofill's 'Walden 7' in Sant Just Desvern, a northwestern suburb of Barcelona. A dead-end in both stylistic and planning terms, it was, and remains, the most literal response in mainstream architecture to the perceived crisis in the normative family. Nowhere else apart from the commune can you see such a clear (and enormous) attempt to do this. Completed in 1977, it invokes B. F. Skinner's book *Walden Two* (of which more in chapter Three), although it is a distinctly

Mediterranean, hedonistic take on Skinner. A large-scale private housing development, it was designed deliberately to frame an alternative to the normative family experience. Barcelona was chosen in part for its relatively liberal bourgeoisie, capable (Bofill thought) of accepting an 'avant-garde experience'.[26] The initial project was for a set of 400 pods of no more than 20 square metres that could be combined according to needs. Walden 7 was nothing less than 'a proposition for a new mode of life'.[27] Bofill drew explicitly on New Left politics to imagine an 'anti-bourgeois and nonconformist society. An existence which celebrated the individual liberated from the traditional couple, but which also provided him with the possibility of living in a group of three, or four, or communally.' 'Each person', he declared, 'must invent his interior in the image of his own interiority.'[28] The resulting multi-storey complex contained 341 apartments altogether, ranging from one-cell units of 30 square metres (70) to the much more generous four-cell units (54 in total). The majority had three cells, by Barcelona standards a still quite generous 90 square metres. There was a lot of public space: two swimming pools on roof terraces, Unité d'Habitation style, and on the eighth floor 400 square metres for unspecified communal activities. The images of show flats indicate a quite conscious attempt to break with traditional boundaries between spaces, with mirrored walls, futons instead of beds and large, rather public bathrooms. Life was clearly to be lived horizontally, on the floor or in the bath.[29] Meanwhile, the building's recurrent motif – a pair of micro-bays, projecting from each unit – could be interpreted anthropomorphically as a human pair. Bofill's vision was an archetypically 1960s one: a radical individualism born of relative wealth, internationalism and an avant-garde desire to break with the past. The critique of the traditional family is built into every unit, and every partition wall. On the Walden 7 website a poem by Pablo Neruda urges the resident to 'procreate, procreate'.

Walden 7 is very much an outlier, however, a one-off in what was in 1977 a deeply illiberal and peripheral place. To explore the erotics of modern architecture in real detail, it was clear that the focus had to be elsewhere, and from the start, the United States was inescapable. Nowhere else had sex been so hotly and consistently debated – and nowhere else had there been so many attempts to visualize in built form alternatives to normative sexual relations. At the same time, nowhere else, arguably, has been so wedded to the idea of the single-family home. The u.s. long had a reputation among European intellectuals for sexual licence, not always justified. Forel interrupted his book *The Sexual Question* to inveigh against the evils of 'Americanism', by which he meant the sexualization of middle-class women, and their increasing exemption from the duties of labour or childrearing.[30] He offered no evidence for this assertion, but as an attitude it is exemplary of a certain European anxiety about the u.s. as regards sexual morality, an anxiety that continues to the present.

Beyond simple prejudice, the u.s. was where modern theories of sexuality were first properly disseminated. As Jonathan Engel described in *American Therapy* in 2008, the u.s. was the place where psychoanalysis really took root, in spite of local suspicions about all things European, intellectual and Jewish.[31] Psychoanalysis's origins lay clearly in nineteenth-century Vienna, but the Second World War disrupted its European application and it remained an upper-middle-class interest, available to those with the money and leisure to explore it. Its transplantation to the u.s. did not make it any cheaper – but it was much more widely spread and discussed. In New York, for the well educated and well off, it was by the mid-1950s perfectly normal. The therapeutic habit stuck and grew in the u.s. far beyond the original constituency of psychoanalysis, allowing any number of therapeutic trends to flourish, some more respectable than others. For non-clients, psychoanalysis was understood sufficiently well to become a key theme in popular culture. The *New Yorker*'s cartoons are incomprehensible without a working knowledge of psychoanalysis (the shrink's couch is a stock motif); Woody Allen's movies likewise make no sense without Freud; and the same can be said of the popular American TV show *Frasier*, which concerned the inability of a successful analyst to deal with his own neuroses.[32] The therapeutic conversation invariably concerned sex.

Kinsey's researches generated a huge amount of media interest, and initiated a tradition of popular sex research in which could be included the work of William Masters and Virginia Johnson, and Shere Hite. All the later sex researchers started from the assumption that an active and healthy sex life was a prerequisite of human existence, an essential component of a successful relationship, and to all intents and purposes a human right.[33] We should not underestimate how much of a perceptual shift this is: at the start of the twentieth century in the u.s., as in the rest of the industrialized world, the absence of sexual desire would be a measure of moral health; by the end of the twentieth century, it would be largely a source of shame.

Contraceptive pill.

Reliable contraception helped these things no end. The female oral contraceptive pill, developed in the 1950s, was easily the most popular form of contraception by the mid-1970s, and had the unprecedented effect of putting women in charge of their own fertility. The pill, crucially, also had no inhibitory effect on sexual intercourse. It could be taken by mouth at a time independent of intercourse, a huge advantage – although also highly confusing for some early users, many of whom attempted to insert the pill vaginally instead of swallowing it.[34] The u.s. was an enthusiastic early adopter of the pill. It was there that the contraceptive pill was first trialled on a large scale, where it was first widely used and – most importantly in terms of the present argument – where its effects on human behaviour were first observed on a large scale.

The u.s. was also distinctive in its conversation about sex in the popular media. Under the editorship of Helen Gurley Brown, who by the mid-1960s had already published two remarkably frank books of sex advice (*Sex and the Single Girl* and *Sex and the Office*), *Cosmopolitan* was transformed from an ordinary women's magazine to one largely preoccupied with sex.[35] Significantly, its presentation of sex was of a new kind. This was not, for the most part, a kind of erotic publication for women (although it did publish a near-nude spread of the actor Burt Reynolds in 1972) but rather a proselytizing magazine, fixated on securing sexual rights for women: the right to sexual pleasure, and the right to control over sexual lives that men had traditionally enjoyed.[36] Cover headlines were sufficiently explicit for the supermarket chain Kroger to require that each issue be sold in a plain wrapper in its branches. *Cosmopolitan* under Gurley Brown's editorship represents how a conversation about sex became public property in the u.s. during the twentieth century. The male counterpart to *Cosmopolitan* was in many respects *Playboy*, started by Hugh Hefner in Chicago in 1953 and which quickly became a global enterprise with nightclubs and multiple media interests; Hefner himself also rapidly became a public figure – although given that he rarely ventured out of doors, a seemingly agoraphobic one. *Playboy*'s contribution to America's public conversation about sex was immense. At heart a pornographic magazine, it also campaigned through Hefner's leader articles on a range of libertarian topics. Hefner believed in sex and the rights of everyone to sexual pleasure. He would claim from time to time that he was a feminist as a result – a bad mistake on his part, although possibly an honest one.[37] As a proselytizer of sexual rights and freedoms in the 1950s, Hefner probably had no equal. *Playboy*'s cultural importance can be measured in part by its circulation, which peaked in 1972 at slightly over 7 million; it was said at this time that a quarter of Americans in tertiary education were readers.

Hefner's recipe of soft-focus porn, literary reviews and lifestyle advice was tired by the early 1970s, by which point *Playboy*'s readership had hit its peak. A range of much bolder publications then threatened its supremacy, most importantly *Hustler*, owned and edited by the mercurial Larry Flynt. Flynt's background and tastes could scarcely have been more different from Hefner's: working class, poor and rural, he had no time for the glossy fantasy of the *Playboy* empire. However, he shared with Hefner both a belief in the centrality of sex to human existence, and a desire to proselytize. As a consequence, *Hustler* became a campaigning publication on a variety of libertarian causes – and as romantically portrayed in the movie *The People vs Larry Flynt* (1996), Flynt himself was never happier than when in campaign mode, railing against the forces of the establishment.[38] Flynt's two volumes of autobiography try, with varying degrees of success, to confirm this reputation.[39]

There are other ways of instantiating this peculiarly American conversation: the popular success of sex manuals, chief among them *The Joy of Sex* (1972), sex therapy, the existence of any number of fictional representations of the discourse, rock and roll music, the gay rights movement, the abortion debate, the Parents' Music Resource Center (PMRC), plastic surgery, prime-time TV documentaries on the porn industry, Benedikt Taschen's publishing empire, Robert Crumb's cartoons, Hitchcock's films and Hollywood in general. In all of this, arguably, the U.S. has been unusually plain in its public conversations about sex, celebrating straightforwardness in an area elsewhere often freighted with embarrassment.

Of course these are gross generalizations that don't acknowledge (for example) the prudishness of American television networks in relation to nudity. It is also important to restate that what is at issue here is a public conversation about sex, rather than those notoriously unquantifiable sexual acts themselves. Kinsey's 1948 Report appeared to describe a particularly active, and polymorphous, male populace. However, the later report, *Sexual Behaviour in the Human Female* showed, if anything, the reverse. And more recent studies have suggested that in advanced industrial countries such as the U.S., the incidence of sexual activity may be, by some standards, actually extremely low.[40] There may be, in other words, an inversely proportionate relationship between the depiction of sex in the public realm and the frequency of sexual acts; the more sexually obsessed a culture appears to be, the less sexually active it actually is. The truth is hard to establish. The task of gathering accurate data about sexual behaviour is notoriously difficult, with under- and over-estimating and flagrant lying endemic. Kinsey's *Sexual Behavior in the Human Male* produced an astonishing amount of data, but its conclusions suggested a sexual culture wildly at variance with the public image – the same is no doubt true now.

So there are good intellectual reasons for the focus on the U.S. My interest was also motivated by a number of powerful visual images, some of particular houses, some from the history of the cinema, some in art and some in cartoons. These varied quite a bit in terms of what they had to say. Robert Crumb's disturbing and hilarious self-portrait is caught neurotically between the urge to reveal and the urge to hide. Julius Shulman's lush depictions of Californian houses, especially the iconic picture of the Stahl House, construct an image of a society apparently at ease with its libido. And Mies van der Rohe's famous chair, designed for Barcelona in 1929 but de rigueur in any mid-century American office tower, had me speculating (I'm afraid there is no other way to put it) about the spread of the architect's buttocks. These, and many other compelling and sometimes strange images, appear in the subsequent pages here, forming a parallel account of sex and buildings to the one in the main text. They don't make up a narrative, but they exist as a visual index of what seemed important for me when I was putting together the narrative. They underline the importance of America, and especially, perhaps, California, as a place in which a frank conversation about sex could be had.

This book is a journey to various places, representing different possibilities at different times in history, with my reflections on what

Robert Crumb, *The Many Faces of R. Crumb*, 1972 (detail). The artist in his studio, pants around his ankles, masturbating frantically over a pile of 78 rpm records while gazing at a page of his own 'sick' pornographic cartoons. Crumb's semen splatters an unseen passer-by below ('Hey!'). The room where Crumb is shown 'hard at work' is a vision of clutter in a 19th-century tenement in a nameless American city. It's a dense, seedy mess. No one else was so preoccupied with the relationship between sex and its surroundings during the 20th century. Crumb's sex is *always* perverse, dirty and shameful, and the buildings likewise.

happened – or more often, didn't happen – in them. In reality, it is a result of repeated trips to the u.s., and particularly southern California, over a period of some years, during which time I got to know some spaces (such as the Schindler-Chace house) extremely well, as well as some images (Shulman's photographs of mid-century Californian modernism). Though my narrative is driven by what may at times seems to be personal whim this book also represents a set of repeated attempts to answer the questions posed right at the beginning: where *is* sex in architecture? And what might a sexually liberal architecture look like? In trying to answer those questions, some readers may find the choice of material frankly perverse. After all, if sex was my central interest, why not go to the places in which I could be certain it was happening: brothels, the sets of pornographic films, clients' cars in areas frequented by streetwalking prostitutes, licensed sex clubs, night-club toilets, gay saunas, sex research establishments, Hampstead Heath? This is a good question, of course, and one that would make another, different kind of book – perhaps a more anthropological one. It would also be one focused on the sex industry, broadly conceived, something which I was keen to avoid. I was sufficiently committed to architectural modernism to want to see how sex might be played out

in a context that was – or more accurately, thought of itself as – normative and universal. The sex I was concerned with was ordinary, everyday and possibly not very exciting – but it nevertheless was the kind of sex that had been apparently subject to any amount of change in a century in the industrialized, developed world. And yet, the outward frame of that sex seemed not to have changed very much at all. That was my primary observation, and the reason why I didn't explore our most obviously sexualized places. I was looking for mainstream, normative, universal concepts of sex, in the knowledge that in the end I might not find anything at all.

Moreover, objective data about sexual lives was, and remains, astonishingly elusive. No other aspect of human existence remains so badly reported, whether officially or in terms of what we know about others, even our closest friends and family. It made no sense to pretend objectivity with a topic that was so clouded by misinformation. So I wrote as an individual, one whose life could not really be more normative – a middle-aged, middle-class, married, male academic with a mortgage and two kids. From that perspective, the work of sexual radicals such as Marcuse or Laing or Reich was a huge attraction, however flawed, because it represented an ideal of freedom that my settled life couldn't provide. I am in no doubt at all that the book would have been different written from another class perspective: from the viewpoint of Dumbiedykes, the social housing project abutting my university, my preoccupations would seem silly and effete. The myth of freedom is immensely attractive when you're comfortably off; when you're not it holds no appeal. My preoccupations were nevertheless authentic ones based on my circumstances, and my geographical and intellectual itinerary was determined in large part by my origins.

The book is organized into eight, roughly chronological episodes. The first three concern spaces from the early twentieth century, in which architects and others imagined sex as what is perhaps best called a regime of health. Then I consider what happens to erotic space in the middle of the century in the u.s. when sex was openly commercialized and commodified, in both hotel design and in

Pierre Koenig, Stahl House (Case Study House #22, 1959), photographed by Julius Schulman, 1960. The most famous image of a California house and one of the most iconic images of the modern city of Los Angeles. Shulman's image was a composite, a 7.5-minute exposure to catch the landscape, and a flash exposure for the interior. The models are amateurs. Mary Melton in 2009: 'Julius Shulman . . . defined Los Angeles since 1936 and exported the city's mythology to the world.'

the form of private dwellings. The last part looks at the way recent challenges to normative sexual identity might have informed design thinking. I was searching throughout for a frank representation of sex in architecture, something that proved surprisingly difficult to find. That it was so hard was a function of the societies I was writing about. In a highly developed market economy, buildings are commodities as much as lived spaces; their cost and enduring value as investments inhibit experimentation. It is worth remembering that it was a comparatively primitive economy, with cheap land and labour – California in the 1950s – which produced some of the most imaginative and experimental buildings. The Case Study houses, the legendary experiments in modern living sponsored by *Arts and Architecture* magazine from 1945–66, were built for middle-income clients, not the super-rich (Pierre Koenig's Stahl House of 1959 is the most famous example). I am in no doubt that a radical weakening of the real-estate market would facilitate radical living experiments, and a general weakening of the single-family household. When housing is not in effect a cost, people live quite differently: look at the rich. The current recession notwithstanding, I don't imagine that scenario as especially likely. However, the questions I ask are still, I think, worthwhile, and they will be worth asking again, repeatedly, in the future.

one

The Care of the Body

IF ANYWHERE STANDS for liberal attitudes to sex, it is southern California. In terms of architecture, the connection between liberal sexual attitudes and local modernist architecture has invariably been made, the physical openness of the buildings believed to signify the loosening of behavioural constraints. In architectural terms, California's modernism still, decades after its first appearance, reads as contemporary, and it is only our noticing outmoded hairstyles or car designs in the periphery of photographs that reminds us that these buildings belong to another time. But to explain the peculiarity of California's culture, it is best to start not with a building, but a person: the remarkable 'Dr' Philip M. Lovell, patron of two Austrian émigré architects, Richard Neutra and Rudolf Schindler.

Lovell was, according to historian David Gebhard, 'a character-istic southern Californian product . . . He was, and he wished to be considered, progressive, whether in physical culture, permissive education, or architecture.'[1] He was a 'naturopath', a practitioner specializing in 'drugless' therapy, conducting his business from 1151 South Broadway, right in the heart of LA's downtown. As well as this, he offered consultations in 'maternity cases', 'general dentistry' and 'optometry, including the fitting of glasses and optical examinations'.[2] By the mid-1920s, Lovell had built up a large, wealthy and influential client base, among whom was Harry Chandler, publisher of the *Los Angeles Times*. In 1924 Chandler offered him the editorship of the popular and influential column 'Care of the Body', and two years later, Lovell could claim, for once in his life with some justification, that his was the most 'widely read health column in the world'.[3] That is about as far as most histories of Lovell go, however. Lovell was certainly a quack – self-confessedly so later on. He had not always been Lovell, having been born Morris Saperstein in New

Rudolf Schindler, Beach House, Newport Beach, California (1926). The glazed areas at the side of the building are porches designed for open-air sleeping.

York City, only adopting the Anglo-Saxon-sounding name of Lovell on moving to Los Angeles: he apparently saw 'Dr Lovell' on a bill-board as he drove into the city and decided to adopt it to conceal his Jewish origins (anti-Semitism was rife in 1920s California). He kept the 'M.', however, as one link with the past. If Dr Lovell was not really Lovell, neither was he really a doctor. The title was an invention, an elaboration of a course in chiropractic he had taken in Kirksville, Missouri, en route to LA. Once in California he quickly established himself, not only with the drugless healing business but also with a very beautiful, somewhat older, wife, Leah, who shared her husband's views on natural health. Lovell's education may have been slight, but he had forthright opinions, delivered with consistency and conviction to both his downtown clients and his readers in the *Times*. Neither constituency was in any doubt about what he stood for. And to be fair to Lovell, his world view was also entirely consistent with that of a number of other theorists of natural health around at the same time. Key to Lovell's thinking was Bernarr Macfadden and his magazine *Physical Culture*, which argued in favour of 'fresh air, exercise, organic diet, periodic fasting'.[4]

The architect Richard Neutra enjoyed Lovell's humour and writing style. His surviving correspondence with Lovell shows great affection and respect, in spite of their very different origins.[5] Lovell and Neutra shared a warm friendship – and a liking for dogmatic, nutty ideas about health. Lovell wrote in *The Health of the Child* (1926), 'All disease is a sequence of the crimes we commit against an over lenient Nature . . . The public is rebelling against the constant drugging and serumizing, and the promiscuous, haphazard, ever-ready use of the surgeon's knife.'[6] Instead of health based on the treatment of symptoms with drugs, health should be a product of (to invoke another contemporary concept) lifestyle. This lifestyle was, and remains, remarkably puritanical: no prescription drugs, no alcohol, no tobacco, no caffeine, no meat, no processed food, nude sunbathing, outdoor sleeping whenever possible, plenty of fresh air and vigorous exercise. Lovell was 'proud of his fitness and virility' and contemporary photographs of him show a sturdy, vigorous-looking man, happiest out of doors.[7] This virility was accompanied by a progressive attitude to sex. But these liberal/progressive attitudes were held at the same time as a set of highly disciplined, even authoritarian views about human behaviour, of which diet was only one component. Lovell's ideas also had a powerfully aesthetic dimension. As he argued in the same book, heath and beauty were continuous. His followers would attain 'the body beautiful, the strong body, the virile body!' And on the following page, Lovell argued for something that smacks now of eugenics: 'the quality of the seed determines the kind of child that is brought forth.'[8] (California was in fact at the forefront of the practice of eugenics in the u.s. in the first half of the twentieth century.[9]) This appears in a section of the book arguing that the health of the parents is instrumental in the health of the child that they produce, a common-sense position in the first instance, but

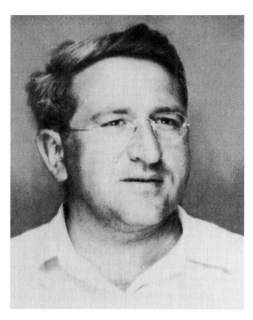

Dr Philip M. Lovell, *c.* 1925. David Gebhard: 'Dr Lovell was a characteristic southern Californian product. It is doubtful whether his career could have been repeated anywhere else. Through his *Los Angeles Times* column, "care of the body" and through "Dr Lovell's Physical Culture Centre", he had an influence which extended far beyond the physical care of the body. He was, and he wished to be considered, progressive, whether in physical culture, permissive education, or architecture.'

overlaid with moral demands: in conceiving a child, the parents should not only observe correct diets, take sufficient exercise and so on, but should also exhibit correct behaviour – which in Lovell's terms is quite precisely defined. From this, not only the child once born but also the foetus, develops correctly.

If Lovell was a sexual libertarian at all, he was by contemporary standards a peculiar one.[10] Lovell's position on masturbation is as negative as can be imagined in a secular society: masturbation, if not a sin, induced madness. *The Health of the Child* argued that (a) masturbation is compulsive, and ubiquitous at adolescence, and (b) fundamentally dangerous to mental health, citing the risk of epilepsy or worse if the practice continues. In *Sex and You* (1940) he went further, citing a case of complete mental breakdown followed by suicide, the direct result of masturbation.[11] Of course, Lovell had a solution. He was convinced beyond reason that constipation was the key. It was really quite simple: in the boy, a full rectum placed undue pressure on the seminal vesicles, leading to the desire to discharge those vesicles; regular bowel movements were therefore essential – 'erection, sex desire, and very shortly masturbation occur. Of course the solution is to "clean house"' (a highly appropriate architectural metaphor, as we shall see). Lovell acknowledged female masturbation too, writing that a similar constipation/arousal mechanism existed in girls, although he declined to explain precisely. He had other anti-masturbation strategies apart from the regular evacuation of the bowels. He thought fresh air, cold showers and vigorous exercise all good. He was also firmly against the adolescent lazing too long in bed ('do not let him linger too long in its cozy warmth'). Finally, he thought (as no doubt did most of his readership) that cultural influences would also play a part: 'the entire problem of masturbation is largely an individual one of training, discipline and home morale. Fast company, loose literature, salacious moving pictures and suggestive magazines – these form an almost irresistible combination.'[12] On marriage, he inveighed against what he called 'ham and eggs' marriages, in other words the marriage in which sex was too easily available.[13]

The Kings Road House

Lovell and Neutra first encountered each other at the Kings Road House (1921–2), a nondescript building by Neutra's friend and compatriot, Rudolf Schindler. Located in an unremarkable Hollywood street, it is the opposite of monumental, and is more or less invisible from the road. In plan it is a series of simple one-storey rooms in concrete and wood, each looking out on to a portion of the lush gardens. It comprises three roughly interlocking L-shapes. In use it was meant to be, as the architect described in an important retrospective account, a 'Co-operative Dwelling'. A shared house for two couples, in the first instance it housed Schindler and his wife Pauline, and their friends Marian and Clyde Chace. The couples were on close terms. Schindler conceived the house after a camping trip, wishing to recover something of the informality and closeness to nature of that experience. So the house is barely enclosed, and the rooms, such as they are, abandon the Western convention of specialization for particular purposes. Instead, wrote Schindler,

> each person receives a large private studio, a common entrance hall and a bath. Open porches on the roof are used for sleeping. An enclosed patio for each couple with an out of door fireplace serves the purposes of an ordinary living room. The form of the house divides the garden into several such private rooms. A separate guest apartment with its own garden is also provided . . . each room in the house represents a variation on one structural and architectural theme. This theme fulfils the

Rudolf Schindler, Kings Road House, Hollywood (1921–2). View towards shared living room. Sleeping porch is visible on the right, upper floor.

     basic requirement for a camper's shelter: a protected back, an open front, a fireplace and a roof . . .[14]

The most striking part of the design was the sleeping arrangements. Instead of enclosed bedrooms, Schindler built rough platforms, more or less open to the elements. There was no wall, or door, or corridor or any other material separation between the two couples as they slept, just a distance of twenty yards or so in the night air, a more or less complete break with the conventions of the bourgeois house with its walls and divisions. The only nods to conventional propriety were the distance between the two sleeping areas, and the fact that the 'L's of the plan faced in opposite directions.

Precisely what occurred between the couples is unclear, although Schindler's erstwhile employer Frank Lloyd Wright described him as an incorrigible bohemian.[15] There were certainly some good parties in the early years. Schindler was also certainly a womanizer, a serial seducer of clients' wives (his libido routinely failed his business sense). Wiry and hirsute, with moustache and long hair, he cut a romantic figure. In a well-known picture of him with Neutra, he stands with legs slightly apart, head thrust back, chin up, grinning, every bit the romantic rascal. Neutra just glowers at the camera, in shirt and tie, aching with propriety. Neutra wrote of his more conventional approach to life in a letter: at the Kings Road House, Schindler and his friends liked to stay up until two in the morning, while he, Neutra, preferred to retire at ten; 'a smoke-filled night is worth less to me than a clear head in the morning.'[16]

The Lovells – especially Leah, given her husband's long hours – were regular visitors by the time the Neutras moved in, and Lovell had already commissioned Schindler to build the Beach House Schindler at Newport Beach (1926) as well as a mountain cabin at Wrightwood.[17] (The latter was badly specified and collapsed under snow.) The same year, Lovell, in his capacity as editor of 'Care of the Body', invited Schindler to describe his architectural philosophy in relation to health. So Schindler took over the column for six successive Sundays, from 14 March to 21 April 1926, writing about ventilation, heating, plumbing, lighting and furniture, and the more general question of the changing role of shelter. In each piece, Schindler centred on the phenomenology of the house: what it was like to use and inhabit, and how it might be improved if the usual conventions about style and propriety could be discarded. The central problem, he argued on 21 April, was that social conventions were now in advance of the architecture that could house them: American house design was preoccupied with outmoded questions of style.[18] Instead, as Schindler consistently argued, the house should become a multifunctional, flexible space focused on delivering as comfortable and practical an environment as possible, making as much use as possible of the natural environment and climate. The house should, in other words, derive from bodily experience and needs, not social convention; inner, not outward experience should be the driver. Conventional distinctions between rooms, and between

Kings Road House, view towards outdoor living area.

inside and outside, should be rethought. On 21 March, for example, Schindler re-imagined bathing as an essentially public activity:

> Instead of being crowded into the smallest possible space, the bathroom will more and more assume the spaciousness due to a room for physical culture. It will have the largest window in the house and be adjoined by porches for sunbaths and gymnastics. The respectable 'Saturday night' bath has developed into showers taken at least daily . . .[19]

Here a state of more or less constant cleanliness is imagined, facilitated by new technologies and new attitudes to the body. Washing the body moves from a more or less private, occasional activity to a primary focus of the home, one of the main activities that it houses. And it is linked with other activities – gymnastics, exercise – in which one's body could be displayed and improved. Such changes, Schindler reflected, would also be manifest in new attitudes to clothing, in which constant, total cleanliness would come to be expected. In the Kings Road House itself, these principles are quite apparent. The main rooms are left undefined, and can be used in a variety of ways; the bathrooms are central to the house, although perhaps not quite as public as Schindler suggested they might be in the column; inside and outside spaces are thoroughly blurred, with the gardens divided into a number of 'rooms' with fireplaces; the sleeping arrangements were the open-air porches already mentioned. Every aspect of the house was directed to the body, its display, to its maintenance, to its experience. The psychosexual dimension to the house is clearly implicit in all this. The rooms of the Kings Road House invite a variety of uses, and there is a clear sense in which walls and imagined uses dissolve. But it has none of the sense of openness of Neutra's work in which everything is literally made visible, and a house's plan is legible from the moment one enters. Kings Road is dark, mysterious and rather secretive: you can hide here. There are aspects, such as the sleeping arrangements, which suppose openness where conventionally it would not exist. But for the most part, this is a romantic and highly atmospheric place, imbued with a calculated sense of mystery.

The bodily character of the house certainly includes sex. It's there in the very concept, a house not for a conventional, hierarchical family but for two active young couples enjoying the freedom of the open air. That is clear enough, as is Schindler's own sexually predatory nature, worn like a badge in his dress and deportment. It also strongly informs the relationship with the Lovells, and through that, the disastrous breakdown of Schindler's relationship with his friend, Neutra. Neutra puts it most clearly, in notes on a conversation with Lovell from 1962:

> I recall that Mrs Lovell, just like her sister, was really very much attracted by Mr Schindler, as have so many other human beings, and especially also ladies. This attraction was very little to Dr Phillip [sic] Lovell's liking who saw in his somewhat older wife, who had some cultured behavior, a sort of mother. She mothered him and then became attached to this young man with a nice little moustache. He was also very much influenced by the

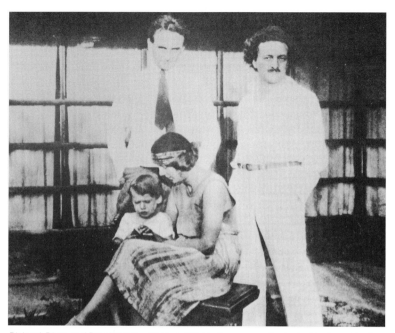

Richard, Dione and Dion Neutra, with Rudolf Schindler, c. 1929. Neutra's oldest son, Frank (b. 1924), born autistic, was rarely photographed.

predilection of Mrs Freeman who was had [sic] also transferred her liking for Frank Lloyd Wright to Schindler.[20]

This retrospective account appears in a letter – one of many – designed to set the record straight about Neutra's relationship with Schindler, and its breakdown over the commission for the Health House. Some of this has been traditionally linked to Schindler's failure to design Lovell's mountain cabin properly, leading to its collapse under snow. But it seems from most available evidence now that it had rather more to do with Lovell's sexual jealousy surrounding his wife's quite public involvement with Schindler. Leah 'fell hard for Schindler' during the Kings Road period; their affair intensified when Lovell was contemplating the Health House.[21] This matters, because the projects represent two distinct models of sexual propriety. In one – the Kings Road House – the model is bohemian, with the dissolution of physical boundaries intensely linked with its author's own lack of respect for sexual ones. There were no rules, except the gratification of the libido.

For all Schindler's intentions, as a dwelling the Kings Road House was mostly a failure: it singularly failed to frame the kind of free sexual life that was imagined in the original design. The Chaces moved out in 1925 after only three years of cohabitation; the Schindlers split in 1926 and Pauline moved north to Carmel with their son Mark in 1927. Neutra, his wife Dione and son Frank (named after Lloyd Wright) moved in, in 1926, and out in 1930 (the family now included Dion, born 1926). At the end of the 1930s Pauline Schindler retuned to live in the Chace section of the house, but barely in communication with her ex-husband – when contact was necessary, they mailed each other (Schindler scrawled in angry block capitals). This peculiar, tense arrangement, far removed from the liberatory spirit of the original house, continued until the architect's death from cancer in 1953.[22] The openness of the Kings Road House supposes an open and fluid sexuality, but in reality the majority of its life as a home was tense and sexless, one in which the primary relationship, that of Rudolf and Pauline Schindler, had irrevocably broken down.

The house is a de facto mausoleum, now, albeit a popular one. Go on a Sunday and you join a steady stream of young design tourists, eager to pick up tips. Stripped back to its essentials, it's essentially a sculpture, in which you contemplate a set of simple forms and materials, arranged in repeating patterns. It is hard to imagine as a lived space now all the mess of living has been removed. The sleeping porches in particular don't easily suggest their use; neither do the outdoor fireplaces, unlit in decades, retain anything more than a trace of their original spirit. But visitors don't just come for the refined aesthetic experience that remains, but for the human story that underpins it and which the house's guardians, the MAK Center (the LA branch of the Österreichisches Museum für angewandte Kunst, Vienna), keeps in the public domain. They come because it represents an experiment in living.

The Lovell Health House

In the contemporary imagination, the Health House has an erotic character thanks to its numerous appearances in the cinema. In *LA Confidential* (dir. Curt Hanson, 1997), the Lovell House is the home of Pierce Patchett, the mastermind of an illegal call girl ring; it features in a key scene and becomes an architectural metonym for sexual vice. The reality, sadly, is something like Kings Road:

a wretched marriage, held together by the shared love of a house.[23] The Health House itself resulted from a tortured commissioning process, which – according to one observer – resembled something from Dostoyevsky, in which at least four families all had an interest.[24] The fallout from the process lasted until the architect's death, well documented in the Neutra archives at UCLA. At stake was Neutra's behaviour vis-à-vis Schindler, specifically whether he 'stole' the commission for the Lovell house. Conceptually the house was quite different from Kings Road: Schindler and Neutra were split not only by a complex set of sexual rivalries but also by quite different approaches to architecture.

The house itself was designed in 1928 and built in 1929, and is located on a precipitous site adjacent to Griffith Park from which it is still, just, visible. The main part of the construction process was done remarkably fast: 40 hours of work time, by Neutra's own estimation, to erect the steel frame, and a further 32 hours to spray the concrete on to the supporting panels.[25] On Dundee Drive, at the top level of the house, is the sleeping accommodation, internal bedrooms and open-air 'sleeping porches' (remember Lovell's mania for the open air). A spectacular glazed staircase connects this level with a middle floor containing the main dining room and guest rooms, these with their own private patio. The lowest floor contains a large pool – about a quarter of the surface of this floor – an open area for children and a laundry. Lovell's world view is represented in the profusion of balconies and terraces, the sleeping porches, the huge extent of glass and a vast kitchen on the middle level, designed for a labour-intensive vegetarian diet.[26] A full third of the house was devoted to the cultivation of the body.

This was no mere house, of course, but an experiment in living. Lovell himself conceived of it as such, and to his great credit he made sure it was understood as a semi-public project. He publicized it well in 'Care of the Body', stating that the day had 'arrived' when he had built 'a home premised on the fundamental health principles and construction ideas' he had described in print.[27] Lovell extended an invitation to the Los Angeles public to visit the house shortly after its completion, and 15,000 showed up: traffic on the tiny cul-de-sac of Dundee Drive must have been appalling. The project obsessed both Lovell and Neutra – a notice affixed to the inside of the house read:

> The demonstration of this building would not be complete
> unless I, as the owner, stated something publicly concerning

Richard Neutra, Lovell Health House, Dundee Drive, Los Angeles (1927–9). This view, from Aberdeen Ave below, is now entirely obscured by trees.

Mr Neutra and his relation to this house. Mr Neutra is perhaps better known throughout Europe than he is here. He follows the modern school of architecture whose most famous exponent is Frank Lloyd Wright, the creator of the Tokyo Imperial Hotel, Olive Hill in Los Angeles, and the Ennis Home which you can see directly opposite on the hill west of here. Mr Neutra has many structures to his credit in Los Angeles, which, considering the scant few years he is here, is decidedly creditable. The architecture he espouses is modern in more senses than one.

Neutra, Lovell Health House.

That is, it is unquestionably the very best combination of
the utmost in utilitarianism and beauty. When Mr Neutra
received the commission for this house he not only spent a
year in the preparation of plans but also made an intensive
study of the social uses to which this house is to be put . . .
Although familiar with every method practised both in this
country and in Europe, he has incorporated, wherever expense
would permit, nearly every feature desirable in a modern
home. The work of an architect should not be finished when
plans are drawn and he exemplified the very best spirit of
architectural cooperation in this construction. Not only were
plans drawn to the minutest detail – far more complete than
for the average house – a necessary procedure by reason of the
unique quality of this home – but he also gave it his constant
supervision throughout the entire year this house has been

under construction. Mr Neutra could be found here every morning until the late hours of the afternoon. Such cooperation is rare and we as owners desire to express this appreciation publicly to him. If we had to build a home over again, or if we had to do any other type of construction, there is no architect in the city we would rather choose than Mr Neutra. We therefore express this as a token of our appreciation to him.[28]

Neutra for his part spent an exhausting year on the designs, and we know also that at the end of the process he took an extended break from work, travelling to Asia and Europe.[29] Lovell describes obsessiveness in the construction process too, with the architect constantly on site directing works. We know in this connection that Neutra was the de facto contractor for the house, having been unable to find anyone he trusted enough in California for the job – a job that was admittedly unusual, the first steel-framed house in the U.S.

The Need to Know

Neutra's obsessiveness about Lovell extended far beyond architectural matters. Neutra (wrote Lovell) 'made an intensive study of the social uses to which this house is to be put. He diligently ascertained the living habits of the family, our likes and dislikes – our prejudices and idiosyncrasies', and built accordingly.[30] Such minute observation became standard practice for Neutra for the rest of his career, but this is the first properly documented instance of it. The precise papers relating to the conversations between Lovell and Neutra were lost in the 1963 fire at the VDL house (the acronym acknowledges Neutra's early patron Case H. Van der Leeuw), so we cannot know exactly what Lovell's 'idiosyncrasies' and 'likes and dislikes' were. But it is enough to know that this minute, quasi-scientific, observation was at stake here and that it was for the client something unusual. Neutra's engagement with the project also seems to have produced something akin to psychoanalytical transference. The relationship with the Lovells involved not only the quasi-anthropological observation of his clients' personal habits, but the adoption of some of those habits too: the Neutras all began to avoid coffee, and eat more salad.[31]

Neutra was certainly eager to please clients. He could also adopt a quasi-therapeutic role, offering to his clients a service that included much more than the design of a shelter. His design mode (with the detailed consultation, the desire to find out everything about a client's life and habits) and the buildings that resulted were, according to Lavin, meant as a therapy.[32] The name Neutra gave to this attitude was 'biorealism', a mode of designing buildings based as far as possible on the needs of the users.[33] It was based on Neutra's long-standing conviction that people were inescapably conditioned by their environment, a process that operated on an entirely unconscious level.[34] It was the job of the architect/shrink to reveal, and subsequently house, the unconscious.

Sex is at the centre of many, perhaps most, psychotherapeutic conversations: but talking about sex, and having it, are two different things, and whatever may occur between therapist and client has to stop short of physical contact. The therapeutic space is a space in which sex *cannot* occur – and indeed for it to occur is in most cases a grave professional transgression.[35] So if Neutra's houses were meant primarily as therapeutic spaces, they could not at the same time be spaces in which sex could occur. Of course, that is, on the face of it, ridiculous. But there is something in the imagination of these houses with their acres of glass, their mirrors, and their light and space that represents a desire to know *everything* and in so doing, actually inhibit activities that require things not to be known. As Esther Perel writes, too *much* knowledge can inhibit sex.[36]

Neutra subjected his clients to a thorough interrogation. According to his son Dion, he would want to know such things as 'when you give a dinner party, do you wash dishes right away? Is it important that they are not visible to guests?' Clients, if they were a couple, were given separate questionnaires, with consultation expressly forbidden.[37] The process could take a long time. In the case of the now destroyed Brown House in New England, the client, John Brown, spent a whole week composing his responses to Neutra. Among the most detailed records of the consultation process are those of the Chueys, a couple for whom Neutra built a house in the mid-1950s. Mrs Chuey's agonies about the design of the house were – in one account – a result of her own anxieties about her fertility, anxieties Neutra seems to have happily fed.[38] What is also apparent from the correspondence between Neutra and the Chueys is a deep and ever-present interest in the phenomenology of the house, in the relationship (or in this case, potential relationship) of the bodies of the clients to the space of the house. Neutra wanted to know everything. After one round of correspondence, he wrote in summary:

I cannot convey to you how deeply touched I was by your most interesting record of your deep feelings and references to your past life. It is really a world – is it not – which one has to express if one seeks to plan for one's future happiness. I have found some differences in emphasis in your two records of course. For example the bedroom assumes a less important role for you, Mr Chuey, than for your wife. You had expressed this verbally, but it is much more apparent now.[39]

The precise topic of these lines – just a fragment of a letter of 3,000 words or so – is perhaps the most intimate space of the house, the bedroom, the room that above all symbolizes and frames the clients' marriage. Significantly, Neutra did not seek compromise here, but identified differences between the couple that could easily have a bearing on their sexual lives. The remainder of the long letter to the Chueys deals with a range of other environmental concerns – Mrs Chuey's sensitivity to cold, for example, and her neurotic dislike of the low ceilings of modernist houses. Neutra also commented on her extreme sensitivity to space, agreeing with her that space was not neutral, but in effect alive.[40] Neutra's presence is far less that of an architect than of a psychotherapist whose knowledge of his clients' habits must be complete.

Nowhere shows Neutra's desire more clearly than the Neutra family home, the VDL Research House in the Hollywood suburb of Silverlake. The original house was destroyed by an electrical fire in 1963, but was rebuilt to largely the same design in 1966, with the design and construction overseen by Neutra's architect son and business partner, Dion.[41] It is a two-storey villa with a small glass-roof pavilion, opening to a terrace with views to the Silverlake reservoir. The rear of the house opens to a small, tree-shaded patio, bounded to the rear by the one-storey, mostly glass, studio: this was the one part of the original house that survived the fire intact. There are small kitchens on the ground and middle floors, an office/study on the ground floor (occupied continually by the ailing Neutra in his later years) and three small bedrooms off a corridor on the middle floor. A tiny, galley-like bathroom is located between the largest of the three bedrooms and the smaller ones. The rest of the house is more or less open-plan: a generous living room, lined with books, defines the middle floor, with views out to the garden and the reservoir.

Everything in this house is in sight or earshot; it has a panoptical character to it, and it is hard not to imagine Neutra as a big physical

Neutra VDL Research House, Los Angeles, exterior, 1966. The house is one of ten built by Neutra on Silver Lake Boulevard.

presence here, tall and authoritative, barking orders to his family and work associates. His powerful, sometimes bullying, presence produced at best a creative tension that was good for work – but the VDL was also a family home, and life with him around was destructive and unpleasant.[42] Without Neutra there, the VDL house/office was a notably quiet place; with him, it was tense and anxious. From any point in the house, Neutra could exercise control. Not only was the house open to a high degree in terms of plan, it was also lightly built so sound would carry; and these characteristics were further underlined by the installation of an electronic intercom system throughout the house, so Neutra could catch anyone at any time. All parts of this house were at his command at all times, a situation he described when he explained how after a major heart attack in 1953 he could quite easily work from his bed: everything, and everybody, was at hand.[43] Further, the intimate spaces of the house are extremely small. The upstairs bedrooms and bathrooms are more like the bunks in a ship or a train. The largest bedroom has what passes for a double bed, of Neutra's own design – but it is tiny by contemporary standards. But these rooms are not places to spend time, to relax.[44] They are sleeping containers which one uses only for that purpose, from which to rise quickly on awaking to join the public life of the house. We are reminded here of Philip Lovell's demand that teenagers resist lingering in bed in the morning; they should be *up*, diverting whatever libidinal energy has gathered in their loins during the night into health-giving exercise.[45] The VDL house literally brings everything out into the open. It is the built equivalent of the psychotherapeutic session; its unintentional consequence is, however, that its invocation of therapy leaves no place in which some of the subjects of therapy can occur; there is no darkness, no mystery, no place to hide, only a quasi-rational setting in which the master architect/shrink can talk things through with his client. There is no private life in this house.

In *Life and Human Habitat* (1956) Neutra wondered about private space in relation to neuroticism. Referring to his personal contact with Freud and his family in his youth, he recalls overhearing from an early age the idea that witnessing sex between one's parents is a primary cause of later psychological trauma: the 'primal scene' in Freud's terminology, and one of the key events in the narrative of the 'Wolf Man' case history. With no evidential base at all, Neutra goes on to argue that primitive societies seem to be far less neurotic, because the boundary between private and public space has no meaning. The 'primal scene' could not exist as the shocking scenario it is in the developed world because there sex would be unconsciously integrated, a part of everyday life:

> After wanderings over the more primitive parts of the earth, I began to wonder why natives in their one-family rooms breed so few neurotics. The answer is perhaps that there can be no question of an occasional shock where the behavior of grown-ups – who are nevertheless childlike people – is quite natural, long before words are used to explain the facts of life (if such verbal enlightenment ever psychically succeeds at all). At any rate, the 'pavor nocurnus', the medically so well known nightmare of the child, isolated and civilized in its own dark bedroom, will be found very seldom in the big, closely sleeping family of the 'savages' or the living together, characteristic of all early cultural circumstances.[46]

Something of this perhaps obtains in the designs for the Lovell and VDL houses, with the reduction of private space to the minimum and the sublimation of the public areas. But the inhabitation of these

Neutra VDL Research House, 1966. View of main living area (top) and single bedroom (bottom).

spaces – especially what we can infer from the anecdotal evidence of the VDL – suggests a space in which openness facilitates, even materializes, the domination of one overly powerful figure. Neutra's desire to know, and to control, were represented powerfully in these houses. In that way, his and Lovell's world views coincide. Both worked exceptionally hard; both desired fame and attention; both sublimated their libidos into professional work; both desired spaces that made material that sublimation. So, in both the VDL and Lovell houses, there are no spaces to hide, no spaces to be lazy or to waste time. Everything has to be public, and productive; everything and everybody must be reconciled with the singular project of these powerful men, whether it is natural health or architecture. The Lovell and VDL houses therefore had sex at their core, but their transparency and openness represented the desire to control, rather than facilitate, the expression of sexuality. Dione Neutra was remarkably open about the difficulties with her architect husband; it is quite clear from her reports that work dominated their life together in the most exaggerated way. The Lovells' marriage was by most standards a disaster, with the Health House's existence in part the result of Leah Lovell's destructive affair with Schindler:

> 'It was a very unhappy marriage', said Dione Neutra, 'and they quarrelled terribly with each other. They had three lovely boys, but it was kind of painful to be together with them because you could feel the tension in the air. And I think that the house Mr Neutra designed for them really kept them together because they both loved the house so much.'[47]

So if we take this at face value, Neutra was instrumental in keeping a tense, sexless marriage together. So it was in the earlier case of Schindler. There, a house with a distinctly libidinal dimension in its design was the frame for much of its existence of the most dysfunctional marriage imaginable.

two

Inside the Orgone Accumulator

CALIFORNIAN MODERNISTS like Neutra increasingly thought their buildings could condition the libido.[1] That idea was given legitimacy by the maverick psychoanalyst Wilhelm Reich, whose work developed a cult following on his arrival in the U.S. in 1939. Reich's highly eccentric work linked sexuality and space in the most explicit way, principally through his invention of the orgone energy accumulator, a device that generated huge popular interest in the U.S., but which also led to his public downfall. For me therefore, the trail of architectural liberation led inexorably east, to Orgonon, Reich's compound in Rangeley, Maine. My interest in Reich had been piqued years earlier by the eccentric English rock group, Hawkwind, and a song called simply 'Orgone Accumulator'. The standout cut on 1973's *Space Ritual*, it consisted of ten minutes of fuzz guitar boogie and space effects against which resident poet and all-round loony Robert Calvert declared his enthusiasm for the orgone accumulator. It remained a mystery as to what the device actually was, but it clearly had something to do with sex.[2] Reading Kerouac's *On the Road* later on revealed the famous fictional portrait of the writer William Burroughs ('Old Bull Lee') and his 'orgone box', a device productive of enormous erotic powers (Burroughs/Lee on its effect: 'I always rush up and take off at ninety miles an hour for the nearest whorehouse, hor-hor-hor!').[3] Later still I came across references to Reich in Robert Morris's idiosyncratic but influential writings on sculpture. In the essay 'Three Extra-Visual Artists' (1971), a parody of a certain kind of art criticism, Morris imagined an artist working with unspecified cosmic forces, via a device 'three times more powerful than Willy Reich's orgone box'.[4] In retrospect Morris's sculpture of the period was close in both concept and execution to Reich's box – boxes, roughly human-scale, made approximately of wood and metal, proliferate. Some were even made to contain a human being.

Like Neutra and Schindler, Reich is a direct point of contact between modern American culture and the sexually curious intellectual culture of early twentieth-century Vienna. Where the architects were merely interested observers of that circle, however, Reich was an active participant, working directly with Freud in the 1920s. Reich's work was, and remains, an essential reference point for the discussion of mid-century modernism; his sexual theories were genuinely popular, and his orgone accumulator became fashionable among American intellectual and literary circles in the 1940s and 1950s. Burroughs had one, as did Norman Mailer and J. D. Salinger, as well as across the Atlantic, the influential head of the experimental Summerhill school, A. S. Neill. Schindler and Neutra certainly knew about Reich – they were compatriots, and moved in the same circles. The architectural historian Sylvia Lavin goes further and suggests that Neutra's work draws *formally* on the accumulator, that his houses in other words are accumulators reinterpreted on an architectural scale. That may be an over-interpretation (as may be other, similar, speculations about Reich and the architect Charles Moore).[5] However, Reich's life and material work were enormously popular mid-century, and they offer up a novel way to imagine sex and buildings. Other buildings in this book merely invite sexual activity; in the case of the orgone accumulator, the building allegedly makes sex happen. Reich's precipitous rise in the U.S. had everything to do with the burgeoning pubic interest in sex. His downfall was equally so, the result of a prosecution brought against him by the government's Food and Drug Administration (FDA) in 1955, a case resting on the doubtful effectiveness of the accumulator. The FDA argued that the accumulator did not produce any of the effects it advertised, and that Reich was therefore a fraud. Reich famously lost the case and was jailed in 1956, his institute fined, his publications publicly burned, the accumulators destroyed and the institute forbidden to distribute any material relating to them, their use or their construction. In short, Reich suffered one of the most complete acts of censorship brought against an individual in a democracy.[6] His work is nevertheless one of the most consistent meditations on sexuality and space that we have.

Reich in Space

However, Reich's interest in architectural space long pre-dated the accumulator. He didn't put it quite like that – he was no architect –

Jo Jenks, portrait bust of Wilhelm Reich, 1949. The bust can be found on Reich's tomb at the top of the museum site.

but from the start he considered the libido to be conditioned by the built environment. He was both drawn to spaces with erotic potential, and drawn to create erotically charged spaces of his own design, including the orgone accumulator. Reich's early interest in the topic is represented by two books published in the 1930s, *The Invasion of Compulsory Sex-Morality* (originally published in German in 1932) and *The Sexual Revolution* (1936). Both refer to the experience of the early USSR, based on a visit Reich and his then wife Annie had made there in the summer of 1929.[7] Here a fascinated Reich saw a series of experiments in communal living. These had begun with the explicit desire of abolishing the family – the nuclear family was after all the basis of capitalism – in favour of youth groups and the commune. Some of these had architectural expression; the Dom Kommuny ('communal houses') were supposed to open up new possibilities for post-family arrangements, including new forms of sexual behaviour.[8] In the new, emergent structure, sexuality was in the service of 'society as a whole', displacing the old patriarchal family in which sexuality served only the desires of a minority. It was the first step to a society in which the family had dissolved, to be replaced with a 'sex-affirmative' set of social relations.[9]

When Reich first came to write up the experience (in *The Invasion of Compulsory Sex-Morality*) he was an enthusiast. By contrast with the sexual ferment of Vienna, there was a curious and not unattractive asceticism about Moscow ('asceticism' is precisely the word Reich uses):

> no sexual importuning in the street; reserve and seriousness everywhere; prostitution still in existence, true, but not seriously affecting the character of the towns; lovers here and there, but not nearly as many as in Vienna or Berlin; at social gatherings an absence of the sexual allusions and smutty conversation characteristic of our circles. In addition one heard curious anecdotes: if a man dared slap a woman's backside or pinch her cheek, as sometimes happens in our part of the world, he might well be prosecuted before the party tribunal if he were a party member. But the question whether one wanted to become a sexual partner was asked more and more openly and unhesitatingly: sexual companionship without any under-handedness, women's genitality a matter of course.[10]

It was far from a sexual free-for-all, but a state of openness in which restraint was an active choice. There is an absence of the sexual traffic that so characterized Reich's cities, Vienna and Berlin; sexual behaviour by men is relatively more respectable, with transgressions both punished legally and looked down upon.[11] And it is a vision organized around urban space. The city street is a vital figure here; the reorganization of sexual life has produced, Reich argues/projects, an entirely new mode of street life. His spatial-sexual critique extends to the private realm too. In an aside he remarks how a girl of sixteen openly offers to 'sleep with X (her boyfriend)' to make way for a family visitor to stay the night.[12] It is a passing aside, possibly an invention of the author, but no less interesting for that, identifying the way in which new patterns of organizing sexual behaviour in space might operate at the most local level.

It's an account strongly informed by a reading of Bronisław Malinowski's celebrated anthropological work, *The Sexual Life of Savages* – and in fact an analysis of this text, or more accurately Reich's fantasies about the text, forms a large part of *The Invasion*.[13] Reich was captivated by Malinowski, finding in this famous account of the matriarchal Trobriand Islanders a wealth of ideas that could be projected back on to Western civilization. Three aspects he particularly liked: the centrality of sex to public life (citing an archaic public orgy, the *kayasa*), the sexual independence of adolescents and the provision of appropriate spaces for sex, the last two concerns being connected.[14] Quoting Malinowski at length, with his own emphases, Reich related the early sexual behaviour of adolescents as driven by the libido, but also quite reasonable. This is again no sexual libertarianism, but a self-regulating ideal, in which fidelity is, if anything, sought after:

> the boy *develops a desire to retain the fidelity and exclusive affection* of the loved one, at least for a time. But this tendency is not associated *so far with any idea of settling down to one exclusive relationship,* nor do adolescents yet begin to think of marriage. A boy or girl still *wishes to pass through many more experiences.*[15]

This general mode of adolescent sexual organization had a spatial expression too, in the form of *bukumatula,* a house for 'unmarried girls and bachelors'. In these houses, or sometimes in the house of an unmarried relative, according to Malinowski, a comfortable corner could be contrived with leaves and mats for sex. Reich confidently asserted that the Trobriand Islanders were 'orgastically potent' in the way that most Westerners were not; and that the frequency of sex was, if anything, lower than in the West, because its quality was so much greater.[16] Here, then, is a 'primitive' ideal, filled with Reich's utopian desires, projected on to the incipient USSR, and when that failed, his own community at Orgonon. Reich was quite untroubled by experience in his account of the Trobriand Islanders – at this point he had never been further west than Paris. But his Malinowski-derived fantasy was certainly vital.

As regards the USSR, by 1936 Reich had more or less completely changed his mind (a capricious and mercurial figure, Reich underwent frequent, and total, changes of direction). His assessment of the country's sexual politics had become far gloomier.[17] The early desire to replace the normative family structure – 'compulsive sexual morality' as he tended to describe it – had been superseded by a comprehensive reassertion of that structure. So the USSR had in fact become as reactionary in sexual matters as anywhere. Reich quoted a ghastly revolutionary pamphlet, *I Want to be Like Stalin* (1947), in which the reassertion of the authoritarian family was complete: 'the most infamous abuse of the child's character for political power purposes that I have seen in thirty years of psychiatric work'.[18] But even in early, pre-Stalinist thinking, Reich detected anti-sex attitudes. Another pamphlet, *The Sexual Revolution in the Soviet Union*, claimed that youthful libido would be sublimated in a 'wave of revolutionary feeling'. Worse, the incorporation of women in the public realm meant their de facto de-sexualization: 'the woman, in experiencing social liberation and becoming acquainted with public social tasks . . . *went sexually cold to some extent*' (Reich's emphasis). Lenin's puritanical attitude to sex was a constant concern for Reich. Lenin: 'though I am not an ascetic, it seems to me that this so-called "new sexual life" of youth . . . is often nothing but an expression of the good old bourgeois brothel. All that has nothing in common with the freedom of love as we Communists understand it.'[19] Reich reported the demand from some USSR youth leaders for sexual abstinence, on the grounds that sex was a distraction from the revolution.[20] And so on. For Reich, one of the most committed members of the Austrian Communist party, it was a disaster. The Soviet revolution seemed to him doomed: its failure to engage the libido fully could only lead to the return of the (repressed) family, and 'compulsory sex-morality', the first step, in the Reichian universe, on the road to fascism.[21]

The Orgone Accumulator: Theory and Practice

The best example of Reich's spatial erotics is his orgone accumulator, the result of another shift in direction. Those unfamiliar with Reich tend to misrepresent it as an orgasm machine, the real-life embodiment of the Woody Allen's orgasmatron from *Sleeper* (1973), or the 'excessive machine' demonstrated by Jane Fonda in Roger Vadim's movie *Barbarella* (1968). Popular culture certainly did the accumulator no favours in this respect. Reich's son Peter recalled with horror as a child finding a magazine in his father's laboratory in which the accumulator was depicted as a straightforward masturbatory machine: 'There was a picture of a naked girl jiggling her breasts in front of a row of accumulators', he wrote. 'There were men staring out of the accumulators at the girl and the story said that the men were masturbating and that the accumulator – only they called it an Orgone Box – was supposed to give them huge orgasms.'[22]

The orgone accumulator is not in fact a machine at all but rather a homespun piece of furniture, bearing some resemblance to a Faraday Cage (a standard piece of scientific equipment used for blocking electrical fields). It has no moving parts apart from the door, and no electrical components, apart from sometimes a reading lamp. The size of a refrigerator, it is made of overlapping organic and non-organic materials, with three or more layers, up to twenty, the number of layers signifying therapeutic power. (Orgonics, one of the few companies in the u.s. actually making accumulators these days, offers a twenty-fold version for $3000; in their words it is so powerful it should only be used 'out of doors, by professionals'.[23]) The outer surface of the accumulator was to be varnished with shellac, not only for durability but also for its capacity to repel orgone-destroying moisture. The accumulator is made from six panels, joined together with screws to make a hollow box, collapsible to allow transport. Reich was relaxed about the precise composition of the materials. He favoured fibreglass for the filling, but suggested that if this were not available, 'felt cotton batts' might be a suitable replacement; likewise the iron panel might be replaced by steel wool held in place with chicken wire.

In fact, the accumulator could be made of almost anything as long as the principle of alternating organic and inorganic materials applied. In correspondence with the educationalist A. S. Neill in wartime North Wales, Reich advised that in an emergency the accumulator could be not much more than a metal sleeve surrounded by a cotton sheet. Neill, although desperate for the healing power of orgone, decided to wait for the real thing.[24] Simple as it was, made properly, the accumulator involved some significant investment: 60 square feet of galvanized sheet iron, 100 feet of pine, several pounds of steel wool. But its simple, rustic quality is key: this is no machine, but a primitive hut. The Reich Foundation's design remains widely available online, giving detailed instructions on how to make an accumulator, plans, information about materials and possible substitute materials, and several pages of advice about its use.[25]

The unproven theory of orgone derived from amateur investigations in the natural sciences that Reich made in 1939. In one of Reich's characteristically manic phases during which *everything* seemed to be connected, he became fascinated by what he called 'bions', sub-cellular particles that appeared to be charged with energy. In an early experiment, Reich described making a 'bion-rich' soup from 'meat, potatoes, vegetables of all kinds, milk and eggs', which he cooked and put under the microscope. Anyone who had seen this, Reich cheerfully admitted, would have thought him insane.[26] He noted movement in these ostensibly non-living forms and speculated that it represented a previously unaccounted for, and universal, form of energy he termed *orgone*, a neologism specifically designed to refer to orgasm. In the human being, sexuality was the key expression of orgone, and Reich's therapies were designed to give it as much free expression as possible, although normally stopping short of actual sex. Orgone also had atmospheric manifestations, Reich thought, claiming that it could be seen as a bluish radiation at night and that it was responsible for the colour of the sky.[27]

The orgone accumulator was designed to concentrate as much atmospheric orgone as possible, and keep it close to the body. As Reich argued, orgone was 'held' by organic materials, and repelled by metallic ones, so the alternation of layers therefore gave 'direction', from the outside inwards. The therapeutic use of the accumulator was as open-ended as its construction. In the construction manual, Reich wrote of the need for regular, daily sessions, and the need to keep one's body at a distance of a few inches from the walls of the accumulator. But apart from that, there were no rules. 'There is no mechanical rule as to HOW LONG one should sit in the accumulator', wrote Reich. 'The sensitive person will, after a while, have "had enough"'. What the 'sensitive person' would feel was equally open-ended. After a certain time, the user would feel 'warmth', 'prickling', 'relaxation', a 'certain reddening of the face', but nothing much more. Reich noted that sensations might become unpleasant if the 'safe' level of orgone was exceeded, noting 'pressure in the head, slight nausea, ill feelings all over, dizziness'. In such cases, 'one simply leaves the accumulator and takes some fresh air and the symptoms of overcharge simply vanish.'[28] It was acceptable to wear clothes, as orgone could easily penetrate natural fibres. Accumulator devotees tended however to take their sessions naked.

James Bell, Orgone Energy Observatory, Orgonon (1948). View of west front and entrance. It has commanding views of Rangeley Lake to the south.

Remarkable claims were made for the accumulator as a therapeutic tool. It could retard cancerous tumours, and treat anything from anaemia to vaginal bacteria.[29] However, what most fascinated Reich, and what most alarmed his enemies, was the accumulator's potential as a device to increase sexual performance. Reich was convinced it could increase what he termed 'orgastic potency', or the ability of human beings to achieve a satisfactorily complete discharge of energy following orgasm. Most people, Reich thought, were 'orgastically impotent', which is not to say that they were not capable of sex, but that their experience of sex was incomplete. Orgastic potency allowed a complete release of energy that could be measured as electrical discharge with appropriate instruments. Therapy using the accumulator was open-ended as Reich indicated, with genuine therapeutic effects only felt with repeated, regular use over a long period, hard to measure or confirm. This was Reich's position in the FDA prosecution; in each case where a therapeutic

Wilhelm Reich, 'cloud-buster', rainmaker device, Wilhelm Reich Museum. In operation the tubes would be angled at the sky.

effect was claimed, Reich could, and did, argue that benefit could only be felt over a longer period.

However, there was anecdotal evidence to suggest more immediate and more powerfully libidinal effects. William Burroughs had been depicted fictionally in *On the Road* as an orgone enthusiast – in real life he was no less keen, relating his experience of a powerfully increased libido after using the accumulator, a state lasting days.[30] The understanding of the accumulator as a sex machine is the subtext to the highly critical *New Republic* article by Mildred Brady, 'The Strange Case of Wilhelm Reich' (1947), which helped initiate the FDA investigation.[31] Brady's view, expressed more sharply still in 'The New Cult of Sex and Anarchy' for *Harper's Magazine*, was that Reich was a fraud whose claims for orgone were unverifiable, and his activities nothing but mysticism. Worse, she argued Reich was part of a professional organization, psychoanalysis, which was dangerously unregulated but also highly protective of its own members, allowing charlatans to practise with impunity.[32] Brady, an economist by training, made powerful, and ultimately successful, arguments against Reich and psychoanalysis in general. However, along with Reich and psychoanalysis, she invoked artists and poets such as Herbert Read, indicating that her argument was as much cultural as it was about scientific truth. Underpinning the *Harper's* piece was a conservative morality, suspicious of an open expression of, or interest in, sex, and it is that morality that ultimately drove the investigation, and to which Reich responded.

Architecture frequently figures in Reich's work as a metaphor of repression – or of liberation. In William Steig's brilliant cartoons for *Listen, Little Man!* Reich's 'little men' of the title are stuffed together in little hutches, but too fearful to escape. Reich's own interests in architecture extended to his extensive involvement in the design of the most substantial building in the Orgonon complex, the Orgone Energy Observatory. It's much less an experimental laboratory, more an example of how to frame a modern life free of repression. Situated on a clear, south-facing slope with spectacular views of the surrounding landscape, it was constructed out of local stone over eight months between 1948 and 1949 to plans drawn up by a New York architect, James Bell. Reich was intimately involved in the design. So access to the open air is critical. It is an intensely physical building, made for the cultivation of the body; everywhere there are balconies and terraces, spaces to take the air, to open windows, to admire views; there is an open-air shower on the roof, beds everywhere. Intellectual work and body culture merge into one; the laboratory becomes an erotic space.

Mysteries of the Organism

Few read Reich in earnest these days, and fewer still make it as far as Orgonon. Reich's public presence consists more in artistic representations: in some eccentric pop music, an exhibition of contemporary art in Vienna and best known of all, Dušan Makevejev's inexplicably popular movie, *WR: Mysteries of the Organism* (1971).[33] Makavejev's film draws together the disparate elements of Reich's career, but also gives it – like Steig – a powerful aesthetic that was influential in modelling a non-repressive society. If you wanted to know what a sex-positive society might look like, then *WR: Mysteries of the Organism* was a good place to start. Formally the film is a collage, owing much to Vertov and Eisenstein, cutting abruptly from one thing to another.[34] It is exceedingly complex and allusive, as one critic put it, 'groaning under the weight of its intertextuality'.[35] Most confusing for the viewer is the mixture of fiction and documentary, blurred further by the fantastical quality of the former: the New York documentary sequences in particular stretch credibility. There, 'real' life comprises a transsexual (Jackie Curtis) from Andy Warhol's entourage, a penis plaster-caster, a portrait painter specializing in masturbation scenes, a naked editorial meeting at the magazine *Screw* and the orgasmic shudderings of a patient in therapy with Alexander Lowen. Against this backdrop of sexual libertarianism, the scene involving Tuli Kupferberg – in which he masturbates a gun, and symbolically shoots at random into Manhattan's crowds – hardly registers.[36]

Interspersed with all this is a reasonably straight documentary about Reich's life and work, including interviews with many of Reich's associates and followers: his son Peter, his daughter Eva and a variety of local acquaintances including his barber in Rangeley. The film gradually becomes fiction, through the New York documentary sequences, to a narrative centred on a young Yugoslav woman, Milena, who wishes to realize Reich's dream of a sexual revolution properly integrated with a Communist one. As the *Guardian*'s film critic Derek Malcolm put it, she, 'riotously, tries to prove Reich's theories in the context of being a party member', producing in the process a satire (but a touching one) of Communism. In one fantasy sequence Milena, in full military dress, harangues her neighbours in the internal courtyard of her apartment building. 'Comrades!' she shouts, 'Communism and physical love must not be in opposition!' Fantasies like these sequences are juxtaposed with newsreel footage from the 1930s or propaganda films, most memorably *The Vow* (1946), a Soviet hagiography of Stalin of (in Malcolm's words) 'unbelievable banality'.[37]

Communism without free love is a wake in a graveyard.

Still from *WR: Mysteries of the Organism* (dir. Dušan Makavejev, 1971).

There is not much of narrative, however, and a great deal of sex. Throughout sex is central to everyday life, normalized and de-eroticized. Close to the start of the film, Reich's biographer Myron Sharaf is interviewed at home where, amid the toys, tools and debris of his garage is located, unobtrusively, his orgone accumulator. 'There is the accumulator', he says casually to the interviewer, as if it were a fridge. The Yugoslav sequences are often framed by Milena's apartment, where her friends can invariably be found, fucking away with abandon. There's an accumulator there too, used to recharge sexual energies, but in the most casual way; Milena herself enters as she returns home from work, in a movement as unreflective as throwing off a coat or making a cup of coffee. What's important in all this is that sex is simply *there*, a human instinct that needs proper acknowledgement and accommodation. It is a film about sex but, as Reich would have wanted, the sex is matter-of-fact, properly housed, integrated with life.

Reich's own sexual life was a disaster. Serially married, in relationships with countless other women, often clients or wives of friends, his sexuality was often destructive, as much the cause of his flight from one place to another as his countless professional disagreements. Were he still alive now, it is unlikely (given employment law and the regulation of medicine) that he would have any chance of either practising or even remaining at liberty. His psychoanalytical work was, it seems obvious now, an attempt to make sense of his own unruly sexual impulses. His theory does that, but he was also a de facto architect, a creator of environments in which alternative forms of sexuality might be imagined and housed. Reich's ability to imagine an alternative reality is the reason his work retains a small following – but it's a following largely made up of artists who at the same time might dabble in the writings of other-cultural theorists like Guy Debord, without necessarily subscribing wholeheartedly to their views. This dilettantism drives the Reich Foundation mad. Nothing upsets them more than an eclectic approach to Reich: you either take it all, or not at all, hence the extraordinary sense of grievance and offence found in the Foundation's communications. Their aggrieved reaction to a large-scale, but highly aestheticized exhibition in 2008 at the Jewish Museum, Vienna, is instructive.[38]

Nevertheless, the Reich people were sufficiently trusting in 2009 to let me spend three days at the Reich Museum in Orgonon, where I stayed in a cabin built by Reich, on the site near Dodge

Pond. In what were possibly the oddest three days of my life, I visited the Observatory, Reich's tomb, hiked in the woods, swam in the lake, cooked steaks on the barbecue and spent a long time in the Orgone Room. Twenty feet square, low ceilinged and windowless, the Orgone Room was lit by a single fluorescent strip lamp, and lined entirely in galvanized steel. Scattered haphazardly were moth-eaten easy chairs and boxes of rubble. Half a dozen accumulators lined the back wall, made to a variety of designs. Some had square holes punched in the door, some didn't, some had lights, one was a quite beautiful piece of joinery, while another was a wreck. There was a small version, apparently for a child. The atmosphere was cold, clammy and airless. It was at first sight a kind of dungeon, or bunker, sealed from the outside world with only a clock marking the existence of the exterior. I felt anything could, and might, happen here. I tried out a couple of accumulators, having been given strict instructions not to overdo it. For the initiate, fifteen minutes, they said, would be enough. I sat with the light on, and apart from a vague sense of unease, felt nothing.

On my second attempt – after a good rest, and a couple of beers – I sat in the dark, having been advised that that way there was a good chance of seeing blue flashes, or a kind of blue mist, evidence of 'orgonotic radiation'. I sat in silence for a few minutes, and was then overcome by frank terror: it was too quiet in there, too dark and just too strange. I groped my way blindly out of the Orgone Room. The five yards to the light switch felt like five miles. I never went in the room again.

What I felt in the Orgone Room I am sure had nothing to do with orgone, but rather the simple fact of being put in radically unfamiliar circumstances, an experience of defamiliarization. Everything about it was peculiar, from the distance from home, to the remoteness from any large city, to the strangeness of the Orgone Room itself (where else do you sit in a windowless room, lined with metal, apart perhaps from an atomic shelter?). Then there was the accumulator itself, and the experience it engenders of being in a tiny space, in close contact with metal. It's not an obviously sexual experience, but it is certainly a bodily one, productive of some quite profound sensations (the coldness of the metal, the sound of one's own breathing, the heat produced by one's body, the strange smell of the metal, the dampness of the atmosphere. That profound bodily defamiliarization has been the stock-in-trade of performance artists for decades, but also more prosaically any

Orgone Room, Wilhelm Reich Museum, 2009. The steel lining of the room is clearly visible.

number of alternative therapies from Hopi ear candles to flotation tanks – in every case, the defamiliarization is sought, and considered valuable. That defamiliarization was the lesson of the orgone accumulator in the end, and I could see how to a 1940s public it could seem to have an erotics of its own. But this was an erotics of space in a generalized and abstracted sense – the body consciousness it produced wasn't obviously to do with sex. And finally, the Reich Museum's pervasive fear about incorrect representations of Reich had a strangely sex-negative quality to it. Nothing upsets them quite as much as the idea that the orgone accumulator is the Orgasmatron.[39] And consistent with this, I struggled to find images with *any* sexual

Orgone Room in the Reich Museum, 2009.

content anywhere in the Museum, which has overall a most unerotic, low-church ambience. Reich's ideas about sexual liberation were and are critical to any sexual history of the twentieth century, and are still in their own peculiar way compelling. Sex is completely, weirdly absent from his Museum.

three

Communal Living

REICH'S DISILLUSIONMENT with the commune was complete after 1936 – but it remained a powerful idea elsewhere. After all, for the twentieth century's sexual radicals, the bourgeois family was simply a prison. The psychiatrist R. D. Laing, for example, thought that the repressive sexuality of the 'normal' family was in fact the cause of many of the disorders he saw. His understanding of schizophrenia was strongly conditioned by the circumstances in which it was found. His *Sanity, Madness and the Family*, written with Aaron Esterson in 1964, describes a set of schizophrenic women whose madness is indelibly connected with the repressive circumstances of their family settings, particularly when it comes to sex. In one striking case, he described a young girl's blooming libido completely denied by her parents, whose strict religious beliefs could not permit its expression. Was it any wonder, Laing argued, that such patients lost their minds?[1] The normative family, in short, was a jail for human nature, a machine for curtailing desire. (Of course, plenty of sex happens in prisons – perhaps more than on the outside. After all, what else is there to do?) Laing was no architect, but his work is full of architectural description: houses whose accumulation of debris from the past prevents the enacting of desire in the present; hoarding as a substitute for sex.

I could empathize with Laing. Laing was in many respects as deranged as his clients, and many argue now that his work on schizophrenia probably did more harm than good. His private life was also every bit as disastrous as that of Reich, and like Reich he seems to have been able to deal with everyone's problems except his own. But as a Scot, he had an acute lived knowledge of the urban environment in which I was writing, the nineteenth-century Scottish city, its streets, its institutions, its tenements, villas and stairs. In his case, it was Govanhill, a respectable lower-middle-class suburb on the south side of Glasgow, close to the slum city of the Gorbals, but a place in which people had aspirations. He understood this landscape, as I did, to be a landscape of repression, all twitching curtains and gossip and rectitude, against which he for one was compelled to rebel. Laing described Govanhill frequently, and in the most striking terms, as a landscape where sex was more or less forbidden. Laing was certainly prone to poetic exaggeration, but it does seem likely that his mother, Amelia, only ever had sex once in her lifetime, resulting in the pregnancy that produced him. So shameful was sex that Amelia hid the pregnancy until it had reached term – and even after his birth denied she had ever had sex with her husband, implying an immaculate conception.[2] As an adult, Laing's career amounted to a long rebellion against the normative family, and his in particular, through whatever means came to hand. It was as complete a rebellion as any.

Once one accepts Laing's analysis of the family, the only way forward is some form of communal living in which the family's tendency to sexual and other dysfunction is attacked with artificial new social structures. Laing in fact did establish a community, Kingsley House (1965–70), in a rented hall in London's East End, to treat schizophrenics in which the boundaries between the mad and the sane, and between staff and patients, were blurred to the point at which they no longer had any meaning.[3] It was an extraordinary and excessive place where all members were encouraged to 'let go' as far as possible, sometimes under the influence of officially procured LSD. The community's extreme character was represented most clearly in the figure of Mary Barnes, a former nurse later to become an artist, who at Kingsley regressed to an astonishingly helpless, pre-linguistic condition, requiring round-the-clock supervision. For months she lived naked, screaming, smearing the community's walls with her own excrement. Laing and his followers had dreams of one day spreading the Kingsley House model beyond the medical environment (they thought that every street ought to have such a place). But the reality was Kingsley was a psychiatric experiment, at heart an attempt to treat a pathological condition in a new way. It was not strictly a commune.

Walden Two

The best-known communes in literature (Thomas More's *Utopia*, William Morris's *News From Nowhere*, Aldous Huxley's *Brave New World*) all had a lot to say about sex – and all in different ways imagine sex removed from the normative family, whatever 'normative' might mean at the time and place of each novel's writing. *Brave New World* is both attracted and repelled by its fantasy of sex wholly removed from procreation, turned into a ubiquitous leisure pursuit, healthy, hygienic and strongly encouraged – a bit like swimming. Huxley's women are 'pneumatic', a mechanistic description that is (I think) meant to be both abhorrent and secretly attractive. The rest of *Brave New World* describes a libidinal utopia, all 'feelies' and 'soma', a landscape in which everything has become eroticized, but at the expense of authentic, uncommodified, life.[4]

Among the most precise communal fantasies is B. F. Skinner's *Walden Two*, first published in 1948, important here for three reasons: firstly, it was published right in the middle of the modernist period and it was very widely read, as influential in its way as *Brave New World*. Secondly, it provides an extremely detailed account of the social organization of a future society, expressed clearly enough to be a blueprint. And third, *Walden Two* says more about sex than most preceding utopian fictions. That's not to say it is a piece of erotica – it is hard to imagine a less erotic book – but that it under-stands the organization of sexual lives as a genuine problem that threatens communal life unless controlled. Unfortunately for the reader, *Walden Two* is a wretched novel, with all the poetic qualities of a tax return. The main characters, the narrator, Castle, a sceptical visitor, and Frazier, the humourless voice of the commune, are ciphers for subject positions. Intellectual arguments are presented in the medium of clunking conversations. Its literary merit aside, however, it is a powerful vision of a commune in which rights and responsibilities are carefully balanced, labour de-alienated, culture made central to everyday life and sexual reproduction carefully controlled. It was seductive enough to inspire the founding of several 'intentional communities' based on its prescription, the most long-standing and successful being Twin Oaks in Virginia, founded in 1967.[5] It is *Walden Two*'s attitude to sex that warrants exploration here, because what is set out is a scenario that for 1948 challenges a whole range of sexual norms but at the same time imagines a time in which sex more or less disappears from the community, except for in reproduction. Each aspect of the community's sexual life has an architectural framing too, so that the creation of a couple is accompanied by 'nesting', the building by the couple of their own private living quarters ('part of the process of being in love in Walden 2').[6] Later stages see the couple routinely adopt separate rooms as a signal of the maturity of their relationship.[7] One of Frazier's main criticisms of conventional marriage is the insecurity it breeds around the basic function of shelter – it connects sex and housing in a way that is abolished by the new community. Several aspects of *Walden* challenge the normative American understanding of sex in the 1940s. Most striking is the advocacy of early marriage. Skinner proposed the effective abolition of adolescence at precisely the moment it came into being as a sociological category. Why delay, asks Frazier. 'What is so unwholesome about sex? Why must there be a substitute? What's wrong with love, or marriage, or parenthood? You don't solve anything by delay – you make things worse.'[8]

Youthful marriages are de rigueur at Walden, as are early pregnancies, on average occurring at age eighteen, but on a downward trend (how far down they would go, Skinner didn't say). But in no way is it advocacy of sex itself, certainly not sex for pleasure. Skinner writes that if sex is permitted to occur naturally, without shame, and in a timely fashion, then its fascination will if anything lessen. Promiscuity would be abolished. By allowing sex to occur early, and in a socially approved context, a 'sane' attitude develops. Failure to do this means (in the leader Frazier's words) 'the sportive element in sex is played up – every person of the opposite sex becomes a challenge to seduction. That's a bothersome cultural trait we're glad to avoid.'[9] Frazier goes on:

> we have successfully established the principle of 'seduction not expected.' When a man strikes up an acquaintanceship with a woman, he does not worry about failing to make advances, and the woman isn't hurt if advances aren't made. We recognize that sort of sexual play for what it is – a sign, not of potency, but of malaise and instability . . . I'm sure there has been the minimum of mere sex without love.[10]

The aim of this is surely the minimization of sex altogether. This is a sex-negative scenario that uses openness about sex as a means of its control. At the heart of Frazier's vision seems to be a desire for sex to disappear except for procreation – the exact reverse of the sex-as-recreation utopia in *Brave New World*. His reporting that in maturity, most married couples do not share rooms any more is presented not as a failure of intimacy (as it might be these days in the West) but a success: sex has been eradicated. And the circumstantial description of Walden is of a place that positively resists seduction.

Frazier's own quarters are a shabby mess, dining is a functional activity done quickly and with the minimum of fuss, and entertainment centres on productive, participatory activities done in public. There is, apart from at the beginning of a couple's lives together, practically no space in which sex can occur. Later on in life, it is assumed, to all intents and purposes, to disappear, to be displaced by more productive activity. Walden is by contemporary Western standards pleasure-free. There is plenty of leisure time at Walden – the new working arrangements allow a working week of just twenty or so hours – but the newly acquired free time is filled with work surrogates. Half the community seem to have become virtuoso musicians, including Frazier, who dismisses his considerable abilities as a pianist as merely an example of the natural order.[11] Everyone has time, therefore everyone engages in some productive pursuit. In sum, the libido has been sublimated into work. Its true expression at Walden is that brief moment in adolescence in which it is required for reproduction.

Down on the Collective Farm

Walden is a fiction, but it is striking how much its puritanical approach to sex is mirrored in real-life communal living projects. This might be expected in the u.s. where the connections between the most austere Protestantism and communal living date back to the very founding of the nation. Among the better-known intentional communities of the northeastern u.s. are those of the Amish and the Shakers, both of whom consciously suppress sex in order that erotic energy be redirected into labour, and prayer. The Shakers enforce celibacy, maintaining sect numbers purely through conversion. Skinner knew these communities well: they were part of the Pennsylvania landscape in which he lived and worked. In non-religious intentional communities, a certain Puritanism of approach is also common. Twin Oaks, Virginia, the community most closely modelled on Walden, is a serious place in which communal ownership, 'income sharing', is the driving principle. The website's advice for potential members stresses the lack of private space and the centrality of productive, communal labour. Their official bumper sticker, available from the website, reads: 'My other car isn't mine either'.[12]

Such American intentional communities suppress sex in a programmatic way. In intentional communities elsewhere, however, even where a liberal attitude to sex is expressed, it remains a real problem. Rarely is the commune an erotic utopia, even when that is partially the aim. In the early USSR, in spite of Lenin's well-documented dislike of sex, several key members of the revolution advocated a reconfiguring of sexual life in direct opposition to the institution of the bourgeois family: the logic was, and is, straightforward – you cannot have a complete revolution without destroying all of the institutions on which the existing order was based. The key figure was Alexandra Kollontai, head of the women's section of the Central Committee Secretariat who pushed through liberal reform of laws on marriage and related areas, and advocated 'free love' and 'erotic friendships' between men and women. To Kollontai's assertion that the satisfaction of sexual desire in a communist society 'should be as straightforward as drinking a glass of water', Lenin is said to have replied: 'thirst has to be quenched. But would a normal person lie down in the gutter and drink from a puddle?'[13] Kollonatai's difficulty in promulgating the sexual revolution any further than her bedroom is encapsulated by another story, in which her decree was taken a little too seriously by the authorities in the southern Russian city of Saratov. The local authorities issued a decree 'nationalizing' women, abolishing marriage and giving men state-sanctioned rights at official brothels. It was not exactly what Kollontai had in mind. In Vladimir a similar decree apparently 'declared all women to be "state property", giving men the right to choose a registered woman, even without her consent, for breeding, "in the interests of the state"'.[14] And as we saw in the last chapter, Wilhelm Reich's observations of communal life in the USSR showed – to his intense disappointment – the development of a profoundly sex-negative society.[15] From an early stage, the revolution appears doomed, at least in erotic terms.[16]

The problem of sexuality in the commune appeared immediately: in many communes sex was effectively prohibited. In the State Library in Moscow, where a full commune was in operation, they even had underwear in common. If one of the communards wanted to wear their own overcoat or underwear, the behaviour was condemned as 'petit-bourgeois'. There was no personal life. It was prohibited to have a closer relationship with one communard than with all the others. Love was outlawed. When it was found that a girl had taken a liking to a certain communard, both were attacked as 'destroyers of communist ethics'. In an account of another Moscow commune of the 1920s, Reich quoted from a communard's diary, in which the writer asks for 'frankness in sexual matters' or sex will take place furtively and unhealthily: 'there will be the desire for secrecy and dark corners, flirting and other undesirable manifestations'. The problem,

Reich described in summary was this (unwittingly paraphrasing Virginia Woolf):

> the commune was confronted with the problem of youth in all countries and all social strata: *the lack of a room of one's own*. Every room was crowded with people. Where could there be an undisturbed love life? In founding the commune, nobody had thought of the multitude of problems which would be presented by the fact of sexual living together.

Later, Reich describes another negative case, another communard, Tanja, writing to her husband:

> all I want is a bit of simple, personal, happiness. I long for a quiet corner where we could be together undisturbed, so that we would not have to hide from the others, so that our relationship could be freer and more joyful. Why cannot the commune see that it is a simple human necessity?

In all of these cases, Reich points to the failure of the Soviet sexual revolution, a failure that is intimately connected with its housing. With its emphasis on industrial production at all costs, the revolution in general had – literally – no space for sexuality, demanding its literal abolition in some cases, or making its expression furtive. From the top (Lenin, and later Stalin) the demand for a social (including sexual) revolution was forestalled by the refusal of the leadership to give literal space to it. So, for Reich, housing and sexuality are intimately connected. The commune by and large cannot accept sexuality as it feels it cannot afford, in times of scarcity, to devote space to it. Marriage might be grudgingly permitted but had to 'remain without offspring', therefore implicitly asexual in these pre-mass contraceptive times.[17] The key problem is 'the lack of a room of one's own', not for the literary life (as it was for Woolf), but for sex.

The experience of the Dom Kommuna in the early USSR overlaps with that of the post-independence Israeli kibbutz, an object of fascination for left-leaning observers everywhere, for whom it represented authentic communism.[18] The kibbutz movement had a lot to say about sex, about family life, about childrearing, and about relations in general between men and women. Where the USSR failed in Reich's eyes because it had not given due attention to sex, the founders of the kibbutzim assumed from the start that sex was an inevitable part of communal life. As such sex needed to be organized – and the organization could be minutely prescriptive. Unlike their counterparts in the early USSR, the kibbutz pioneers were mostly well read and middle class. They were well acquainted with the literature on psychoanalysis, Freud's writings in particular. An early pioneer, quoted in one study, stated: 'we came upon psychoanalysis and it was as if Freud had written specially for us'.[19] So the kibbutz's innovations in social structure were developed in relation to Freud's conclusions about the sexual life of the Viennese bourgeoisie. But it should be said that the pioneers responded to Freud's analysis rather than his conclusions, for the father of psychoanalysis, whatever his thoughts about the difficulty of family life, never advocated a departure from tradition.

The key features of the kibbutz's sexual experiments were 'free love', the de-eroticization of everyday relationships between men and women and the replacement of the conventional family with a system of communal childrearing. None of these innovations were universal, or entirely successful, and the later history of the kibbutz describes the more or less complete normalization of sexual relations.[20] But in the early years, the experimentation was real enough, and the subject of much informed debate internationally for the implications it held for normative family life everywhere. How it all worked in practice varied. 'Free love' was an aim of most kibbutzim, but meant not polygamy or polyamory, but simply the free choice of sexual partner, and the acceptance as normal of sex outside of marriage. There were in some places more exotic experiments. In 1956 Melford E. Spiro described the attempts by some kibbutz pioneers to reinvent sexual relations from the ground up:

> they were convinced . . . that it was possible to create a relationship between the sexes on a sounder and more natural foundation that that which characterized 'bourgeois' marriage and they experimented with many substitutes including informal polygyny and polygamy.[21]

More regularly, the kibbutz's commitment to free love meant simply marriage based on love and sexual attraction rather than the extraneous social factors determining bourgeois marriage. One writer declared of the early kibbutz: 'sexuality should be anchored in spontaneous love. Marriage was to be a voluntary union between free persons . . . who place a strong emphasis on personal autonomy and erotic gratification.'[22]

So even if the kibbutz did not experiment with sexual extremes, it was a decisive attack on the bourgeois family. The architectural organization of the kibbutz universally reflected this: couples were entitled to a room they could share together. But no larger architectural unit was permitted, no architectural form that might represent, or house, the forbidden nuclear family. The couple became a mere love association, based on spontaneous sexual attraction.[23] All other kibbutz relationships were to be communal.

The second sexual experiment in the kibbutz was the de-eroticization of male/female relations, in the hope that it would make more efficient use of kibbutz labour. In other words, if kibbutz members were not distracted by sex (in what were often physically challenging circumstances), they could channel their libidinal energy into the development of the commune, and by extension the new Israeli state. The early youth movements were often actively hostile to sex for this reason. However, given that the youth movements were nerdy and angst-ridden, it is hard not to surmise that this was a post-hoc rationalization of their own sexual hopelessness. In the pre-kibbutz phase, the youth movements even condemned flirting between the sexes. They were 'too serious' for sex. In any case, there was a serious demographic problem: the two to one ratio of males to females. In architectural terms, as various writers have noted, the de-eroticization of male–female relationships was represented by the institution of a mixed shower, and attempts to challenge 'sexual shame'.[24] This experiment, reported in various kibbutzim, and in various age groups, was striking but rarely welcomed. More successful in de-eroticizing relations was the near-universal adoption of mixed-sex dormitories. Other related innovations included the widespread adoption of male clothing by female kibbutz members.[25]

The kibbutz's most dramatic development was perhaps a system of communal childrearing, a direct challenge to the status of the nuclear family, a major topic for sociologists.[26] At birth babies were reared communally, and babies forbidden from sleeping with their parents until the age of six months. Children would sleep, be educated, and socialize more or less entirely separately from their parents, with living accommodation provided by mixed-sex dormitories. For the child, the nuclear family was replaced by the dormitory group, and parental relationships by a series of more or less professional adults. The new system involved a high degree of micromanagement: from birth parents were discouraged, and sometimes forbidden, from putting their children to bed. Time with birth parents was possible, but limited, although it became more common and accepted with the loosening of certain controls on the kibbutz. As one (feminist) kibbutz member noted: 'All we have left is our children, and we don't even have them for they are in the children's house.'[27]

There is an odd tension in these remarks between the asceticism of the commune seen in the American experiments and a genuine engagement with the problem of sex, which is not. The kibbutz therefore arguably represents asceticism, but not Puritanism; there is a wish to control sex, to put it in its place, but not proscribe it. The prehistory of the kibbutz suggests a strongly sex-negative attitude, analogous to what Reich found in the USSR. Yet the instigation of the communal shower, whatever the stated aim, carries with it an undoubted erotic charge.[28] It is indicative of the curious nature of the kibbutz that it should deal with sex head on, but that it should also somehow fail. It is a neurotic, ambiguous relation with sex, enshrined in architecture.

A similar tension can be found in the organization of child-rearing. Its communal organization supposedly freed up couples for other things, while marriage was driven by free love. These aspects of the kibbutz's social organization should have made sex more central. But sex was curtailed by the tendency to organize labour irrespective of private relationships. Married couples would frequently find their time together curtailed by labour practices that could see them work different schedules, with different times for leisure. Unsurprisingly, the birth rate in the early decades of the kibbutz movement was *lower* than in normal Israeli society. In spite of the outward liberalization of sex, there was simply not the time, nor the energy, nor space to do it. The emphasis on physical labour produced some common kibbutz neuroses. Women fretted about ageing. The loss of sexual attractiveness mattered deeply, wrote one commentator, for 'the marriage bond is based only on love'. Kibbutz marriages, in other words, lacked the 'extraneous factors that conspire to perpetuate a marriage in our society long after love has passed'. Along with these organizational factors was a residual puritanism in the kibbutz, strongly opposed to both promiscuity and homosexuality. Both are in theory permitted, but for cultural reasons both were rare. Sexual relations seem frequently to have an undercurrent of shame: 'Couples attempted to keep the special ties between them as a secret as long as they could', she writes.[29] The same sexual conservatism is reported in other studies too. Variations seem temporary and local, with the kibbutz culture in general strongly opposed to anything resembling

promiscuity.[30] The kibbutz, in other words, may have had the infrastructure for an alternative sexuality, but it was in the end rarely any
more a sexual paradise than the Puritan communities of Pennsylvania.

Drop City Blues

Forward to the western u.s. in the mid-1960s, and images of sexually
libertarian communities abound. Aided, for certain, by the invention
of female contraception, the hippy communes produced an image of
sex completely separated for the first time from reproduction – and
also separate from the regime of health. Sex might – or might not –
be good for you health-wise, but it was fundamentally an *experience*
to be consumed as liberally as possible. As good a place as any to start
is Haight-Ashbury, the district of San Francisco where the hippy scene
evolved. Many of the key figures in the scene lived communally: the
rock group the Grateful Dead were a good example, their lead guitarist
Jerry Garcia presiding over 710 Ashbury Street, a rambling nineteenth-
century house that also served as the scene's unofficial headquarters.
The Dead also lived communally for a while in a big adobe mansion
with a pool in an idyllic ranch, Olompali, on the Marin peninsula,
about ten miles north of San Francisco. Here, during the summer of
1966, they lived and played what in retrospect much better describes
the so-called 'Summer of Love' than the Summer of Love itself. It was
a perpetual party, fuelled in large part by the productions of the Dead's
sound engineer and one-man drug factory, 'Bear', aka Augustus
Owsley Stanley III. In one version of events, the 'pool was filled with
naked maidens, and under it was a mountain of Bear's best and
shiniest electronic equipment. There was also a jug with Bear's best
and shiniest chemistry and it all made for a happy day.'[31] In 1967,
following the Dead's return to San Francisco, Olompali was leased
by Don McCoy who founded a more serious commune, The Chosen
Family. The Dead did however memorialize their stay at Olompali
with a strange and compelling photograph by Thomas Weir on the
back of their 1969 album *Aoxomoxoa*.[32]

 In retrospect, however, the Dead were more interested in
music and drugs than getting laid. Far more sexually libertarian
was the Haight-Ashbury offshoot of Morningstar, a ranch commune
founded in 1967. *Time* magazine featured Morningstar in July 1967,
and for readers the most shocking aspect of the community was the
general state of nudity.[33] The article was sensationalist in tone – but
retrospective accounts of the place in the words of a member, Pam

Grateful Dead, *Aoxomoxoa* (1969). The circular image, reproduced the same size as the vinyl record the sleeve contained, depicts the band and much of its entourage in the setting of the Olompali ranch. Those depicted include Jerry Garcia in the background with a horse, and Pigpen (Ron McKernan) reclining in the foreground wearing his trademark cowboy hat. To his right is a 5-year-old Courtney Love.

Read, and the commune's founders Louis Gottlieb and Ramon Sender are no less lurid, describing a chaos of drugs, pregnancies, accidental deaths, hopeless farming, made-up religions, dysentery, crabs, militant vegetarianism, nudism, sun-worship, police harassment – and lots and lots of sex. More than anything, sex seems to have been Morningstar's *raison d'être*. It was here that any and every sexual possibility was tried out and debated. At one end of the erotic spectrum was a group of neo-medieval celibates, who flatly resisted desire.[34] Somewhere in the middle were monogamous couples who remained somehow faithful to one another amid the libidinal chaos. But according to most of the surviving accounts, the ranch's defining character was a freewheeling polygamy. For

Olompali ranch, c. 1966.

the most part this meant a regular trade in sexual partners, with 'open marriage' the norm.

Pam Read, a commune member who became a minor celebrity after being photographed nude in *Time*, described the situation in relation to her own partner, Larry:

> By mutual agreement, we had an open marriage before the idea was generally bandied about as a bold new experiment. Morningstar people were refreshingly open about the matter. There were much more judgmental vibes about food on the set in those days than there were about sex.[35]

(The communards' diet, all concur, was wretched, and produced widespread poor health.) According to Bill Wheeler, another Morningstar resident, a typical experiment in polygamy involved two couples trading sexual partners each night.

If any generalization could be made about the family on
Open Land, it was that the traditional model of father, mother
and child was the exception rather than the rule. The nuclear
family rarely stayed intact when bombarded by the intense
interpersonal energies of alternate culture. It seemed as if
greater affiliations and loyalties were being demanded of us
than those of the blood level. Couples attempting to stay
together would give each other the freedom to have outside
relationships, ultimately shattering the marriage.

Morningstar's founder, Lou Gottlieb, in fact refused to perform
marriages after a time because he felt he was 'merely erecting a
No Trespassing sign'. There were also periodic orgies, 'but they
were more of a joke than anything else . . . someone always had the
clap'.[36] And there was the Phantom Fucker, an enigmatic nocturnal
visitor. A resident, 'Friar Tuck', wrote: 'On at least one occasion,
almost everyone I knew at Morning Star [sic] was visited in the
middle of the night by the Phantom Fucker. Whether it was the
same Phantom Fucker or not I don't know, but I doubt it.'[37] The
architectural frame for this was informal in the extreme – simple
lean-tos or A-frames that gave Morningstar the look of a Depression-
era 'Hooverville' slum.[38] Sanitary arrangements were somewhat
primitive – at best 'one took a shovel in hand and a brief walk in
the fresh country air to select the perfect spot for a donation to
Mother Earth'.[39] This method did not suit those with urgent needs,
or the plain lazy, and one ongoing battle with local buildings inspect-
ors concerned the disposal, or not, of human faeces. Morningstar so
upset Ronald Reagan in 1967, then running for office as California
Governor, that he made an election promise that there would be 'no
more Morningstars', a promise achieved in 1973 during his second
term, although more likely the result of the commune's own implosion
than any concerted political action.[40]

The colourful, but excellent, first-hand accounts of Morningstar
published on the web underwrite *Drop City* (2003), a novel by T. C.
Boyle.[41] It describes a California commune with a charismatic leader
('Norm Sender', modelled directly on Morningstar's Ramon Sender),
which decamps to Alaska with predictably disastrous consequences.
Sex is ever-present in Boyle's novel – it's a sacrament, an article of
faith, more important than anything else. It's also sex that ultimately
brings the commune down. The flight to Alaska follows a series of
catastrophic sexual allegations, and an outbreak of crabs finally seals

the communards' fate. The death of the most objectionable (and predatory) character, Ronnie, is accompanied by an intolerable scrotal itching, in one of the book's many tragi-comic moments.

However, Boyle's use of the name *Drop City* referred to another, quite different, commune – and in fact the libidinal chaos of his fictional commune provoked the wrath of several of the 'real' droppers.[42] The 'real' Drop City was founded in Trinidad, southern Colorado in 1965 by two hippies from New York City, Gene Bernofsky and Clark Richert, along with Gene's wife Jo and Richard Kallweit. Peter Douthit ('Rabbit') was the most vocal of the later residents. The commune lasted until the early 1970s, but its high point was the June 1967 Joy Festival, when the commune became a key node in the global hippy network. It wasn't technically an offshoot of Haight-Ashbury but was, albeit briefly, on the grid. For the architectural historian Felicity Scott, Drop City, along with Olompali,

> formed an interconnected field of experimentation in new forms of social and political participation. Withdrawn from an identification with 'America' they set out (like the Roma) to create their own modes of citizenship and belonging within a post-national territorial organisation connected by an informal network.[43]

The Grateful Dead's experiments in communal living were friendly but haphazard. By contrast Drop City had a plan. Bernofsky and Richert, former art students, had seen Buckminster Fuller speak at the University of Colorado, and concluded that his geodesic dome was what they were looking for. Drop City's name alluded to then current hippy slang – to drop out, or to drop acid (LSD), the psychedelic drug most commonly associated with the movement – but it was also an allusion to the founders' experiments as art students in which they would routinely drop unlikely objects from high windows to observe the reactions of passers-by. Fuller approved of their ideas for the dome, and in 1966 sent them an award, plus a cheque for $500.[44] But Drop City departed considerably from Fuller. It was a ramshackle settlement made from whatever came to hand. The chief materials were wood salvaged from nearby mine workings, and the roofs of cars which the early settlers discovered could be had for free – or at most 40 cents a piece – from local scrapyards; they evolved a technique with an axe for cutting them free of the car body. It was crude, but effective. A story of the droppers slicing the top off a parked Cadillac outside a Colorado bar was probably apocryphal, but it illustrates both their opportunism and industriousness.

So much for the domes. Drop City was a sexy place. Its inhabitants were young, good-looking, keen to throw off as much of the baggage of ordinary society as possible, and its members (some of them, at least) set to exploiting the erotic potential of the new arrangements. Rabbit wasted no time, writing pornography with his commune partner Poly Ester, which he had printed up (with some reservations from other commune members) in the first issue of the *Drop City Newsletter*. He also made a short art film depicting Poly Ester performing fellatio on him, which along with communally made painting, was one of the main exhibits at a Santa Fe art gallery in 1966, an event Rabbit also masterminded. Its screening at the opening led to the immediate closing of the show by the police, an action that gave the event a notoriety out of all proportion to its scale.

Meanwhile, back at Drop City, Richert (now become 'Clard') was given to speak of the ambitious Theater Dome in erotic terms. Speaking to John Curl ('Ishmael') on the occasion of the latter's arrival in Drop City, he described an immersive environment of strobes, electronics and film loops, designed to produce 'constant orgasm'.[45] Curl, fresh from New York's Lower East Side, was mightily impressed. Aspects of the design of Drop City at least help frame this impression: the domes themselves were tiny for the population they eventually housed, and barely subdivided – privacy barely existed in conventional terms. Rabbit's dome in particular was densely populated, with a steady turnover of sexual partners. The informality of Drop City was conducive to libidinal thinking, with no explicit pressure to organize, just a vague sense of being part of an art experiment. And as Curl reported, there were certain sexual experiments involving multiple partners – though these were few, and seem to have arisen as much out of necessity, as the result of the shortage of available partners, as anything else.

For the most part, however, Drop City conformed to sexual convention. A BBC2 documentary of 1966, fronted by Jacob Bronowski, described an earnest bunch of idealists, pioneers in a historic sense, re-invoking an old American tradition. They were earnest, resourceful and hard-working; nothing at all was said of either their drug use (unexceptional, it turned out) or their sexual behaviour. Bronowski rather approved.[46] Accounts of the sexual politics of Drop City paint a picture a long way from any kind of libidinal excess. In fact the close proximity of residents coupled (in the case of female commune

DROP COME CITY

JOY FESTIVAL JOY

COME   COME

JUNE, 9
-10-11

DROP-IN

BRING:
sleeping bags
tents
FOOD

poetry·painting· ·music· BANANAS-FEDS
lite SHOWS·droppings·   dance·films

NEWSLETTER VOL. II   NO.   TRINIDAD, COLO. 81082

members) with some half-digested feminist theory seems to have produced some awkward moments for visitors expecting the ready availability of sex. This was certainly Curl's initial experience: the production of new behavioural norms not wholly unlike those that they ostensibly replaced. Reflecting on the awkwardness of his first interactions with the Drop City women, he described how 'primary relationships' seemed unaffected by the commune environment. 'Everybody still maintained, or wanted a special relationship with one other person, just like in the big outside world.[47] Gene Bernofsky wrote:

> it was kind of a straightforward middle-class deal. The sexual politics were pretty conservative and strait-laced [sic]. We talked about how we wanted to keep that part of our lives simple. Not to get involved in fiery cross-relationships. We disciplined ourselves so that it didn't go on. We were mostly college graduates and had a little maturity, and we realized how complicated and difficult life would be with any partner trading. That was one of the disciplines we had that helped us in our achievements on the land.[48]

If Drop City reproduced some helpfully stabilizing characteristics from the outside world, it also reproduced a lot of its more negative characteristics. So for female droppers, the sexual revolution could simply seem fraudulent – a means for otherwise undesirable males to get laid, claiming refusal of sexual advances as refusal of the revolution itself. This is a major theme of Curl's history. He quotes a commune resident, Miss Margarine: 'the truth is, this whole so-called sexual revolution is really something made up by guys and for guys. It tells women we're suppose to feel liberated by having sex with all of you. It just doesn't work like that, at least for women.'[49]

Worse still, Drop City and the other hippy communes that followed could reproduce the sexism that existed in the real world, with well-documented division of labour between men and women. As one woman reported to Matthews, how come it was that only the women had to cook at Drop City?[50] Even worse was the implicit racism – in a recent account, Drop City represented a highly sophisticated example of so-called white flight.[51] Bernofsky's sexual conservatism was perhaps a form of denial, or submerged regret: 'If there was any

Drop City, Joy Festival poster, June 1967.

Alex Hartley, reconstructed Drop City dome at Occupy London protest, Finsbury Square, 2012.

sleeping around or trading partners I didn't know about it. And it didn't go on as far as I could tell.'[52] When Drop City held its Joy Festival in June 1967, Bernofsky retreated to his dome, refusing – in stark contrast to Rabbit – to join the revelry. He left Drop City shortly afterwards, implying in interview that the Joy Festival in effect marked the end of the commune as a valid project. It certainly marked the end of the project as something that could be controlled by Bernofsky himself. In a curious parallel with the fictional *Drop City*, the Trinidad commune's demise seems to have been presaged by a decline in sexual morality; later arrivals could be unsavoury, including an older (male) sexual predator whose sole interest in the commune seems to have been its supply of young girls.[53]

Drop City has had a curious afterlife in the 2010s via the Occupy movement. Here the British artist Alex Hartley built a dome adapted from the Drop City design, lived in it for the duration of his Victoria Miro Gallery exhibition in the winter of 2011–12 and donated it at the end to Occupy, who used it as a shelter in Finsbury Square. In image at least, Drop City's libidinal utopia survives.[54] The dome was removed in mid-June 2012 along with the rest of the camp, some of which reappeared on Hampstead Heath. Hartley transported his dome back to his studio in Devon where it became clear it had been a place of some excess – the interior was coated in vomit, and the remains of an exploded beanbag, concealing a good scattering of used sex toys and condoms. A period of disinfecting and decontamination ensued.[55] Hartley's re-enactment of Drop City in the gallery's garden was a fascinating, but essentially polite project based on a genuine affection for and knowledge of the original. His enthusiasm for Drop City was evident to visitors, and the experience of recreating it helped explain – in a straightforward architectural-historical sense – how the original had actually worked. It was a historic recreation in a long, worthy tradition, a counter-cultural Colonial Williamsburg.[56] In the hands of Occupy, it became a zone of dystopian excess, an apocalyptic party space. The transformation from one to the other parallels many things in this book (the plot of Ballard's *High Rise* is one). But it also curiously parallels Drop City's own history. A high-minded utopian scheme in the beginning, it was brought to earth by Eros. Peggy Kagel, one of the original droppers, wrote of sex at Drop City: 'we call it the evil black snake. It just tears everyone apart.'[57]

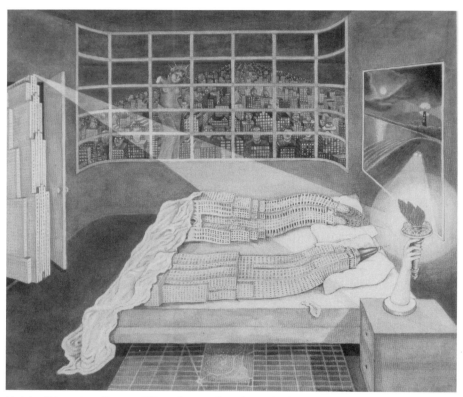

Madelon Vriesendorp, *Flagrant délit*, 1976, aquarelle and gouache. A post-coital bedroom scene; note the deflated Goodyear blimp on the edge of the bed.

four
Phallic Towers and *Mad Men*

NEUTRA, SCHINDLER, Reich, Laing, Skinner, Drop City 'dropouts' – they are diverse characters, but all defiantly avant-garde. Important in their own estimation, and among their immediate circle, they stood in critical relation to the mainstream. Schindler built hardly anything, Reich and Laing were intellectual mavericks whose reputations fell as quickly as they rose, Drop City a short-lived experiment that attracted, by accident rather than design, a lot of press attention. Yet mainstream modern culture was as preoccupied with sex as the avant-garde, especially in the U.S., so I needed to ask where *that* popular eroticism was represented in buildings. It is a real enough phenomenon, measurable in the millions of copies of soft porn magazines shifted on a monthly basis by Hugh Hefner and others, by the sudden appearance of women's magazines like *Cosmopolitan* that dealt with sex head on, with the development by the end of the century of a gigantic porn industry. This popular fascination with sex has some connection with the sex industry, but I was interested in where it might be in relation to the ordinary built environment. To put it another way, if sex became by mid-century a popular and open fascination, then where was sex going to *be*? It certainly wasn't going to be in a Reichian Orgone Box, not after 1956; nor was it likely to be in an austere modernist house by a middle European intellectual; and it definitely wouldn't be in a commune. Skinner's austere Walden Two was for most Americans as much a parallel universe as the cyberpunk landscape of Drop City, and neither would represent a sexy environment in the slightest.

So what would? The answer might be found partly in the pages of the architectural magazines, where from the mid-1960s in the work of Venturi Scott Brown & Associates, Reyner Banham and others there was a re-evaluation of the popular built environment,

with the avant-garde-baiting conclusion that it was probably all right. None of this work was about sex, exactly (and looking at mid-1960s images of Banham, and his calculated, tweedy eccentricity, there's something faintly grotesque about even making the connection). But Banham's celebration of the ordinary landscape of '60s LA, or the comparable work in Las Vegas by Venturi Scott Brown & Associates, is full of commercial imagery that is openly libidinal. The cover of most editions of Banham's *Los Angeles: The Architecture of Four Ecologies* is the most famous of David Hockney's swimming pool paintings, while the equivalent for the Venturis' book is a billboard of a woman in a bikini advertising tanning lotion. Both covers, and their contents, celebrate rather than criticize the blizzard of pop cultural imagery, much of which was openly erotic. The avant-garde tended to suppress the body – now it was everywhere.

Phallic Towers

In the popular imagination, the most shamelessly sexual building form is the tower, an idea so widespread it is beyond cliché. Towers are invariably, inescapably phallic symbols, standing proud, firm, erect (or on the case of a splendidly surreal image by the Dutch artist Madelon Vriesendorp, in a state of obviously post-coital droopiness). In 2003, *Cabinet* magazine, a respectable academic journal, held a competition to find the world's most phallic structure, the winner being an 1890 water tower in Ypsilanti, Michigan, known locally as the Brick Dick.[1] The competition was held after a minor controversy caused by the assertion by one of their contributors, Jonathan Ames, that the 1927 headquarters of the Williamsburg Bank in Brooklyn, New York City, was the world's most phallic structure. The ensuing competition among *Cabinet* readers produced 61 submissions, and a variety of building types. Memorials and monuments were prominent. Among the suggestions were the Washington Monument, the George Washington Masonic Memorial in Alexandria and the Liberty Memorial in Kansas City. There were also TV towers (the Fehrnseeturm, Berlin), shopping malls (the Smáralind in Reykyavík), industrial structures (the Lead Shot Tower, Bristol) and a plethora

William R. Coats, the 'Brick Dick' Water Tower, Ypsilanti, Michigan (1889–90). The world's most phallic building, as voted by readers of *Cabinet* magazine. It is a truly astounding building, a huge, overbearing, downright rude structure in an otherwise delicate Victorian college town.

of postmodern office towers (inevitably 30 St Mary Axe, London).
Some of these were quite astonishingly phallic, such as the winner.
Not only did this stout, cylindrical structure sport a pronounced
glans, being a water tower, it was also routinely full of liquid.

Cabinet's readers would have been well versed in the long
tradition of describing buildings as phalluses. They would have
known of that extraordinarily striking passage by the architect
Louis Sullivan, much quoted, on the (demolished) Marshall Field
warehouse in Chicago:

> here is a man for you to look at. A man that walks on two
> legs instead of four, has active muscles, heart, lungs and other
> viscera; a man that lives and breathes, that has red blood, a
> real man, a manly man, a virile force.[2]

They would also have most likely known of the *The Fountainhead*, an
equally extraordinary 1943 novel by Ayn Rand in which masculinity
and modernity are completely synonymous. It narrates the career
of an uncompromising young modernist, Howard Roark, and his
interactions with both a reactionary peer group (represented by the
character Peter Keating) and unscrupulous clients. The sexual narrative concerns Roark and Dominique Francon, daughter of Guy, a
pillar of the conservative architectural establishment. Dominique is
emotionally and ideologically Roark's match, and as a consequence
their relationship does not follow any conventional pattern of
romantic courtship, but is a battle of wills with episodes of cruelty,
sadism and, finally, domination. Dominique's desire to dominate
Roark, for example, leads her to engagement to Roark's (then)
nemesis, Gail Wynand, a corrupt newspaper proprietor, and then
an actual marriage with his professional rival Keating, in both cases
the relationship merely serving as a means of antagonizing her lover.
Dominique and Roark's first sexual encounter is in effect a rape, a
fact that has drawn much criticism to the book over the years with
its apparent validation of domination by physical force.

Architecture is central to *The Fountainhead*, not merely as a
vehicle for a narrative about professional rivalry, but as a set of highly
sexual images. Roark's body appears, from the first line, as an object
of architectural fascination. He is all structure and so it is with his
buildings, which pointedly eschew decoration. The tension between
structure and decoration is particularly clear in the film version of
The Fountainhead, in which every scene can be clearly located on one

side or another. The identification of Roark's body with architecture is particularly strong in any of the early scenes in which Roark, for lack of funds, is forced to work in Francon's stone quarry. Here, stripped to the waist, like Jacob Epstein's figure sculpture *Rock Drill*, Roark is all phallus, a hard body literally penetrating the earth.

Shortly after, Rand writes of Roark's physical power over the materials in the quarry. The rocks, thinks Roark, 'are here for me; waiting for the drill, the dynamite and my voice; waiting to be split, ripped, pounded, reborn; waiting for the shape my hands will give them.'[3] In the later encounter between Dominique Francon and Roark in the quarry, a key scene, the sexual tension between them is seemingly intolerable. Dominique, riding out to the quarry on horseback, becomes obsessed with the semi-naked Roark, but is unable to withstand the hold he now has over her. In an astonishingly sadistic moment, she horsewhips him before galloping off.

The Fountainhead (dir. King Vidor, 1949).

The quarry scenes represent an elemental sexuality that is later sublimated into formal architecture. It is no accident – nothing is accidental in this most programmatic of novels – that Roark's eventual victory is made material through the erection (in every conceivable sense) of a Wynand-commissioned tower, the tallest in the city. Neither is it accidental that in the final scene of the book and the film, Roark's subjugation of Dominique is staged at the tip of that tower. Keating's figurative and literal impotence is meanwhile symbolized by his attachment to ornament and his stylistic vacillation. His bending to the whim of the client for short-term gain is shown to be opportunistic, and ultimately an expression of sexual failure. Roark's sexual potency is located in his building and his unbending relations with clients, as much as his physique. This is a stereotypical male identity, located in erotic power.[4]

Mies's Masculinity

In the real modern world there is one inescapably phallic tower, not so much for its form as the way it embodies masculinity in its every detail.[5] This is the 1958 Seagram Building by Ludwig Mies van der Rohe, which rises 38 storeys from a pink granite plaza on New York's Park Avenue. Built for the Canadian distillers Seagram, the choice of Mies had in fact most to do with the intervention of the chief executive's twenty-something daughter, Phyllis Lambert, an enthusiastic modernist then living in Paris. Lambert encouraged her father first to dump the initial design of 1954 by Pereira & Luckman, already dismissed by *Architectural Forum* as resembling a cigarette lighter. She then sought advice from Philip Johnson at MOMA, who recommended – not without self-interest, it seems – Mies. It had three main innovations: the half-acre plaza on Park Avenue, for the time a highly extravagant use of space; the absence of setbacks in the tower form, in marked contrast to conventional New York practice of the time; and the use of bronze cladding and topaz-tinted glass. In plan, it is not the uncompromising slab it first appears, having a distinct front and back. From Park Avenue, it is so, but it is connected to a much more complex, lower building to the east. Even the slab itself is not straightforward: it splits into two sections, joined asymmetrically at the rear – five-by-three bay design on Park, and then a three-by-one section at the rear. Louis Kahn caustically

Ludwig Mies van der Rohe, Seagram Building, New York City (1958).

Mies van der Rohe in his Chicago apartment, 1964. He is sitting on one of his Cantilever chairs, designed in 1927.

described Seagram as 'a beautiful bronze lady in hidden corsets'.[6] You can see what he meant, but there is hardly a less feminine building in existence. In a review strikingly reminiscent of Louis Sullivan's remarks on Marshall Field, W. H. Jordy insisted on Seagram's weight and materiality, as if it portrayed Mies's own considerable bulk. The idea of weight is continually stressed. Seagram 'meets the earth firmly on heavy, two-storey stilting', Seagram's 'very darkness' gives it weight, its 'massive columns' giving 'a sense of weight, of a building resting solidly on the ground, rather than tethered to it in a fit of airy levitation, as has been the effect with some of Mies's imitators'. Seagram has 'density'; it is a 'play of masses'; it has a 'hierarchy of massing'. Finally, Jordy gets to the point, and quotes Sullivan: 'it stands as the oration of one who knows well how to choose his words, who has something to say, and says it – as the outpouring of a copious, direct, large and simple mind.'[7]

Mies was indeed a big man. Not fat, but well covered, a 'large, lusty man' as his obituary in the *New York Times* described.[8] More specifically, as almost everyone who came into contact with him noted, he had an enormous head. He was, in one account, 'a large and impressive figure', his head looked 'as if it had been chiselled out of a block of granite' and his face had 'the massively aristocratic look of a wealthy Dutch burgher by Rembrandt'.[9] His social awkwardness was well known, especially on his translation to the u.s. where poor English crippled his public existence. But in spite of this, he drew attention to his physical appearance. He was a bit of a 'dandy', with a taste in clothes that exceeded the sobriety dominant in photographs of him. The materials were rich and well cut, and there were always carefully chosen flourishes like the silk handkerchief. His clothes and accessories in fact all fall into the category of Freudian phallic objects – homburg hats, pipes, tightly rolled umbrellas, cigars, trench coats, walking sticks – things that in the psychoanalytical universe unequivocally connoted maleness. The dandyishness was there in the buildings too: his *New York Times* obituary wrote of Seagram's emphasis on 'pure line, fine materials and exact detailing outside and in. Special attention was paid to the room numbers, doorknobs, elevator buttons, bathroom fixtures and mail chutes, as well as the furniture.'[10] The window blinds were a source of both wonder and frustration, Mies insisting on a mechanical system that would hold them in only three positions (fully open, halfway, and fully closed) to avoid the unacceptable disorder of the ordinary office tower.

All this is perfectly clear in a photograph by Werner Blaser of Mies in his Chicago apartment at East Pearson Street in 1964, some five years before his death. Here he is relaxed, sitting in his Brno chair, puffing on the cigars that he smoked with such appetite – twelve to 24 daily.[11] Mies leans back, looking ahead in a pose of relaxed contemplation. But it is a peculiarly masculine kind of relaxation in which Mies, in a dark suit and tie, is actually dressed with a high degree of formality; a white handkerchief emerges carefully from the top pocket. This is an image of a particular kind of masculinity that was barely legible *as* masculinity any more.

Mies, in this 1964 image, represents a much more static form of masculinity; maleness expressed through stasis, in which the man remains immobile, contemplative, often silent while others scurry around and do the work. The body – unlike Roark's – remains hidden, but it is, vitally, there. This is a man who possesses space and those around him, who is listened to (however little he has to say), who expresses power through stillness and lack of physical activity. That form of masculinity may no longer be in fashion but it has an epic lineage from Buddha to Hitchcock and is, in its own way, highly sexual even if it does not express itself in relentless sexual activity. The most sexually charged of Mies's client relationships, with the Illinois doctor Edith Farnsworth, was powerfully manifest in the nature of the building which he designed for her, powerfully about putting the female on display. But their relationship was almost certainly not physically sexual. As Alice Friedman has written, what they might have done otherwise with their bodies was expressed through work. Farnsworth's description of meeting the architect for the first time in November 1945 is also indicative of Mies's sexual power over her. She described the effect in terms of sexual sublimation. It was 'tremendous, like a storm, a flood, or other act of God'.[12] It is powerfully expressed in the Barcelona chair, a chair for sitting *in* as much as looking at, and in the spatial qualities of his architecture.

Mies van der Rohe, Barcelona Chair (1929). Low, buttoned-leather chair on a scissor frame in stainless steel, designed for the architect's pavilion at the 1929 International Exposition. An industrial design icon, still in production, it describes a particular kind of comfort. The cushion is 75 cm in width, and the cushions themselves are thick and well sprung. The art curator and writer James Johnson Sweeney, on meeting the architect in 1969: 'He invited me to his office. When my wife and I entered we both saw at once the answer to a question that had been troubling us for some time: why was the Barcelona seat so wide? As we opened the door we realized. Mies was seated on one and it just comfortably accommodated his breadth.'

Detail from 'The Many Different Lives of an Office Building', *Life* (February 1957).
The executives are listening to a radio advertisement.

Life on Madison

Mies didn't build that much in New York City, but his style was
phenomenally influential. In fact, by the time Seagram was complete in
1958, there was plenty of sub-Miesian work to be seen in Manhattan's
mid-town business district, Mies before Mies as it were. A great
example is 260 Madison Avenue, built in 1952 by Sylvan and Robert
Bien, arranged in the form of a nine-storey block, a de facto podium
for three set-back storeys above. Squat rather than soaring, 260
Madison's main face was a curtain wall with ribbon windows; the
treatment of the facade off the main street had the ribbon windows
only, and a much plainer effect. The Biens built another building
directly opposite, taller and more dramatic in its massing but with

the same facade treatment.[13] In and of itself, 260 Madison is of limited architectural interest. However, for *Life* magazine it was an archetype, representing in an article of February 1957 by the photographer Walter Sanders, 'The Many Different Lives of an Office Building'.[14]

Organized both chronologically through the day and spatially, it's a fascinating piece of photojournalism surveying life in all parts of the building from the lobby through to the elevators, the office floors, the boardrooms and dining rooms. On the first spread there is an aerial shot of the Madison facade from the building's neighbour, 261. Then the lobby where a middle-aged man in hat and overcoat, cigar ablaze looks with barely suppressed contempt at the names listed in the lobby directory. The second spread introduces the ancillary workers – the 'elevator girls' with their proscribed hair colour ('black or red . . . they get free hair treatment every two weeks to keep correct color'), the news-stand proprietors, the secretary, the window cleaners hanging precipitously from the outside of the building.[15] Then comes a double spread of larger, but bolder images with more close-ups: the boardroom of the Mathes advertising agency with three pensive-looking executives listening intently to a reel-to-reel of a radio ad for instant stock cubes. A lighter image from the board level has two executives show off a new undershirt 'based on a Norwegian design'. The design, more hole than shirt, dangles between two smirking executives. Over at Cunningham & Walsh, another executive stares hard at a proposed ad for coffee, his office lined with endless sketches for another ad selling razors. At the bottom of the spread, a highly abstracted, cropped image shows the conversation between two men at Communications Corp. behind a glass wall; represented as fuzzy outlines only, the seriousness of the scene is in no doubt. All the images on this page reinforce the strapline, 'A constant call for decisions'. The final spread lightens the tone: 'conviviality and a shower' shows groups of women secretaries in lighter moments of socialization (coffee with friends, a surprise shower of gifts for one of the group), and on the right-hand side of the spread a six-image, semi-humorous narrative details the 'thwarted escape' of a Reigel Paper Corp. secretary, whose exit at the end of the day is forestalled by her boss having found a mistake in an order she had earlier processed. The final page depicts the night watch in two bold, dark images: a lettering artist at his drawing board late in the night, and the night dispatcher for marine operations at Merritt-Chapman & Scott, dozing at his switchboard.

My boss gets around! (He's got The Hertz Idea)

Right! Her boss has found you can save time on business trips when you leave your car at home, go faster by plane or train, then rent a Hertz car when you get there!

That's The Hertz Idea. You can make more calls, get back home sooner, too. What's more, you have a car to drive as your very own—a day, a week or longer!

All you do is show your driver's license and proper identification. You'll get the keys to a bright, new Powerglide Chevrolet Bel Air or other fine Hertz car. Cost? The low national average rate is only $8.00 a day plus 8 cents a mile (lower by the week). That includes all gasoline, oil and proper insurance. In addition to the Hertz charge

card, we honor air, rail, Diners' Club and most all hotel credit cards. So to be sure of a car at your destination—anywhere—use Hertz' free reservation service. Call your local Hertz office. We're listed under "Hertz" in *alphabetical* phone books everywhere! Hertz Rent A Car, 218 South Wabash Avenue, Chicago 4, Illinois.

More people by far...use

HERTZ
Rent a car

Hertz—largest and finest rent a car service—has more of the kind of cars you like to drive—like Chevrolets!

The sexual politics of this *Life* feature are always explicit. This is a world in which men are active, and women passive, in which men do things, and women support them. Men wear suits and hats, stand upright, smoke and make decisions; women are the figurative and literal bustle around them. If the Seagram was the ideal built representation of the normative sexual politics of the era, an upright male figure, surrounded by attentive females, then here is the mundane reality of that representation. Men are always bigger, taller, harder, more assertive and visually bolder. Women are the rococo detailing, pretty but not structural. This visual rhetoric does not appear in isolation, of course, but is itself supported by a whole world of representations. So elsewhere in the same issue of *Life* are advertisements that enact exactly the same politics; on page three, a uniformed commercial pilot draws on a Philip Morris Long Size, fired by a slim female hand proffering a match. Veto Deodorant (page 72) has a close-up of a girl, eyes closing in orgasmic ecstasy with the accompanying text: 'isn't it a *fabulous* feeling to know he'd rather be close to *you* than anyone in the wide, wide world? Don't let anything mar this moment.'[16] An ad for Green Giant Peas has a tired, suited executive come home to a dish of peas prepared by an eager wife and daughter. For Hertz (page 104) the strapline is 'My boss gets around!', the main image depicting a blonde secretary in red lipstick adjusting her make-up while gazing up at the reader. The 'getting around' in theory refers to the mundane business of car rental, but the image speaks of nothing but sex. Underwear ads bang up against articles on Sunday schools; a full-colour spread on an anti-bomber defence system jars with an advert for spaghetti sauce. Men are the doers in all of this, making the decisions, holding the meetings, getting the girls. Women feed, decorate, entertain and support. All this is visually coded, from the excessively phallic dress of the exec on page one of 'The Many Different Lives' (homburg, overcoat, umbrella, cigar clenched in teeth), to the tight uniform dress of the elevator girls, to (for one feminist critic) the very reflectivity of the International Style facade.[17]

From Madison to *Mad Men*

To anyone who has seen *Mad Men* (2007–), Matthew Wiener's AMC television series, 'The Many Different Lives of an Office Building' is

'My Boss Gets Around!', advert from *Life* (February 1957).

only too familiar.[18] The series is set in a fictional Madison Avenue advertising agency and its title, *Mad Men*, appropriates the vernacular of the time to describe not only the geographical location but also the libidinal reputation of the business. The *Life* piece depicts the same rigid divisions of space into masculine and feminine, the same rigid dress codes, the same hierarchies, the blueprints for a range of characters. However, where 'The Many Different Lives' merely alludes to sex – like the rest of the magazine – *Mad Men* enacts it. *Life* stops at innuendo; *Mad Men* does not. And in so doing it makes real what *Life* could, in 1957, only hint at, and what was only known through gossip and suggestion. Whatever the quality of the TV series, it performs an important role in making visible the sexual life of buildings. More broadly, it represents the modern office as a lived experience, one that was perhaps known about through hearsay, but rarely if ever, represented.[19] Those graph-paper buildings might have been supposed to teach rationality, but they housed the same animal instincts as any other. And its attention to period detail makes it in effect a work of architecture in its own right.[20]

Mad Men has been a huge enterprise: to date a five-series, thirteen-episode per series drama, nearly 50 hours in total, shot with the resources and budget normally associated with a full-length feature film. It is of a scale equivalent to 30 or so movies. It is extraordinarily successful too, especially given its origins on a cable network, AMC. It has also been, overall, a critical success, not surprising in view of its high production values and attention to detail. The quality of its surfaces demand sustained attention, and repeated viewing. There is in fact a good deal of repetition, plot-wise especially around the key character of Don Draper, the enigmatic creative director. Draper's narratives are almost exclusively about sex. There's typically a female client, with whom there is a mutual attraction, and the story is motivated by the question of when, and where, they will have sex. The 'where' is of particular interest here, as it is invariably not the socially correct place for sexual activity, normatively the home, but some other place: a car, a hotel room, a rented apartment in a seedy location, the office. Draper's spacious accommodation, along with that of his peer group, has sofas and privacy, and unlimited booze. More often than not, business at the show's fictional setting, the ad agency Sterling Cooper (later Sterling Cooper Draper Pryce), takes place horizontally.

The physical setting of Sterling Cooper is an amalgam of various Madison Avenue towers, one of which may be 260 Madison, the setting of *Life*'s account of office life.[21] There are occasional hints of exterior location, such as the view from Pete Campbell's window depicting a long axial view northwards along Madison towards Central Park. A wide-angle shot of the tower's facade (most likely 275 Madison, not 260) appears occasionally as a transition device, marking the shift from one subplot to another. But it is the interior that stays in the memory, describing with marvellous clarity the complexities, subtleties, and sexual politics of the modern open-plan office.

In the case of *Mad Men*, the office set, in all depicted locations, has four distinct zones: an open-plan, public zone occupied by exclusively female secretaries and reception staff; a private zone of individual offices, occupied by (almost) exclusively male executives; a female switchboard room (and associate bathroom) and a (mostly) male art office. These are supported by zones exterior to the office itself, equally coded: the suburban house (female), the Oyster Bar (male), the commuter train (male) and certain zones in which ritual-ized interaction between the sexes may take place (the country club). Of these zones, it is the interaction between the public (female) and private (male) parts of the Madison Avenue office that are most critical. As with Mies, there is a play of transparency, of the inter-penetration of spaces. So the private and public zones share the same ceilings and recessed lighting, and part-translucent screens separate them. The doors are often open. There's continual traffic between the two zones as meetings start and end, and as secretaries bring messages for executives inside. There's also a formal ambiguity about the private zone in that its individual component offices all face on to the public world of the street, albeit at some remove. But despite the traffic, and the translucency, and the public-facing aspect, the private zone lies behind a de facto wall, the transgression of which is a serious matter. The zone is protected by individual (female) secretaries whose principle task is to limit as far as possible contact between the two zones. Unannounced demands for contact with the interior are regarded as crimes.

The private zone itself is formally different too, an expression of a specific form of masculinity. There are critical elements here, all in Freudian terms 'phallic' if not specifically phallic objects: the desk, a big, immovable, powerful object used as a form of defence, or to bolster power; the drinks cabinet, incessantly deployed. (Every meeting between executives, every moment that hints at celebration, regret, disappointment, satisfaction, anticipation or in fact *any* emotion at all is cause for a drink.) There is the view out. The ribbon

windows of the Madison Avenue building frame the chief protagonists like a movie screen, continually projecting them as actors in an urban movie – which they are, in reality, but in this setting the building fictionalizes them, romanticizes them, making them into actors on the grandest of urban stages. There are the cigarettes, and less usually, cigars, criticized in some quarters for the glorification of smoking, deployed here as defiantly phallic objects. There are the softer furnishings: chairs, in which the executive can sit, held in a position that is both relaxed and authoritative. There is the couch, a piece of furniture with domestic connotations, as well as those of psychoanalysis, but deployed here as a site of masculine repose, of creative work, of sex – and sometimes all three at the same time.

Mad Men is great at showing interiors used erotically in ways that could only be hinted at elsewhere. In the first episode of the first series there is a scene that defines masculinity, a moment of celebratory reflection where Draper relaxes with a fat cigar in an easy chair, while his associate, Roger Sterling, pours a drink by the window.[22] It's an intimate scene, but one charged with masculinity: all the signs are there – the suits, the cigars, the whisky, the toned bodies, the lined faces, the wood panelling, the venetian blinds. It's a moment of intimate reflection that strongly alludes to a post-coital moment, coming as it does after a period of tension and uncertainty, in which finally, after a struggle, a deal is orgasmically brought off. The cigars and booze facilitate a space of relaxation and transition before the next battle. That image from the first episode is about sexuality in the broad sense. However, *Mad Men* shows the office is not simply a place where sexual identity is constructed, but where sex is had. In representing sex itself, the makers of the series don't do anything new in terms of what might be acceptable on mainstream TV, but they do stretch the way architecture is represented, as the screen sex links closely with a fetishized approach to the setting. To put it another way, the sex (its location, duration, nature, form) is strongly conditioned by its surroundings; the office becomes in effect a sexual device, defining whatever activity actually occurs, and it is distinctly different from the sex that occurs in others of the series' locations. In episode eight of series one, Pete Campbell, the most aggressively ambitious of the younger staff members, pounces on the enigmatic Peggy Olson. The scene uses all the key elements of the office. It

Mad Men, Don Draper (Jon Hamm) with Roger Sterling (John Slattery) in the background, series 1 (2007).

opens with a demonstration of the gender divisions of the interior, with Peggy on the outside, public side of the divide, Pete on the inside. He beckons her in, and is initially seen behind the desk, that emblematic barrier of executive power. He moves around to approach Peggy, symbolically closing the door between the private and public realms. The sex itself is rough and joyless, and takes place, Pete on top, on the small couch placed against the translucent wall. The public part of the office is at this time free from other staff who might see – apart from a janitor, pushing a mop; hearing muffled grunts, he looks towards the translucent wall of Pete's office, where Peggy's vertical legs, heels still in place, are silhouetted unmistakeably against the light. The janitor's indifference says it all: the sex is as normal as the cleaning of the floors.

A far nastier episode occurs in series 2, episode twelve, when the office queen, Joan Harris (née Holloway), is raped by her husband late one evening, in Draper's office. Here again the scene is powerfully motivated by the architecture. Joan's husband, Greg, a doctor, has in a previous scene found himself sexually humiliated by Joan when she, uncharacteristically in their relationship, initiates sex by climbing on top of him. His blunt refusal mixes aggression with insecurity. The office scene has him enact a series of spatial transgressions aimed at re-establishing his potency: first the entry into the forbidden territory of Draper's office; then Harris's refusal to accept his wife's wishes; then his brutal forcing her to the ground and penetrating her in an act she in no way enjoys. The scene is over quickly, but it disturbs, because it inverts Joan's usually unassailable status: here she is literally brought down. As with the previous depicted instance of office sex, the office's interior architecture plays a key role. Here, the act of sex itself is framed by the inarguably powerful, male accoutrements of Draper's office: the dark wood furniture, a stainless-steel ashtray, the venetian blinds gridding the view of Madison's towers by evening. Joan's face, with a most uncharacteristic expression of fear, is framed by the furniture. With her red hair and purple dress, not to mention her spectacular figure, she's an exotic creature brought to earth. It is a spectacle of sexual domination in which the architecture is complicit.

For readers now, the sexuality invoked by *Life* magazine is unbearably coy, all innuendo and inference. *Mad Men*'s architectural achievement – regardless of its quality as TV – has been to flesh out the sexuality of the International Style and make explicit what it means for human beings living and working and loving in these buildings. Since the heyday of the International Style, the designers of towers

Mad Men, Joan Holloway (Christina Hendricks) in the office, series 1 (2007).

have arguably become more overt. Foster + Partners in London have been responsible for some of the most flagrantly phallic buildings ever designed, supreme among them the building known as 30 St Mary Axe in the City of London, politely referred to as the Gherkin. There is any number of claims from the designers that the building's form was determined by the minimizing of wind shear. None of these really convinced the critics, or the general public, who have generally *only* understood the building as a giant phallus. That is not to detract from the Gherkin's considerable architectural qualities, rather to acknowledge that as *image* it only reads that way. Foster's work in fact has long had a powerfully masculine aesthetic, drawn from areas

Foster + Partners, executive washroom, Commerzbank, Frankfurt (1991–7).

of activity that are largely male preserves – aviation, motor racing, the factory floor. At a detail level, the attention to the washroom, an area of the most intimate male activity, is remarkable – it is always designed generously and with the utmost attention to surface quality. There is one supreme example of this sexualization of modernism, the Commerzbank, Frankfurt, also designed by Foster + Partners, where there is a washroom for male executives on the top floor with a urinal fixed to the exterior glass. Standing to relieve his bladder, cock in hand, the Commerzbank executive has an unparalleled view of the city as he pisses. In urinating over the entire city, it's also an enactment of an archetype of sexualized male power, a fact hardly lost on the urinal's users. Freud invokes pissing on the fire as the archetypal beginning of male sexual competition.[23] The reference to that here is clever, neat and funny, reiterating, but also sustaining, the myth of male authority.[24] There is no female equivalent, at least not yet.

five

Pornomodernism

ONE OF *Mad Men*'s attractions for its audience was the opportunity to experience, albeit vicariously, a whole set of forbidden pleasures (an early puff piece for the series claimed 'You'll Love the Way it Makes You Feel').[1] Alongside smoking and drinking, a lot of those pleasures were sexual in nature and had to do with experiencing roles that in real life for a largely middle-class audience had become unacceptable – but nevertheless carried an erotic charge. For such audiences, the power relations between men and women could be deeply unacceptable, but also attractive. The Draper character is both evil and compelling. Perhaps its appeal was possible because many of the behaviours it described were so firmly attached to the past. Something similar happened with pornography at the same time. An industry in frank decline at the time of writing, pornography likewise became an object of middle-class fascination, and in its retro form – for example in Taschen's publication of facsimiles of the first quarter-century of *Playboy* – respectable and even chic.[2] The same audience who might have read, approvingly, Andrea Dworkin's anti-pornography tirade *Pornography: Men Possessing Women* in 1981 was conceivably enjoying a television series on the anal porn entrepreneur Seymour Butts, or considering via some serious academic studies that *Playboy* circa 1962 was as much a vehicle for social liberation as it was of female repression.[3] And there's a good chance their coffee tables might have groaned under the weight of such respectable porn as Taschen's *Big Penis Book*, or the equally tombstone-like *Big Breast Book.* Erotica became big in the publishing world, via some remarkable first-person accounts.[4] And there were films celebrating a 'golden age' of porn in the 1970s, in which all was innocence and good fun.

Of these films, the best-known were *The People vs Larry Flynt*
(Miloš Forman, 1996) and *Boogie Nights* (Paul Thomas Anderson,
1997). Both were visually and spatially spectacular, situating early
1970s pornography in a set of precise architectural locations. In this
revised understanding of pornography, the genre was not simply
about bodies, but bodies in spaces which themselves carried erotic
meaning. The protagonist of *Boogie Nights,* the colossally endowed
Dirk Diggler (played by Mark Wahlberg) inhabits a series of immacu-
lately realized clubs, bars and houses, the designs of which themselves
connote sex. The house Diggler purchases with the proceeds of his
first movie is a studied exercise in 1970s baroque, whose pool, den
and spectacular bedroom, everything festooned with animal prints,
are all suggestive of sexual excess. What has been created in these
movies is what I think we should call 'pornomodernism'. This is
modernist space that has come to have, one way or another, specifically erotic connotations. This has happened almost entirely through
visual representation (in films, magazines, photographs) rather than
by design. It may not mean to, but in every case, pornomodernism
subverts, or undermines critically approved, *echt*-modernism. It's
a debased, mannered, baroque variant that challenges all the usual
assumptions about modernism's purity.

Nobody has understood this better than the German publisher
Benedikt Taschen, whose entire list brings together sex and buildings
through the medium of photography.[5] He publishes extensively on
modernist architecture at the same time as producing a very well
developed list of erotica – from the gay porn of Tom of Finland, to

Boogie Nights (dir. Paul Thomas Anderson, 1997).

expensive photographic surveys of middle-American swingers, to
Playboy reproductions. All of the erotic output is conditioned by a
powerful aesthetic in which the architectural setting is critical. The
outrageous scenarios drawn by Tom of Finland are outrageous because
of their lovingly depicted transgression of their urban settings. Naomi
Harris's recent book about swingers is as fixated on the minutiae of
middle-class American interiors as it is on the bodies of the swingers
themselves.[6] Likewise, Taschen's treatment of architecture is highly
selective, and sexualized, even where it uses well-known photographs
and photographers. When Julius Shulman photographed the Case
Study House #21, a small steel and glass bungalow by Pierre Koenig,
I doubt he thought too hard about the figures he used to populate it
– Shulman worked fast, intuitively and with what and whoever came
to hand. In Taschen's hands, however, Shulman's work becomes
pornomodern: the Taschen book on Koenig takes an unusually loaded
image for its cover, depicting the architect (toned, crew-cut, full of the
Right Stuff) in a room with an unusually good-looking, unidentified
woman. In the context of Taschen's list – and the physical context of
Taschen's LA store, stuffed with high-class erotica – it is impossible
not to read this image in sexual terms.

   In pornomodernism we are concerned primarily with visual
images rather than structures. As well as images, there is a great deal
of bad taste, a sometimes barmy sensibility in interior decoration,
the wilful misappropriation of otherwise restrained buildings and
a lot of fakery. Fantasy rather than reality, it's nevertheless vital to
the way modern architecture was disseminated and understood in
the U.S. Wherever one stands on pornography, whether consumer
or critic, one has to accept that American modernism has been
conditioned by it. Modern houses were so few and far between,
even in a modernist hotbed like LA, that their reception was far
more likely to be through the photographic image than any other
way. Of the producers of pornomodern fantasies, none is greater
than Hugh Hefner's magazine *Playboy*. Hefner understood better
than anyone before Taschen how sexual fantasies (albeit of a male,
heterosexual and conventional kind) might be enhanced, or even
created, by architecture. Architecture was an enduring topic for
Hefner, whether in the pages of the magazine he created or in his
own architectural creations. The *Playboy* lifestyle is inconceivable
without its architectural setting.

   Playboy in fact had an architectural manifesto: a plan for a
modern town house to be located on the Gold Coast, an upmarket

area of Chicago. It was never built, however, due to planning difficulties and Hefner's sudden enthusiasm for the house that became the first Mansion. However, it is vital in terms of *Playboy*'s imagination of what constituted an ideal modern house. The plan resurfaced as a nine-page spread on the 'Modern Town House' in the May 1962 issue, and it strongly influenced the subsequent design of the Playboy Clubs.[7] The proposed house had four storeys, five baths, a '24-ft entertainment wall' and was to cost $150,000.[8] Assertively modern, its horizontally oriented plate glass and concrete facade maintained the building line but otherwise contrasted with its surroundings, transparent where the adjoining brownstones were opaque. It was designed around pleasure, with the pool and entertainment walls set as key features. And in both the textual accounts and the images, it was a place very clearly meant for a single man rather than a family. Humen Tan's perspective sketches that appeared in both *Chicago Daily News* and *Playboy* articles showed a Jaguar (E-type X-KE) sports car parked in the basement-level parking garage; understood then as now as the most erotic car ever designed, its nose alluded to both male and female sexual organs (the radiator grille of the Mark 1 is a vulva, the front wings double cocks).

The Town House had other libidinal inventions: a glass wall in the pool, elaborating an idea Hefner had seen in his friend Harold Chaskin's newly built modern house in Miami, allowing the voyeur unimpeded views of the 'underwater activities'. There was also a generous 'rec room' (quite what the 'rec' was, was left undefined) on the same level, and a roof deck for 'summer simmering'.[9] The most memorable architectural feature of the proposed Playboy Town House was The Bed. Again a feature built into the actually existing Playboy Mansions from 1965, The Bed was circular, motorized, fully revolving and replete with all available contemporary communication devices. It also a clear sign, if ever one was needed, of its inventor's tendency to apparent agoraphobia – but by bringing the world to him, Hefner managed to turn this debilitating condition to his advantage. In Tan's detailed perspective sketch, The Bed appears to have been recently vacated. Full-length windows in the bedroom reveal its relationship to the dining area and the outside world. (Glimpses of the public world are possible, as everywhere in

Pierre Koenig, Case Study House #21, Wonderland Park Avenue, Los Angeles (1959). Also known as the Bailey House, after its original owners.

the House. The ceiling treatment is suggestive of the public world too, concrete spans forming a grid of recessed cuboids reminiscent of ceiling design in contemporary public buildings.) The bedroom is the centre of the playboy's operations, not a retreat from the world. Tan's image shows it at a critical moment in the evening: it has been electronically turned on its 360-degree base to take full advantage of a romantic fire. The drapes, glass door and skylight have been drawn back so that the star-flecked sky is almost our ceiling. The carousel-striped coverlet has been turned down. We've poured a brandy nightcap from a bar concealed in the rotating headboard, propped up our pillow, and push-buttoned several hours of balladry to add the proper final notes.[10]

The bedroom leads on to a bathroom, 'an enclosure of Olympian proportions', meant for more than one occupant:

> its focal point is a tiled tub whose size is akin to a miniature swimming pool, three feet deep and six feet square: its thermostatic controls keep the water in the tub at a constant temperature. Counterbalancing the tub is a ceramic-tiled vanity with twin lavatories and a wide mirror.[11]

Every part of the Town House was organized around seduction. Even the communications equipment, such as the telephones with their built-in answering machines, were designed as much to manage a complex, polygamous sex life as they were to deal with work.

The Playboy Town House and its variations, both built and unbuilt, offered a powerful corrective to the suburban orthodoxy that characterized American urban thinking in the 1950s and 1960s. Even if the playboy, like Hef, never left his pad, his was a defiantly urban, as opposed to suburban, mode of living; the pad was both in and of the city. Among the key images of the Town House is a perspective of the roof terrace, showing a party against the backdrop of the metropolis. Equally important was Tan's perspective sketch of the living room in which the nineteenth-century facades of East Bellevue fill the windows. Hefner's agoraphobia may have prevented his – and the magazine's – fullest engagement with the urban scene, but the city is a vital context, providing a set of images, allusions and aspirations that fed seduction, and could not be provided elsewhere. The scene portrayed here indicates an intensely visual relationship with the city, one that was of itself deeply voyeuristic. Hitchcock's *Rear Window* was released in 1954 and became an instant classic,

Rear Window
(dir. Alfred
Hitchcock, 1954).
First appearance
of 'Miss Torso',
as described by
'Jeff' Jeffries
(James Stewart).

supplying images that linked the urban apartment with sex through vision.[12] *Playboy*'s Town House draws on precisely the same context.

The model of sexuality represented by the Playboy houses was certainly questionable. As the novelist Martin Amis wrote in an interview with Hefner from 1985, the Playboy world presented itself as a new kind of model family. Unfortunately it was a 'family in which Poppa Bear gets to go to bed with his daughters' and in which 'the turnover in daughters is high'. Here 'no tensions, resentments or power struggles are admitted to or tolerated. At Playboy, everyone is happy all the time. Of every conceivable human institution, a family is what Playboy least resembles.' Hefner's somnolent lifestyle resembles nothing so much as a state of 'terminal depression'.[13] That said, as we have seen here, the Playboy world provides a clearly defined alternative to the suburban model, centred on the single-family home and childrearing. However flawed it may have been, it was an ideal that was highly influential despite, for practically *Playboy*'s entire readership, its unattainability.

If the Playboy Town House was never built, Hefner did incorporate many of its refinements into the first (Chicago) Playboy Mansion. Among them was a cave-like underwater bar with portholes into the pool from which swimmers could be observed. Decorated with photographs of favourite playmates, it was a space both imagined as, and used for, sex. As one magazine employee wrote, 'lots of screwing went on in the underwater bar and in the games room, on the pool table and under the pool table. There wasn't much to do in the house except do that.' The Town House's oversized bathtub – big enough to hold (as Hefner gleefully reported) 'half a dozen naked ladies' – was elaborated on a huge scale in the Playboy Mansion West in Los Angeles, which Hefner purchased on 3 February 1971 for $1,050,000. Located in Holmby Hills, an affluent district of Westwood, the house had 30 rooms before Hefner started his conversion. After renovation, the house was rather larger, and had acquired a basement grotto, illustrated in a rather gruesome *Playboy* photo spread in 1976. Here, Hefner wrote, 'he knew he could throw parties equal to those held anywhere in America or the world'. It was a complete world, providing Hefner with everything; he would never need to leave.[14]

The Porno House

The grotto's image has been much tarnished of late, not least by the suspicion in 2011 that it was the source of an outbreak of Legionnaire's disease – another wonderful, tragi-comic story of the Fall enacted through sex.[15] The Mansion was only one aspect of *Playboy*'s interests in architecture; it had favourite architects which it would happily misrepresent in its ever more refined search for the ideal bachelor pad. John Lautner was one, an architect who, it would appear, despised everything *Playboy* stood for but was nevertheless content to be written up in its pages – perhaps because he had so alienated swathes of the American architectural profession through sheer rudeness that his houses couldn't be reviewed anywhere else.[16] His houses have an extravagant, baroque character that appealed greatly to *Playboy*, although less so when their complex features failed to work as advertised.[17]

Lautner never meant it to be like this. A native of Michigan with a liking for natural materials, traditional craftsmanship and the outdoor life, he became celebrated as the creator of some of the most erotically charged modern spaces. Rather than providing the setting for art-house films, Lautner's work provided the frame for both James Bond and pornography, in both cases representing erotic values normally absent from modernism. Lautner's advocates – especially the architect Frank Escher, who has looked after his archive during its transition to the Getty Foundation – have worked hard to re-establish Lautner's modernist credentials, presenting him as an artist whose work speaks of sensitivity to nature, moral integrity and emotional restraint. The exhibition 'Between Earth and Heaven' says much about this process of re-evaluation through its title alone.[18] Lautner himself in no way courted his reputation: his spectacular, eccentric work emerged from a puritanical upbringing that he did not ever entirely leave behind. His most iconic houses were made for family life, for clients with young families. The sexualization of his work happened retrospectively, and via third parties, from the fictional spy James Bond to a pornographic movie director, artists and Taschen. This legacy is something his advocates have struggled to overcome.

Key to understanding Lautner is Midgaard, a family home built on the shores of Lake Superior to his mother Vida's interpretation of a traditional Norwegian design. Lautner was intimately involved in the design and construction of this cabin from 1921–8. According to Barbara-Ann Campbell-Lange, he helped his father raft logs across the lake and together they built a slipway up the side of the hill to the house. Here 'he learned the mechanics of the windlass and the practicality of handling rough timber – physical contact that spawned an innate confidence in materials and making.'[19] The house was, however, much more than a hobby: it was effectively a manifesto for a primitivist way of life, grounded in European philosophy. The cabin's name itself – Midgaard, the space between earth and sky in Norse legend – describes a philosophical bridge between spiritual and material life. Each summer during the cabin's construction, local university students would be hired as labourers, and their work would be accompanied by long conversations led by Lautner senior on 'philosophy, anthropology, education reform and the nature of civil society'.[20] Vida carved and painted the interior, with assistance from her children. Midgaard was therefore far more than a summer cabin. It was a project designed and built by a family as a collective, built, as it were, on a view of society with the family unit at its centre, and individual freedoms balanced by collective responsibilities. It is difficult to imagine a clearer statement of, by extension, the sublimation of the libido into healthy work.

The existence of Midgaard and its crucial role at a formative stage of Lautner's childhood motivate the nature-oriented account of the architect in the exhibition 'Between Earth and Heaven'. It very much affirms Lautner's own sensibility, evident in his frequent, career-long trashing of Los Angeles, the city where he nevertheless spent practically all his life. LA was 'too rotten to imagine', and a place of 'indescribable ugliness', he declared on moving there; in despair about it, he considered moving back to Taliesin where he had been in practice with Frank Lloyd Wright, to Boston or even Rio de Janeiro. This early view does not seem to have much changed. Writing in 1990, he gloomily referred to LA as 'Junkland . . . fast food, fast deals, fast everything'. Life there was simply protracted 'exile' from the health-giving landscape of Midgaard.[21]

Unfortunately, Lautner had so alienated the U.S. architectural press that his work had no other outlet than the popular media, and

John Lautner, Elrod House, 1968. View of main living area, looking towards pool.

for good or ill, it is as much a product of those media as anything else. It was a disaster for Lautner's reputation as a serious architect – but it gave him plenty of business from people who didn't care about such things. One client was Arthur Elrod, an interior designer with whom he collaborated on a 5,700-square-foot complex – 'house' is far too prosaic a word – above Palm Springs. It was a technological tour de force, with Playboy Bed-style controls for 'everything' from the sleeping quarters, while materially it was a tough, masculine take on its extraordinary desert setting. *Playboy* wrote of the 'seclusion and panoramic setting of an eagle's nest'; *House and Garden* wrote

Elrod House, view of master bedroom.

of 'rugged materials' that could 'take the desert climate without flinching', 'used in massive quantities'.²² Most famously the Elrod House was used as a set for the James Bond film *Diamonds Are Forever* (1971), and became inextricably associated with (admittedly stylized) sado-masochistic violence. *Diamonds* is the campest and most overtly sexualized of the Sean Connery movies: the main action takes place in and around the gaming rooms and floorshows of Las Vegas, the female leads are 'Pussy Galore' and 'Plenty O'Toole', the henchmen are a weirdly mismatched queer couple, milking their role for laughs. The Elrod House scene occurs about halfway through the film, at which point Bond has been kidnapped and rendered unconscious by arch-enemy Blofeld and brought to the home (in reality, the Elrod) of Willard Whyte, a young entrepreneur. On awaking he is beaten by two highly athletic women, 'Bambi' and 'Bumper'. The fight makes splendid use of the house's circular living room and pool; the women, themselves physically spectacular, emerge from the rocky topography of the house itself as if their overt sexuality is somehow a product of the house. Bond is first surprised and then badly beaten in a scene that reverses the normal expectation of male power – although highly sexualized they are also androgynous, and they are racially mixed too. Bond's fortunes seem to be on the wane, when he suddenly gains the upper hand, and in the final part of the scene holds them both at bay in the water as they pant orgasmically for breath. *Diamonds* is perhaps the best-known visual representation of Lautner's work, one which the curators of 'Between Earth and Heaven' struggled to come to terms with, turning a serious piece of architecture into a film set of no greater reality than Ken Adam's work for the Bond series (if anything it looks less plausible than Adam's work in the same movie).

Of all Lautner's houses, it is probably the Sheats House – now the Sheats-Goldstein House – that best represents the transform-ation of Lautner from the architect of nature to the architect of porn. Located at 10104 Angelo View Drive, high up in Beverley Hills overlooking Century City, the house was built in 1963 and has since the 1980s been substantially modified under the present owner, Jim Goldstein. Set on a precipitous, thickly wooded hillside, the house has a complex plan on two levels, comprising two roughly interlocking triangles. The western triangle houses the guest bed-rooms, accessed by a concrete walkway; each room is a kind of concrete cell, faced in glass, entirely visible from the outside. Moving eastwards through the house, the other triangle contains a high living area with a pyramidal concrete ceiling, studded with 750 drinking glasses that provide the space with a gentle, dappled light. The living area extends seamlessly out to a concrete deck containing the pool that reflects the city. Built underneath the main living area is the master bedroom suite with some remarkable features: two large, leather-covered beds, one triangular in form aligned directly with the full-length windows and the spectacular view over Century City; an entirely glass bathroom, open to view from the deck outside; windows on the wall directly above the main bed providing a view into the swimming pool. Throughout the house,

'Bumper' and 'Bambi' in
Diamonds are Forever
(dir. Guy Hamilton, 1971).

spaces flow into one another; mirrors reflect the inhabitants, and glass allows inhabitants to see and be seen.

This house first came to public attention in a *Playboy* piece, written just a year after its construction. It refers to a house with a special design of pool: 'the master bedroom literally faced on the pool – not looking down on it, looking *into* it – on the other side of the glass was water. You peered through the panes and saw the bodies of the swimmers from underneath.' It was an effect that the author 'was later to observe in the underwater bar of Hugh M. Hefner's Playboy Mansion'.[23]

Lautner would have detested the comparison. He understood the house as the sublimation of the nuclear family, absorbed in luxuriant nature, and protected from the horrors of contemporary LA. His original client was Helen Taylor Sheats (1910–1999), a reasonably successful artist, who worked closely with Lautner on the project. Her memorial website describes her as a collaborator on the house, and on three other projects attributed to Lautner of which one – the Sheats apartments – was built.[24] Sheats was politically liberal, active in the civil rights movement and sometime board member of the Highlander School in Tennessee, a radical non-segregated school. In 1942 she had married an educator, Paul Henry Sheats, then employed directly by Los Angeles City Hall, but subsequently a professor in the Faculty of Education at UCLA. Both were powerfully committed to the principle of free access to education. The couple had two children, and the house was conceived of as a family home, first and foremost, never a bachelor pad. The rhetoric of 'Between Earth and Heaven' underlines the natural imagery. The device of the roof with its drinking glasses is analogous to the forest of upstate Michigan, writes Campbell-Lange. This 'primeval' space is the one Lautner discovered as a boy, 'for which he continually

John Lautner, Sheats-Goldstein House (1963 onwards), photographed in 2009.

yearned, and which he strove to rediscover through the techniques of architecture.'[25] Its effect is 'like trees in the forest'.[26]

This impression – the house as ethereal and abstract – is flatly contradicted by its existence since 1972 when Jim Goldstein bought it. Goldstein, a flamboyant multimillionaire with a fortune based – probably, though no one is quite sure – on real estate, has developed the house constantly from 1980 onwards, first with Lautner's own input and after the architect's death with Lautner's business partner Duncan Nicholson. The latest addition is an installation by the light artist James Turrell below the main

Sheats-Goldstein House, master bedroom in 2009.

bedroom. The precise nature of Goldstein's success remains unclear, a mystery that he himself is keen to maintain. His public persona, including that of the residence, which is maintained like a semi-public museum, could not be more clearly drawn, however. Goldstein's interests as declared on his business card are 'Fashion Architecture Basketball' and besides his development of the house, he is well known as a fanatical follower of NBA games, attending upwards of a hundred per season; his simultaneous devotion to fashion sees him attend all major European fashion shows. Goldstein's attire is legendary, and plenty of examples of it can

Sheats-Goldstein House, dressing room in master bedroom with view into pool, 2009.

be seen in the house. A typical outfit is a python-skin suit with matching hat; his patronage of fashion designers has been as extravagant as that of architects. His taste in clothes overlaps with his taste in other areas, including architecture. This is an unusually sexualized wardrobe for a man now in his seventies – animal skins, tight trousers and jackets, shirts cut low to show off the body, a certain flirtation with androgyny (long permed hair, silk scarves), but of a kind now most securely located in heterosexual male culture. His look is in fact that developed in the early 1970s by

Sheats-Goldstein House, ground-floor bathroom, 2009.

Mick Jagger, and perfected a decade later by Aerosmith and Van Halen. Goldstein makes no attempt to conceal this. In *Interview* he describes in some detail his taste for tall, skinny girls (Californian girls, he complains, are too short and have breast implants) in much the same terms as his taste for Gaultier's fashion designs, or Lautner's architecture.[27]

So what, then, has become of the house under Goldstein's direction? If the house was ever legible in purely formalistic terms, there is little hope of that reading now. This is a house that celebrates the body, and that puts bodies on display. Its theatrical nature is inescapable. It is a heterosexual male fantasy house from the plan up, full of spaces to watch women, a realization of many of the ideals of the Playboy Town House. Its decoration by Goldstein in its current form only emphasizes this character. The walls form in effect a photographic hall of fame showcasing Goldstein's past and current sexual partners. Goldstein has since 1980 made a series of additions underlining the new character of the house. In 2009, he completed a pavilion by the light artist James Turrell, adjacent to the main house. A minimalist, chapel-like space with a skylight cut out in the roof to observe the changing effects of daylight, it is in most senses a standard iteration of the artist's work. But it has been 'improved' with the addition of a second skylight (Goldstein thought it looked better), a powerful music system and most importantly a great leather-covered bed, turning what was in Turrell's imagination no doubt an ascetic space of contemplation into another bedroom. Goldstein's work on the house has also included the creation of a master bedroom underneath the pool, with two beds, one facing directly outwards with views over Century City. The other bed lies by the pool windows; from the bed one can look up into the pool. The bedroom flows into a large open-plan bathroom area, which has among other features an outdoor shower on a public terrace. Inside, there is comparable sublimation of the bathroom area but this time with mirrors: an almost entirely mirrored space. Here one's entire body is reflected, made into image.[28]

Every aspect of this extraordinary house sublimates the body and puts it on display. However, the revealing and concealing of the body operates firmly within the regime of a furtive sexuality rather than health. This is a house for a voyeur, where bodies can be observed furtively, at a remove – the dark, cave-like space of the bedroom is a remodelling of a semi-public space; now it functions as an extremely private zone from which the swimmers can be seen. The voyeuristic qualities of the house have pedigree: the device of the pool windows is perhaps lifted from Adolf Loos's unbuilt project for a house for the African American jazz singer Josephine Baker. Here, Loos envisaged a basement room from which (male) visitors to the house could watch Baker swimming, an explicitly erotic, exotic spectacle.[29] Sheats-Goldstein presents sexuality as essentially furtive. While it provides ample opportunity for the display of the body, and numerous spaces in which sex might occur,

Sheats-Goldstein House (1963–), interior, 2009.

its jokes (of which there are many) depend on understanding that sexuality is *normally* kept hidden. So the most sexualized spaces of the house, in the master bedroom, all play with voyeurism and/or exhibitionism, a duality that depends for its effect on the assumption that seeing a naked body, or being seen naked, is of itself extraordinary and, by extension, arousing.

There's a porn film directed by Andrew Blake, *Possessions* (1997), in which the house is inhabited by three surgically enhanced, stiletto-clad women who engage in a variety of lesbian sex scenes with each other in various parts of the house.[30] The title of the movie, and the fact that for the most part the only characters are women, makes clear the sexual politics and power embodied in the house. *Possessions* and the Sheats-Goldstein house were the subject of a later art installation by Dorit Margreiter, where the movie is projected behind a green door through which the viewer is invited to peek.[31] The inference is clear – whatever the heritage of Lautner's work in the sexual liberation and experimentation of modernist LA, sex is imagined here as something essentially repressed, something that functions precisely because of its secret nature. Goldstein himself participates in this dynamic, routinely opening his home to visitors; such visits can be arranged via his website, and are a significant part of his activity. Part of their attraction consists in the play with boundaries of public and private, the opportunity, in other words, to see the private world of a public figure; and there is no significant barrier to what the visitor may see or not see during a visit; the house is more or less completely open to view in an exhibitionistic scheme, in which Goldstein undoubtedly derives pleasure from his admirable openness. But what this makes clear, underlining the physical trans-formation of the house under Goldstein's ownership, is the extent to which the house is now only interpretable through the lens of sex, rather than that of naturalism. Whatever the desires of Lauter's advocates, the house now much more readily corresponds to the pornomodernism of the Playboy Town House than it does to the Midgaard of the architect's childhood.

I made it to several of Lautner's houses, including Elrod and (most memorably) Sheats-Goldstein. In the latter I was taken around by a member of Goldstein's entourage, well used to dealing with foreign visitors; she was flirtatious in a well-drilled way, but very charming with it. Goldstein's openness was impressive and unusual. I wandered at will through the house for hours, jumped on the beds, inspected his wardrobe and his antique Rolls, admired the photographs of friends and lovers, and of the man himself – nothing, it seemed, was off limits. What remained at the end was a strange emptiness, though, as if once everything had been exposed, there was nothing left. There's a photograph on what passes for a mantelpiece of Pamela Anderson emerging naked from Goldstein's pool, so supernaturally enhanced and glistening she no longer seems exactly human. That, curiously, was the image that stayed with me afterwards – an image in which everything pointed towards sex, but remained at the level of fantasy. Sheats-Goldstein is an occa-sional residence, but like most examples of Californian modernism, it mainly exists to provide a fantasy of an erotically liberal state, a fantasy that earns the building's keep. So it's literally a stage set that can be rented by the day, a venue for upscale parties, or at its dullest merely a space for corporate events. For a few moments you really believe the fantasy – but like pornography itself, the reality is more prosaic.

six

The Hotel

OF ALL THE architectural types in this book, it is probably the hotel that most readily connotes sex. I spent a lot of time in hotels writing it, and a lot of time consequently thinking about sex, though sadly nothing more than that (I was occasionally kept awake in various parts of the world by *other* people having sex, of course, one of the hotel's recurrent hazards). The hotel is the space where marriages are traditionally consummated, where extramarital affairs take place, where old sexual relationships are rekindled and where new ones may be formed. The sex industry is never far away, whether in the form of prostitution or in the routine provision of pornographic films for private viewing. The hotel alludes to sex in its interior decoration; the bed is the key feature, exaggerated with extravagant cushions or pillows, or by sheer size. After all, you commonly rent a room based on the size of the bed, not the efficiency of the air conditioning or the pile of the carpet. Its decor may be overtly sexual, even in otherwise sober establishments. In one Amsterdam hotel I stayed in, the rooms were decorated with life-size images of a young couple engaged in foreplay. In a disconcerting *trompe l'oeil* move, they seemed to emerge from the bed.[1]

It's in the movies that the hotel's sexual connotations are most powerfully represented. In Alfred Hitchcock's iconic movie *Psycho* (1960), two hotels frame the action. In the first, the female protagonist, played by Janet Leigh, is introduced to the audience in an aerial shot of a Phoenix hotel at midday; zooming in through the window, we find her in bed with her (married) lover in an illicit daytime tryst. Desiring to formalize the affair but prohibited by the likely cost of her lover's divorce, she steals the then huge sum of $40,000 from her employer; this leads, in due course, to her fatal stay at the Bates Motel. In the first case, the hotel represents the site of illicit sex, an anonymous downtown building whose purpose is seemingly to frame such activity (Hitchcock's aerial shot, steadily zooming in on the tryst, carries the implication that the Janet Leigh/John Gavin scene is just one of any number of these scenes). The second case represents the consequences of such behaviour, a hotel whose psychosexual dynamic is fatal for the main protagonist. In both, the hotel, and sex, are intimately connected, the building the perfect frame for the act, the latter a peculiarly perverse and horrific one. Hitchcock understood this connection perfectly. In many ways it is his imagination of the hotel as a sexual space, with its attendant morality, that now frames our own understanding of the hotel's possibilities.[2] The hotel in Hitchcock is *always* erotically charged. In the hotel one may easily become someone else; the transitory nature of residence makes temporary liaisons easy and possible; the simple anonymity of the space (all those corridors, lack of natural lighting, closed doors, repetition of simple elements) make it easy to hide. Now all of this implies a particular conception of sexuality. Our understanding that these anonymous, temporary, exceptional spaces connote sex *at all* says a great deal about Western concepts of sexuality. In other words, for it to operate, it must be hidden. The hotel is perhaps the best example we have of the tension between our public and private values: 'Sexual desire and good citizenship don't play by the same rules', writes Esther Perel. Civility might be what we outwardly proclaim, but it makes for boring sex. We perhaps need those spaces of exception for sex to function at all.[3]

The Love Hotel

In many countries there is hotel form that has developed precisely for sex, not least, in an unlikely piece of convergent evolution, in Japan and Brazil. The geographical locations of these buildings differ, but in other respects there is strange commonality.[4] The principle is the same in each case: a hotel room that can be rented by the hour, at any time. The main market in each case is established couples, married or not, who simply lack space and/or time to be together, alone; both Japanese and Brazilian middle-class urban living can be crowded. The Japanese situation also has unusual time pressures, with exceptionally long and arduous commutes to the family home; the love hotel provides a means of intimate space close to the workplace as well as, not unusually, a place for exhausted salarymen to sleep if they have failed to make it home. Although for the most part

Opening scene from *Psycho* (dir. Alfred Hitchcock, 1960).

both Japanese and Brazilian hotels provide space for licit sexual activity, they also go to some lengths to ensure a much greater kind of anonymity than that normally provided by regular hotels. The Japanese version provides an almost completely automated service: rooms are chosen from a standardized menu, interaction with reception staff is minimized and if car parking is provided, a curtain-like device known as a *noren* covers the registration plate at the front of the car to prevent identification.[5] The hotels are normally located in secondary zones – by motorway underpasses, or railway stations, or in back streets – rather than in public areas. And their facades are normally blank, windowless, offering no view on to the street. The love hotel is thus a secretive form, a mode of spatial organization designed, as far as possible, to ensure the outward propriety of the clients. Despite this secretive character, the love hotel has always been, and remains, in spite of some decline in recent years, immensely popular. Sarah Chaplin writes (in 2007) of 30,000 love hotels in the country as a whole, of a ¥7-trillion-per-annum business (about £30 billion at the time of writing), of half Japan's sexual activity taking place in a love hotel of one kind or another and a large, though unquantifiable, part of Japan's entire population having been conceived in one.[6] The love hotel exists, she argues, to address very real deficits in intimacy – as well as the threats to intimacy posed by working cultures and by cramped living conditions, more than 15 per cent of Japanese couples do not, apparently, share a bed, further reducing the possibility of intimacy.

In spite of the overwhelming normality of the love hotel and
its centrality to Japanese sexual culture, the *form* of the love hotel
is pure fantasy. The most spectacular case cited in the study is the
Meguro Emperor, a fantasy of medieval Europe with distinct allusions
to northern Germany.[7] Outward appearances are, however, generally
muted by comparison with the fantastic possibilities of the interior.
The act of choosing the room, a ritual part of the experience, is
essentially a choice between fantasies. Cute domestic style ('Hello
Kitty') clashes with the more expected sadomasochistic imagery. But
more common are themes that by Western standards do not connote
sex at all: Mount Fuji, New York City, outer space. In some senses
any imagery has erotic connotations given the right cultural context,
a fact underlined not only by the prevalence of touristic imagery
but also by the excitement potentiated by the mere presence of a
Western-style bed. The bed was, Chaplin writes,

> thought to be the quintessential ingredient in a love hotel
> interior, effectively turning the bed from a place to sleep into
> a rotating erotic stage or adult toy with pornographic and
> kinaesthetic potential, explicitly signalling the bed's primary
> purpose for sex.[8]

The Brazilian example has some similarities. In Brazil, the love hotel
is a *motel*, but here the term exclusively connotes a place of short stays
for sex and is understood to be quite different from the standard
hotel, the *pensão* (small, family-run lodging), and also from the *hotel
'suspeito'* ('suspicious' hotel), which is to say a hotel where prostitution is tacitly allowed.[9] In the case of the *motel*, certain characteristics
stand out. First is (like Japan) the length of the stay, a matter of an
hour or two normally, and a consequent business model based on
an extremely high turnover of rooms (*alta rotatividade*). Second
is (again like Japan) the care devoted to assuring the anonymity of
clients. The hotels are located, invariably, on the urban periphery,
close to main highway exits, allowing rapid access, relatively unob-
served. The registration procedure is extremely attenuated, involving
minimal interaction between client and staff.

In their classic 1982 study of the phenomenon Dinah
Guimaraens and Lauro Cavalcanti also describe a curious culture of
anonymity between clients, such that those who know each other and
who accidentally choose the same time to visit the *motel* conventionally choose to ignore each other's presence. Anonymity, as in Japan,

is also effected through the treatment of the car: parking is hidden, and car passengers routinely hide themselves on entering the motel complex, only emerging once safely by the door of the suite. The *motel* seems to have paid particular attention to the use of mirrors, not conventionally to increase the sense of space in a cramped interior but to allow the users of the room to see themselves as they have sex. Guimaraens and Cavalcanti illustrate this well. Summertime, a hotel in the well-to-do neighbourhood of Barra da Tijuca, is photographed to show the bed with an adjacent mirror covering one wall; it clearly leans inward towards the bed, making the reflection an inescapable part of the scene. Through such mirroring, the scene, as it were, is transformed into visual representation, allowing a distancing that is very likely of itself erotic.[10] And the life-size dimensions of the image, and its proximity, produce the illusion of human presence, literally doubling the scene, turning a tryst into an orgy, a scene clearly also erotic for most clients. Fourth is the *piscina* or swimming pool – although the tiny size of these precludes any swimming. Usually part of an interlinked network of tiny *piscinas*, the pool is symbolic rather than practical, connotative of sex in much the same way as it is in California: a space that implies nakedness. But its use here is mainly symbolic given its small size, and the urgency of the bed. The facade fantasy consists mainly in the evocation of an exotic other, distanced in time and place. The most elaborate example in the Guimaraens and Cavalcanti study is perhaps medieval France ('Le Chateau'), Egypt ('O Vale dos Reis'), Africa in general ('Safari'), Hollywood ('Love Story') and the Playboy Mansion ('Playboy').[11] The love hotel and its equivalents in the rest of the world is a fascinating, pragmatic solution to a pressing problem. It is however a fleeting phenomenon – the Guimaraens and Cavalcanti study of Brazil was done 30 years ago and even then has a sense of nostalgia about it, as if (as it in fact now is) it was a culture at the beginning of a long decline. As Brazilians have become richer and as their attitudes to sex have relaxed, the need for such secret spaces for sex has declined. The same pattern can be seen in Japan, where the love hotel has started to take on a somewhat quaint character.

The Westin Bonaventure Hotel, Los Angeles

However, everywhere, there will always be a demand for fantasy. Back in the U.S., the small-scale fantasies of the Brazilian motel are inflated to absurdity in Las Vegas, a city whose entire existence is predicated on a free market in fantasy. Albrecht and Johnson write: 'today's hotels are not just places to sleep' but 'offer escapist experiences in faraway worlds. Eroticism and escapism continue to charge the fantasy hotels of architects and artists today.'[12] What they describe, to put it another way, is the mainstreaming of tendencies in small-scale hotel building that might have been widespread, but were small scale, localized, and artisanal in mode. In contemporary Las Vegas, fantasy has been industrialized on the grandest imaginable scale. And it all has to do with sex. So in Las Vegas, the local design tactics seen in the love hotels of Tokyo or Rio are developed on a global scale: heavily themed rooms, suites with all imaginable amenities, rapid, impersonalized service. Not only that, but the fantasies played out through images in the love hotels are *precisely* the same as those in Las Vegas: New York City ('New York, New York'), Egypt ('Luxor'), Venice ('The Venetian'), ancient Rome ('Caesar's Palace'), Paris ('Paris Las Vegas'), the South Pacific ('Tahiti Village') and outer space ('Stratosphere'). This appears to be, to put it another way, a global language of fantasy. Vegas has huge industries at whose core is sex: prostitution is a major industry, as are weddings. The hotels are in some ways merely the sex industry's factory floor.

I was tiring of fantasy, however. As a case study hotel, I wanted one in which the erotic potential had been considered in design terms, rather than as surface fantasy. To put it another way, I was looking for a hotel that tried to make things happen in space, rather than merely providing images of these things: hence the Westin Bonaventure, Los Angeles, a 112-metre-tall, 35-storey atrium hotel designed and built by the architect-developer John Portman between 1974 and 1976. Located downtown at Bunker Hill on South Figeroa Street, it now lies close to a range of major cultural facilities (the Walt Disney Concert Hall, the Museum of Contemporary Art) but at the time of its construction, it was an exceptional development in a landscape of decline. It's important for various reasons, not least its scale, which is hard initially to comprehend – 1,354 guest rooms and 135 suites. The Bonaventure was conceived before the large-scale fantasization of the hotel seen in Vegas, but it is vastly more than a box with rooms. Then there is a rich literature around the building, including a famous, very flawed, critique by a philosopher, Fredric Jameson. And then there is the erotic character of the building itself. Portman's best work has been essentially erotic in that it provides spaces in which users' desires can be enacted. The Bonaventure is visually and spatially extremely rich – there are spaces all over this hotel to watch and be watched, to put oneself on display, to see without being observed, to be seen and then be moved (mechanically) out of sight; the erotics of this space are fantastically complex.

Portman (b. 1924) was responsible for the invention and, later, propagation of the atrium, a form that now defines countless hotels, conference centres and office complexes worldwide. However, his critical status is ambiguous. As he set himself up explicitly as an 'architect-developer', creating a company to build what he designed, he crossed the usual professional boundaries, in the process effectively removing his work – not that he personally would care all that much – from the category of art. So the architectural-critical reception of Portman's work is very like that of Disneyland – awed fascination mixed with outright disgust, with the latter predominating. At best, critics discuss Portman in the same terms as Venturi Scott Brown & Associates discussed the Las Vegas vernacular. There is an engagement with it, but an understanding of it as distinctly 'other'. Archigram's Peter Cook wrote in precisely these terms in a 1967 article for *Architectural Design*. 'The Hotel is Really a Small City' describes, in slack-jawed terms, the Peachtree Center in Atlanta, a scheme that in its form and location might as well have been, for an Architectural Association-trained Englishman of the mid-1960s, the moon.[13] Cook's admiration for the audacity of the atrium was tempered by his horror at the kitsch decor, a tension incomprehensible to the hotel's users, but for him, irresolvable. The principal French journal *L'Architecture d'Aujourd'hui* finally got around to discussing Portman in 1977, giving over ten pages to a profile and two building reviews. Troubled deeply by Portman's commercial success, it concluded, grudgingly, that he was a function of America's peculiar liking for commerce, and that in spite of that, he had produced some progressive work.[14]

Portman's status as pop culture rather than art is underlined by a famous photograph by the German artist Andreas Gursky depicting the atrium of Portman's Embarcadero Center hotel in San Francisco. Here Gursky turns his awed gaze to what is for him yet another manifestation of spectacular capitalism equivalent to his other subjects: stock exchange trading floors, sports stadiums, music festivals, horse races, discount supermarkets. The choice of Portman as subject is highly indicative of his perceived critical status, especially by the European profession. It is precisely Portman's engagement with what 'high' architecture normally disdains that makes him interesting. Unlike the mainstream modernists who provided his architectural context, Portman does not imagine the user of his buildings as a disembodied pair of eyes. His users have physical bodies; they eat, drink, shop, socialize, display, and the buildings provide spaces in which all of these things can happen.

Perhaps Portman's critical status is also coloured by the fact of his commitment to the city of Atlanta, where he studied at Georgia Tech, and has remained ever since. Disparaged by most architecture critics, Atlanta – like Las Vegas and other sun-belt cities – registered astonishing rates of growth at precisely the same time that northeastern cities were in frank decline. Portman's decision to concentrate on his home turf made good business sense. His first major project was the Regency Hyatt House on Atlanta's downtown Peachtree Street. This hotel complex, completed in 1967, was the first iteration of the atrium hotel. At 24 storeys and 103 metres in height, it was not especially tall, but its atrium reached the full height of the building, provoking astonished reactions from early visitors. A revolving restaurant, the Polaris, in the unmistakable form of a flying saucer, topped the otherwise unremarkable exterior facade.[15] The Regency Hyatt was accompanied the same year by the Peachtree Center a few hundred metres to the north. This office complex had no atrium but it did have an extensive pedestrianized area at its base, performing some of the same functions.

For 1967, both the atrium at the hotel, and less ostentatiously the pedestrian plaza at the foot of the Peachtree Center, were manifesto-like statements of intent, in which buildings were redefined around their social life. The official photography of these spaces is sometimes brilliant, showing off the potential of the space in casual lunchtime encounters. The Regency Hyatt made the movement through the interior into a spectacle: something that could be experienced *as* an experience. It was a reaction, Portman later recalled, to his experience of Atlanta's existing modern architecture, built on a dense, tight grid and comprised largely of blocks of cells with virtually no space for circulation or socialization. Outwardly, the Regency Hyatt gives no clue as to its interior – it is a slab not very different from those that surround it – but its low entrance suddenly gives way to a vast interior space whose dimensions cannot be guessed from the outside. This calculated shock effect is then elaborated by the complexity of the space itself: a baroque arrangement of balconies and open walkways, with elevators moving up and down: up, counter to any existing intuition about the correct behaviour of hotel elevators, *through the roof*. It is a space of ceaseless animation that of itself sustains the

John Portman, Peachtree Center, Atlanta (1967). Photograph published in 1976.

visitor's interest – at least the visitor of 1967, before, thanks to Portman, such things became common.

The attention to the body of the visitor in this early work is critical. The surrounding buildings of Atlanta's downtown, apart from a few scattered remnants from the nineteenth century, were largely sub-Miesian offices, whose aim was simply to project an image of modernity. The idea that buildings might constitute spaces that could be animated by the presence of people did not figure. Portman had different ideas:

> People enjoy watching a changing scene. This is very obvious.
> I learned from visiting the Tivoli gardens in Copenhagen that
> one of its main attractions is the opportunity to watch other
> people . . . Some people enjoy watching other people more than

they enjoy having other people watch them; others like to be on the stage, part of the passing parade.[16]

Scopophilia, or the pleasure in looking, is a key theme in Freud; he also repeatedly invokes and explores things we would now call voyeurism or exhibitionism; in Lacan, later, the concept of the gaze links looking with the expression of sexual power; Laura Mulvey more recently has explored how, in mainstream culture at least, cultures of looking invariably put women at a disadvantage.[17] One doesn't need to be a psychoanalyst or a cultural historian to understand this: the sexual potential of the gaze is what drives nearly all popular visual culture. Portman's concern for people-watching is underwritten by a larger concern for social space. Motivated by a visit to Brasília in 1960 (he was there for its inauguration), an experience he found horrifying, he resolved to make human activity the core of his buildings. 'Buildings should serve people, not the other way around', he wrote in 1977.[18] In interview later with Paul Goldberger, chief architecture critic of the *New York Times*, he elaborated:

> architecture has suffered from a concentration on things and not on the innate reactions of people to environmental circumstances. Therefore we have attempted to focus on people – to create spaces for human enjoyment.[19]

So how precisely might this eroticized social life show itself? Back in Los Angeles, the Bonaventure is terribly unpromising at first sight: a bunker of a building, defensive and inward-looking, in which the main access would be via the parking garage. The Bonaventure occupies a whole city block, and at ground level is defined by a huge, two-storey podium in *béton brut* (raw concrete). Below this, underground, are several levels of car parking, with elevators taking drivers up to lobby level. The main pedestrian entrance, such as it is, is a small hole punched in the Figueroa Street facade – no grand declaration, nothing of the old porte-cochère, nothing to mark ceremonially the passage from the street. The main part of the building, a cluster of five towers in bronze glass, occupies the northern half of the podium, freeing up the roof level of the southern half for a good-size swimming pool and an area for sunbathing. The towers themselves are clustered in a symmetrical arrangement, with four 30-storey towers clustered around a 37-storey core. Each one is cylindrical; there's something inevitably, boringly phallic about the forms and their relation to the

John Portman, Westin Bonaventure Hotel, Los Angeles (1976). Pedestrian bridge crossing South Flower St.

base. Finished in bronze glass, the towers give nothing away, merely reflecting their surroundings. This is a defensive building, an idea that tends to be confirmed by the other allusion the towers seem to make, to a cluster of missiles and a launch pad.[20] Rising eight storeys above the podium, although not easily distinguishable from the main structure, is a glazed structure around the base of the towers forming the internal atrium. The eight elevators rise through this structure, as at the Regency Hyatt, to burst through the roof, continuing on up the side of the central tower to arrive at a revolving restaurant. On top of this is a helipad. The four smaller towers house the guest rooms.

The atrium holds the greatest interest. Here, as at the earlier Regency Hyatt, Portman makes a calculated contrast between the entrance and the spectacle of the atrium. Here it is if anything more exaggerated, partly because (and here we must begin to invoke one of the chief complaints about the building, its confusing layout) it is so hard to find. A maze of dark, low-ceilinged corridors lead suddenly on to the atrium, which is simultaneously big and complex. It is its complexity that marks it out from the earlier hotels. Unlike the Embarcadero, or the Regency Hyatt, this does not appear at first sight to be a single space at all, but a constellation of interlocking spaces, only some of which can be seen at any one time. It has, in

Westin Bonaventure Hotel.

other words, precisely none of the panoptical qualities of the earlier spaces in which guest-room doors open directly out on to the atrium (one of the qualities that so fascinated Andreas Gursky – you can see who goes in, and who goes out of the hotel rooms, a quality with voyeuristic dimensions, but also potentially inhibiting). This is a furtive space, whose essential character might be said to be that of a *forest* – dark, complex and impossible to perceive as a totality. The ceilings are low; the space dissolves into numerous alcoves and break-out areas. Then the next three levels have shops and restaurants, famously difficult to find, for they cluster around the towers,

Westin Bonaventure Hotel, details of atrium. Note gym equipment in pods.

Westin Bonaventure Hotel, view from revolving restaurant looking northwest.

and given the symmetry of the whole design, orientation is difficult. The stores and restaurants have the quirk of being open to the atrium in the manner of street cafes; occupants can see out into the atrium and be seen, although they also provide cover for more intimate spaces. The walkways around the towers linking these spaces of consumption also have a number of quirks. They are punctuated vertically by the elevators, which are transparent, cylindrical and festooned with circus lights. And horizontally, the walkways are punctuated by ovoid balconies jutting out from the tower cores. There are a lot of these, and they're well appointed with pleated leather benches, proposing a leisurely stay. That in reality they're not much used is more a function of the relative failure of the commercial aspects of the atrium – of which more later – but they are important in terms of the argument about people watching. Here are the ideal spaces to do it: comfortable, excellent sightlines and practically obscuring the viewer if necessary. The opulence of these balconies and their sightlines, and their clear relation to Portman's argument about people watching indicate that we should consider them in terms of an erotic economy.

The sudden appearance of a $90-million hotel in the centre of LA produced commentary on topics ranging from Portman's

Westin Bonaventure Hotel, seating pod in atrium.

regeneration strategy ('what this country needed was not new cities but a restructuring of our old cities') to the scale and variety of food on offer ('I have dined in the future and it is somewhere at the Bonaventure').[21] There was also some commentary on the style of the project, with some difficulty in locating it in terms of architectural history. Paul Goldberger's postmodern comparison of the Bonaventure with its close neighbour the Biltmore (constructed 1923, but refurbished at the same time as the Bonaventure's construction) held that the older hotel, with its simple interiors, white decor and art by Jim Dine, was actually the more contemporary design. Portman's new hotel by contrast, full of nooks and crannies, seemed to belong to a different time. The imagery of the Bonaventure was futuristic, *Brave New World* a frequent shorthand reference point, but the very invocation of Futurism spoke of a moment long past.

Confusion is in many ways the hotel's leitmotif, which for left-leaning intellectuals was described most clearly in Fredric Jameson's essay 'The Cultural Logic of Late Capitalism' (1984). Jameson uses the figure of the Bonaventure to describe, and critique, a state of affairs in which capitalism has evolved urban structures beyond the capacity of human beings to understand them. The well-known argument derives from Jameson's own confusion in the space of the Bonaventure hotel, an experience that – for a philosopher – is described at some length. He starts with the entrance, or rather, entran*ces*, none of which is the correct one, seemingly. To enter the building by foot involves a whole series of reversals, so that to reach the registration desk you have to descend counter-intuitively from what appears to be a lobby. The great central atrium itself no longer reads as a single space, but something far more complex, full of distractions, seemingly busy when it is in fact quite empty. Among the distractions are the glass elevators, constantly rising and falling through the glass roof. Functional in part, they are also symbolic, Jameson thinks, of a space that has mechanized even the simplest processes, in so doing denying visitors even the most basic control over their movement. 'Here the narrative stroll has been underscored, symbolized, reified and replaced by a transportation machine which becomes the allegorical signifier of that older promenade we are no longer allowed to conduct on our own.' No matter that the 'promenade', for which Jameson is suddenly nostalgic, was itself subject to any number of social, if not mechanical, controls: the elevator here means the subjugation of free will.

Then there is the account of the commercial aspects of the plan. The hotel may be popular, Jameson concedes, but the confusing layout, in particular its symmetry, led to profound navigational problems. For each store, 'even if you once located the appropriate boutique, you would be most unlikely as to be fortunate a second time.' The result is a building that has produced an entirely new kind of space, analogous, he speculates, to the changes wrought in late twentieth-century global capitalism. The confusion wrought by the space of the hotel and the incapacity of the human visitor to perceive it intelligibly as a whole can, he writes,

> stand itself as the symbol and analogon of that even sharper
> dilemma which is the incapacity of our minds, at least at

present, to map the great global multinational and decentred communicational network in which we find ourselves caught as individual subjects.

The precise manifestation of this at the Bonaventure is what Jameson terms, in a neologism, a 'hypercrowd', an agglomeration of individuals, moving independently in all directions, contained by the same building, but unable to perceive themselves as a collective.[22]

Jameson's piece is extremely well-known, less for what it says about the hotel than for the way it appropriates it as a symbol of global capital: a baffling network, imperceptible as a whole, evading the understanding of mere humans. As it happens, Jameson was rather late in on the act. 'The Cultural Logic of Late Capitalism' in fact draws on a widespread popular view of the hotel, widely propagated since its opening: the Bonaventure as spectacle, but a somewhat confusing one. Almost all observers regard the hotel with a kind of detachment: its futuristic imagery, its allusions to space flight (the elevator/rockets blasting through the roof/sky), the mirrored glass silos repelling the inward gaze, the massive concrete bunker at ground level protecting the core from its dangerous surroundings – almost everything about the hotel seems designed to create, first and foremost, a sense of otherness, and the critics responded accordingly. So Jack Smith, in a Ballardian piece for the LA Times, wryly depicts the building in the same terms as 'the utopian cities promised in the sci-fi comic strips and movies of the 1930s', or later 'the fertile new world to be built for us in outer space'; looking up from the main floor of the atrium, Smith observes 'overhanging rings of concrete which, like Saturn's rings, circle the centre tower'.[23] Lois Dwan, a food critic, described an extraordinary landscape with 'craggy walls, juts and crevasses', a 'Broom Hilda' landscape, referring to the popular syndicated cartoon strip about a 1,500-year-old witch with a voracious appetite for men.[24] Paul Goldberger came to much the same conclusion:

> There is no way to gain one's bearings in this futurist paradise: if two people were to arrange to meet in the lobby there would be no way for them to rendezvous unless each one came equipped with a compass . . . the Bonaventure is all futurist, brave new world imagery, and there is less concern than there was in the early Portman hotels for what a hotel actually exists to do in the public realm.[25]

For Smith, the adventure has a distinctly libidinal form. His amiable *flânerie* around the hotel's lobby finds him not only a decent liverwurst sandwich, but also the attentions of a pretty waitress, with whom he has an extended discussion about the colour of the interior decor. Disappointed at first by her attire (too 'demure') he is delighted to find her long beige skirt 'slit down the front . . . every step she took delivered a flash of leg'.[26]

Did the Bonaventure work? Did it become a libidinal paradise, a space of relentless flirtation? Well no – at least not on any of the occasions that I have visited. One area in which Jameson was certainly right is – still – the failure of the commercial units, which decades on still struggle for tenants. I wondered if there was a hidden life to the hotel, an existence in which the very unintelligibility of the layout might permit – like an eighteenth-century masked ball – a temporary suspension of social norms. Or, like Ballard's *High Rise*, had it become an exceptional space, sealed from the world, subject only to its own libidinal laws? Or maybe it was a space for furtive gay cruising, all those nooks and crannies providing endless scope for impromptu semi-public sex? Sadly I didn't see any of these possibilities, but it was good to think about them over a martini in the revolving bar. Portman thought about these things too, I'm sure, or he wouldn't have built in the way he did. People and their interactions with each other in space fascinated him. The results of his experiments have been found in hotel design everywhere ever since.

seven

What Would a Feminist City Look Like?

I FIRST LOOKED at architecture seriously while an art student in London during the 1980s when the Canary Wharf office development was under way. Then Europe's largest construction project, it piqued my interest, and it being close to Goldsmiths, where I was studying, I took to cycling around it at weekends. During the week I asked teaching staff a few questions. If I had been studying on an architecture programme, perhaps someone could have answered them, but the responses were negative in every way: Canary Wharf was proscribed territory from which we were forbidden to take an interest. It was, I could only infer, Thatcherite, to do with private finance, and most importantly it was built by and for men in suits. Further, it was clear in the strange climate of the time that no right- (or, rather, left-) thinking person should take an interest in architecture at all, for it was all, only, the representation of capital. I later found a quotation from H. G. Wells that expressed precisely this thought – leaving a meeting in early twentieth-century London he looked up at the huge, surrounding buildings and declared them representative of the scale of the task that lay in front of his comrades in order to achieve socialism.[1] Socialism was one thing; feminism was another, in retrospect far stronger, element in the ideological mixture of the time. Canary Wharf, and by extension all architecture, was not only a product of capitalism but of male capitalists, and we all had absorbed enough Andrea Dworkin to know that men were evil and would in some future society be redundant. Along with men would go architecture; to be replaced by what? It wasn't clear exactly, but almost all radical movements of the time had outward forms that were temporary, mutable and low-key. If there weren't buildings to represent the radical future, there were certainly a lot of soft fabrics. I knew plenty of radical, sometimes separatist, feminists, and true to form they spent a lot of time knitting and quilting, and wearing the results. Their architecture was, as it were, best represented by the quilt: a flexible, cheap, home-made shelter that could be worn, and if pushed, lived in. I knew – I'd seen it often enough at festivals.

Now my memory of all this is uncertain, but the feminist antipathy to architecture was real, enough to dissuade me from studying it properly. It was only much later, thanks to the sociologist Sharon Zukin, that I understood it was possible to take an informed interest in the built environment *and* take a sympathetic interest in radical politics. Zukin's approach, more pragmatic than that of her colleagues on the European side of the Atlantic, understood buildings as complex facts that demanded to be understood rather than simply dismissed as politically incorrect. My revisiting the feminist question was out of real curiosity to understand better how architecture and feminism could have become so hostile to each other in the 1980s, and two sub-questions – was it really all as sex-negative as I remembered? And what did a feminist architecture look like?

The problem was clear enough. Even the greatest enthusiast for architectural modernism would have to concede that its greatest productions were made by men, for women to inhabit: women were informed clients at best.[2] But even in buildings they had helped design, women could find themselves remarkably compromised, the Farnsworth House (Mies van der Rohe, 1945–51) being a fine example. An architectural icon, it was criticized by both critics and the client on completion for its lack of compromise as regards the living arrangements; the way in particular the house put the client on display, especially at night when the interior lighting and lack of window decoration (forbidden by Mies) turned the house into a beacon. It was briefly a public attraction too, further discomforting the client. Elizabeth Friedman quotes Farnsworth's own summary of the lived experience of the house: 'do I feel implacable calm? . . . The truth is in this house with its four walls of glass I feel like a prowling animal, always on the alert.' The problem was, Friedman explained, 'the way the house foregrounded Farnsworth's single life and her middle aged woman's body struck at the heart of American anxiety.'[3] Perhaps a latter-day Farnsworth would have achieved different results, but in any case what is at stake in the account is the idea that men build, and women inhabit the results.

It has often been noted that architecture tended to be built by men and inhabited by women; the building and the inhabiting were different things, nowhere clearer perhaps than in the formal example of the skyscraper.[4] In fictional form, such a statement of rigid sex roles defines *The Fountainhead*.[5] And so on. None of this sits well in a world of putative sexual equality, enshrined in equal opportunities legislation since the 1960s. If feminism has determined (and continues to determine) the nature of sexual relationships between men and women since the 1960s, it follows that it also helps determine the way those relationships are housed or otherwise represented in built form. However, architecture at the time of writing remained structurally sexist. In the U.S., architectural training at the time of writing was equally balanced between men and women, but the industry remained male dominated. In 2010, according to the U.S. Bureau of Labor statistics, over 70 per cent of the U.S. profession was male.[6] Given the nature of the architectural profession, this chapter is less about recovering a line of hitherto neglected female architects. Following the line taken by the art historian Linda Nochlin, when she famously asked 'Why Have There Been No Great Women Artists?', I doubt there is such a lineage, with obvious exceptions such as Lina Bo Bardi or Denise Scott-Brown.[7] The questions here are more structural: how did feminism and architecture relate to each other, if at all? And how did feminism imagine sex in relation to buildings, again, if at all?

Feminist Space

Feminist architecture by and large does not exist – at least in nothing like the same terms as, to give two comparators, feminist sociology or feminist art. Feminist architecture's existence is for the most part not a material practice, but a set of discourses. One starting point is the language used by feminists to describe the condition of modern femininity, language often architectural in nature (the home as a 'prison', domesticity as 'captivity', the 'gilded cage'). These places of intersection also include, more specifically, the burgeoning conversation about suburban life, from the pre-feminist Jane Jacobs in the early 1960s to Betty Friedan and to Dolores Hayden and her important 1980 polemic 'What Would a Non-Sexist City Look Like?'[8] In this context we also need to assess the prevailing cultural representations of the suburb as one of the prime sites in which female sexuality is housed, typically registered as a site of female *dis*empowerment. I wonder here if the de facto displacement of the city by the suburb in the developed world since the Second World War is actually representative of something else – of the comprehensive erosion of patriarchal power, and the loss of practically all the sites of the city in which a normative masculinity might be enacted. In this respect, the relative absence of women from architecture is really of little consequence, for in the suburban world the (male) architect matters much less than the (mostly female) specialists in interior furnishing.[9]

It is a commonplace of American culture to depict the suburb as sinister, dysfunctional – and female. Alfred Hitchcock's depiction of Santa Rosa, California (in truth a small city rather than a suburb) in *Shadow of a Doubt* (1943) set the tone for more than 70 years of culture, not least most of Hollywood's domestic production. Key cinematic and TV examples of this vast genre include *The Stepford Wives*, *American Beauty* and *Mad Men*, which consistently juxtapose a female suburban world with a male urban one.[10] This highly critical, even apocalyptic, understanding of suburban life is curious in its timing as the dominant representative trope, as it has become so at precisely the moment at which America became suburban. In one of the largest population migrations in history, after the Second World War, American cities hollowed and sprawled, producing over time the phenomena of exurbs and edge cities, suburban settlements which lacked any meaningful relation to an original *urbs*. All this is well documented. The American experience is the one best understood, due to its scale and its centrality to American culture, but similar migrations occurred all over the developed world, taking similar forms and occurring on a similar scale in northern Europe, with smaller but still significant manifestations in southern Europe and South America.

Suburbia, for its many critics, was supposed to define and limit the female libido. The suburban house, for those critics, told women what they were and were not supposed to feel, and how they were to look and behave. If there was a founding text for this argument, it was Betty Friedan's *The Feminine Mystique*, first published in the U.S. in 1964.[11] Like her contemporary Jane Jacobs, Friedan read suburbanization as an ideological, rather than natural, process, with wide-ranging political and business support. Her own background in inner city Chicago meant that she could see the suburb as *other*, while at various times in her life also participating actively in it, both raising a family and conducting suburb-oriented research.[12] Friedan is important in any discussion of American feminism, but here especially so because of the way she managed to link the outward material form of the suburb with a marked psychosexual character. If she did not say outright that the suburb *produced* the psychosexual life of its inhabitants, she let it be strongly implied, leaving it for more radical architectural critics such as Dolores Hayden to spell it out, and devise some alternatives.[13] One of the difficulties of the cultural landscape of the suburb is that a lot of what is conventionally understood as fact, in fact now describes situations of the distant past. So Friedan's analysis strongly conditions contemporary culture – for example, the television series *Mad Men* – yet what it describes is the generation of women who reached maturity immediately following the Second World War. Their experience is powerfully informed by the war, experienced either directly or by proxy through relatives and loved ones. The experience of death or loss through the war is a theme that runs throughout *The Feminine Mystique*, and it is at various points said to condition directly the form of the lived experience, the desire (for example) to recreate a childhood home post-war that may not actually have existed previously.

More complex is the effect the war may have had on birth rates and marriage age. Where conventional (cultural) understanding of the post-war suburb suggests an inexorable liberalization of sexual behaviour in post-war America, Friedan makes clear the existence of a positive boom of normative sexuality. Marriage rates shot up. Not only that, but the average age of marriages dramatically fell and the birth rates exponentially increased. Teenage marriages and huge families were commonplace in the 1950s, which statistically better resembles that of a poor developing state than the leading industrialized one. That said, that pattern of development set in train in the 1950s long persisted as an ideal, even if the precise patterns of female fertility and employment had altered.

Friedan's project, like that of Jacobs, was short on quantitative research, long on anecdote (in academic circles it's what might now be termed an 'emotional geography'). Its subject, the lived experience of the suburb, was insubstantial, and hard to recover: its most representative aspect was after all no more than a *feeling*, of alienation that ought to have been banished by the material wealth. As Friedan wrote, the basic material quality of suburban life was exceptionally high – never in human history had so many people been housed so well. So for a suburban woman to complain openly about it might readily seem ungrateful or even immoral, especially when the suburb seemed to breed a dangerous degree of sexual competition among women. To uncover such negative views perhaps required smart tactics, and a high degree of trust from Friedan's interlocutors. The responses Friedan collected from residents often indicate a great deal of uncertainty, hesitancy and embarrassment about desires that they feel ought not to be felt. But the volume of responses also indicates a major phenomenon, albeit one that resists easy analysis.

How was the problem made manifest? 'I saw the same signs in suburban ranch houses and split-levels on Long Island and in New Jersey and Westchester County', wrote Friedan, 'in colonial houses in a small Massachusetts town; on patios in Memphis; in suburban and city apartments; in living rooms in the Midwest.' It was essentially one of entrapment:

> the American housewife is once again trapped in a squirrel cage. If the cage is now a modern plate-glass and broadloom ranch house or a convenient modern apartment, the situation is no less painful then when her grandmother sat over an embroidery hoop in her gilt-and-plush parlor and muttered angrily about women's rights.

Ibsen's fictional character Nora, from *The Doll's House*, frequently makes an appearance in the book. Nora complains of being always a doll, a 'doll-child' for her father, a 'doll-wife' for her husband, and the progenitor of 'doll-children'.[14] An intelligent proto-feminist woman, her dissatisfaction with her comfortable bourgeois life and outwardly kindly husband is a source of psychological torment. Ibsen was one key cultural reference point, as was Freud, castigated for providing the psychoanalytical armature for suburbia life. Alfred Kinsey was also invoked at this point to give substance to a reactionary ideology enshrining women in their roles as childbearers.[15]

Where Friedan is most convincing, however, is in her account of the lived experience of suburbia. Repeatedly, highly educated women were depicted in states of apparently terminal frustration, absorbed in routine menial tasks, or reduced to a state of depression that left them exhausted and near-comatose:

> I seem to sleep so much. I don't know why I should be so tired. This house isn't nearly so hard to clean as the cold-water flat we had when I was working. The children are at school all day. It's not the work. I just don't feel alive.[16]

Others, described towards the end of the book, manifested hyper-sexuality, a condition enacted outside the marriage, during the long day in the husband's absence. A Tennessee Williams-like scenario was depicted at one point, with suburban housewives developing a taste for rough sex with more or less feral youths.[17] Friedan's tone could be overly prim in places, but the point was well made: the suburb was, effectively, a jail, responsible for any number of negative behaviours, from obsessional neurosis to depression to nymphomania. The American suburb was therefore not merely a place, but the systemic embodiment of reactionary ideology aimed at keeping women in childbearing roles, supported by tax breaks, labour markets and real-estate trends. A 'progressive dehumanization' in Friedan's words, it is nothing less than a 'a comfortable concentration camp'.[18]

The dystopian suburb with its negative psychological effects is precisely that portrayed in *Mad Men*, where a Westchester County suburb frames a wide range of female neuroses, principally those of Don Draper's complex wife, Betty. Betty herself manifests an uncontrollable shakiness, brought on by what might now be termed Generalized Anxiety Disorder, and she sees a psychoanalyst to deal with this, her low libido and her peculiar relationships with her peer group. Her friends are pathologically competitive; the prepubescent son of another friend is sexually obsessed with her, an obsession periodically shared; and Betty's own daughter, caught masturbating in front of the TV one evening by her mother, becomes the subject of a harrowing, neurotic row. Everyone is crazy in this place: sexually frustrated, obsessive-compulsive, self-harming, violent and sometimes all of these things at the same time. *Mad Men*'s architectural template draws on a wide range of established sources, so the suburb (as opposed to the Madison Avenue office of Sterling Cooper) connotes exclusive femininity. Men's absence is not only physical (they are simply not there most of the time) but also cultural. The houses are all soft furnishings and nostalgia, the bedroom a well-defended retreat from the world rather than an erotic space. For all their conventional erotic signification, *Mad Men*'s suburban bedrooms *never* facilitate successful sex: they've become far too neurotic for that.[19]

Mad Men draws on a set of familiar suburban archetypes in which suburban space is depicted as neurotic and female. In common with more recent representations of suburbia, it equates femininity with weakness – so emancipation cannot really occur without the dissolution of the suburb. There are alternatives. Camille Paglia, for example, in her various readings of Hitchcock's movie *The Birds*, ascribes huge power to the female characters, not only the powerful lead in Tippi Hedren, a brash debutante, but what she describes as

The Birds (dir. Alfred Hitchcock, 1962). An early scene: Melanie Daniels (Tippi Hedren) meets Mitch Brenner (Rod Taylor) in a San Francisco bird shop.

'malevolent nature', an insuperable female force that overturns male civilization at a stroke, and reveals its insubstantiality.[20] She's a chthonic force like the mythical Lilith, capable of incalculable destruction. The power of the (female) suburb is likewise depicted in both the book (1972) and film adaptations of *The Stepford Wives* (1975 and 2004), similarly in the immensely popular Cherry Productions series *Desperate Housewives* (2004–12) and in the Sam Mendes-directed movie *American Beauty* (1999) – in each case the male characters are emasculated and alienated by an environment that they implicitly may have helped to create, but which now controls them.[21]

'What Would a Non-Sexist City Be Like?'

Jane Jacobs's *Death and Life of Great American Cities* (1961) had an incalculable and continuing impact on American urban design. So what did feminism do to design theory? The key text here is not Friedan, but Dolores Hayden's critique of suburbia, 'What Would a Non-Sexist City Be Like?', published in 1980 in a journal of feminist sociology, *Signs*.[22] Hayden started by asserting that a male-dominated architectural profession has assumed that a woman's place would be the home, and built accordingly; the car-dependent, suburban freeway landscape is this idea in built form. The introduction of large numbers of women to the labour market challenged all the assumptions accompanying that form of settlement. What was needed, Hayden argued, was nothing less than 'a new paradigm of the home, the neighborhood, and the city; to begin to describe the

physical, social, and economic design of a human settlement that
would support, rather than restrict, the activities of employed women
and their families.'[23] Hayden described, like Friedan in 1965, the
production of a hungry consumer around the single-family home,
the wife/mother as homemaker and the marketing of devices (vacuum
cleaners, washing machines, dryers, refrigerators, cars) that made such
a lifestyle possible and indeed desirable.

However, Hayden went much further: the suburban dystopia
she pictured was not only wasteful, creating (as Friedan had also
described) a whole range of time-hungry domestic tasks that never
previously existed, but worse, isolation, alienation, mental illness and
domestic violence. In less than a page, Hayden moved her argument
from the familiar history of the development of a consumer culture
to violence; the reader could only infer that the suburban house is
the cause of the violence: 'there is no doubt that America's houses
and households are literally shaking with domestic violence'.[24]
Hayden's view to some extent resembles Andrea Dworkin's at the
same time. As Hayden critiqued suburbia, Dworkin took on a range
of patriarchal targets from pornography to the act of sex itself.[25]

Hayden's solution was a set of alternative housing forms that
attacked the highly individualized, privatized space of the suburb
(she gave examples of already existing projects in Sweden, Germany,
Denmark and the UK in which not-for-profit housing has been
provided on a more egalitarian basis, and with communal facilities
designed to benefit women living alone, or alone with children).
Her most radical solution, however, was the projected retrofitting
of an American suburb, proposing a radical densification with a
standard 1,400 square foot open-plan house re-planned as a duplex
or triplex. At the same time, she proposed reordering the space
between houses for productive communal activity: in place of
gardens, an interior yard would accommodate

> community day care, a garden for growing vegetables,
> some picnic tables, a playground where swings and slides
> are grouped, a grocery depot connected to a larger neigh-
> borhood food cooperative, and a dial-a-ride garage. Large
> single-family houses can be remodeled quite easily to become
> duplexes and triplexes . . .[26]

All this aimed at nothing less than a socialist transformation of the
U.S., in which female domestic labour would be revalued to occupy

a much more central place, a demand that has echoes of the urban-istic proposals of the early USSR. Hayden's vision involved a radical attack on the assumptions that divide private from public, men from women; her reordering of the most divided of spaces is also a reordering of gender.

> Women had to transform the sexual division of domestic labor, the privatized economic basis of domestic work, and the spatial separation of homes and workplaces in the built environment if they were to be equal members of society.[27]

Hayden's 1980 proposal, like Friedan's analysis of the 'problem' in 1965, placed gender politics at the heart of suburban life, and in both cases, an alternative gender politics is dependent on a radical reorganization of space. In both cases, the solution seems to be something denser, more co-operative and (particularly in Hayden's case) more European, to the point at which (despite the vehemence of the argument) it seems in large part an argument about taste, as it so often is in debates about suburbs.

Peace Camping

Hayden cited a number of European projects that offered alterna-tives to patriarchal American suburbanization, but they were few and isolated in the context of an indisputably male-dominated and (then) sexist architectural profession. It is no surprise to find women architects largely absent from the best-known histories of modern architecture and urbanism, even ostensibly left-leaning ones – such as those by Charles Jencks, Peter Hall, Kenneth Frampton.[28] It is more of a surprise to find no acknowledgement of the profession's structural sexism here, or in one of the better-known anthologies of 'radical' architectural thought.[29] Even feminist architectural writers such as Alice Friedman are forced by the sexism of the very category of architecture to consider para-architectural practices rather than architectural design per se. In her case, architectural creativity came to reside in a collaborative tension between clients, designers, builders and, ultimately, residents – a multivalent process in which (female) clients can be shown to be fully active.[30] But as Friedman would certainly admit, to recover a meaningful place for women in relation to modern architecture meant to draw on discourses that are largely private, informal and outside the public sphere.

It's a measure of the problem feminism has with architecture that to find built examples of authentically non-sexist environment it's necessary to look outside of formal architecture altogether. But that is arguably the case, and why we now jump spatially, geographically and typologically to the Greenham Common Women's Peace Camp in Berkshire, England. However different this place is from any formal project, for over two gruelling decades, it played out in the most public way what it meant to build feminist space. The camp takes us a long way geographically from the typical American suburb, but curiously it abutted a transplanted one: leased by the USAF, official Greenham had, behind the fence, American suburbia's stores, post offices, housing, the cars and the cops. More curiously still, the protest camp, that is, unofficial Greenham, ended up playing out many of the problems Friedan had seen in the suburb: how to deal with childcare, how to deal with men and male authority, how to establish hierarchies of power among women, how to achieve fulfilling sexual lives. But as the suburb seemed to be designed to enforce convention, the camp with its dissolute outer form seemed to give permission to dissolve it. For many, Greenham was a sexual experiment as much as a political one.

The Greenham camp's origins lie in a small, but well-publicized march in September 1981 from Cardiff to RAF Greenham Common to protest against the installation of American Tomahawk cruise missiles, nuclear weapons designed for use in western continental Europe against a putative advance by the USSR.[31] The initial camp developed from the Cardiff Peace March, and was both relatively small and mixed. But after a few weeks, the camp changed character radically, becoming more or less permanent and (most significantly in the present context) female only. The camp remained in place in one form or another for a further nineteen years. It survived the introduction of cruise in 1983, when 96 missiles and associated pieces of infrastructure were located at the base; it survived the removal of cruise missiles eight years later after the end of the Cold War; and it saw the re-creation of Greenham as a genuine public common. Over the years, numbers of protestors fluctuated wildly. The permanent presence averaged a few dozen in the early years, but it was boosted considerably by day visitors, and especially by special events such as 'Embrace the Base' in 1982, which brought an estimated 16,000 to the camp. The final days saw only a handful present, the ones for whom Greenham had become life itself: there was nowhere else to go.

The camp was in fact several, organized around the colour-coded entry gates to the base ('green', 'blue', 'yellow' and so on), with each believed to have a different character. Ages and social backgrounds varied widely, and the gates became a means of differentiating the various factions: Blue Gate, for example, quickly became the place with the most clearly defined lesbian identity, as well as the site where a party could usually be guaranteed. Other gates had distinctly middle-class character, with enthusiastic knitters, quilters, cooks and fans of Radio 4 – elements that showed a basic commonality with the town of Newbury outside. The camp's capacity to arouse feelings of disgust, however, was remarkable: this was no ordinary protest, but something that involved the basest emotions. As Peter Stallybrass and Allon White described in a much-cited book on the carnivalesque, the camp did something extraordinary to otherwise ordinary people's insides, producing a sense of highly sexualized, bodily disgust.[32] One camp resident said:

> all the women arouse a degree of hostility far in excess of any inconvenience they may cause to soldiers, policemen, or residents living near the base. Shopkeepers and publicans refuse to serve them; hooligans unexpectedly join forces with the establishment and actualise the verbal insults by smearing the benders with excrement and pig's blood . . . this spontaneous and voluntary association of females, without formal leadership or hierarchy, seems to threaten the soldiers, the local gentry, the bourgeoisie of Newbury and even its hooligans far more than the missiles, although the latter would be a prime target in the event of a nuclear war.[33]

Greenham was initially mixed sex. Formally, it was a travellers' camp on the lines of those at music festivals, particularly in the south and west of England. A small, but significant travelling culture had evolved from the remnants of the hippy movement and associated protest movements. Much harder than hippy culture, it took in mainstream protest movements such as CND, but had a pronounced anarchist wing, and fellow travellers could include the Hell's Angels. It was tough, self-reliant, and defiant, its tactics were those of the urban guerilla. Often successful in frustrating the police, its aims were usually little more than to be left alone to enjoy music and drugs it its own eccentric way. Greenham emerged from this; its structures (improvised wigwams, or benders, and old buses) were now the established form of such camps. Understanding this background is important to make sense of the later decision to make the camp women only: the emergent traveller culture had more in common with the Angels than anything else. Dominated by figures such as Sid Rawle, it contained a significant number of ex-servicemen who'd been unable to adjust to civilian life.[34] Many of its (male) members liked a fight, and its tastes were noisy and urban. Drawing on the traditions of the Angels as much as Ken Kesey's Merry Pranksters, it was radical in its attitude to authority, but in its internal organization and sexual politics could be anything but.

The traveller community was one source; another was the mostly unconnected explosion in left-wing culture. The early 1980s in the UK saw an extraordinary efflorescence of radical thought from infinite forms of protest, to comedy and even music: the target (Mrs Thatcher) was as clear as it could be; the battle lines were drawn. However, despite the high profile of feminism within the left's con-stellation, political culture was often masculine and belligerent, and the miners' strike of 1981–2 was a good example, taking the form of a pitched battle between two armies of men. The idea of a women-only camp emerged from a context in which political conversation was widely felt by women on the left to be overly masculine in style; politics happened by conflict, and in a curious way, patriarchal politics was as evident in the left protest movements as it was behind the wire at the Greenham Common airbase. One Greenham protestor, 'Clare', put it: 'I felt pissed off with the left and the peace movement . . . What pissed me off? Loud, bearded men making pronouncements.'[35]

The establishment of the women-only camp was its most defining single feature – but it was also the most controversial. The decision was made after a heated meeting in 1981 and produced a well-documented and violent reaction from several male protestors, But the women, some of whom invoked Luce Irigary's notion of 'tactical separatism', well understood what they were doing.[36] The removal of men from the immediate conversation was a short circuit to a different kind of conversation about cruise missiles. Contemporary literature produced by the camp makes clear both the problem, and how they envisaged an ideal politics. A leaflet from 1983 speaks of female disenfranchisement from the spaces of protest:

> The Peace Camp was a women's initiative. One of the women who started it said that she wanted to find a way in which 'ordinary women like myself' could express themselves. The Camp involves women of different ages and backgrounds, many of whom have never taken part in political action before. It has

always been difficult for women to organise and make their voices heard. Usually men assume a dominant role, leaving women to follow passively. At Greenham women have challenged this. They have created a new way of voicing their total opposition to Cruise Missiles and have grown through this in confidence, strength and trust.[37]

That makes the rationale clear enough: the women-only rule was a way of achieving participation for an effectively disenfranchised group, whose voices would be drowned in a typical mixed context. The violence of the reaction to the women-only announcement confirmed the validity of this approach – one male protestor went berserk, destroying a hot water boiler he had rigged up, at some risk to himself and fellow protestors.[38] (I doubt there was anything premeditated about this, but it's interesting the object destroyed was a machine designed to bring a modicum of civilization to the camp. Its creation and destruction by a man, it could be said, points up the masculine dominance of that civilization.)

But his reaction suggested that the separatist protestors were right in that a mixed protest had the tendency to remain caught in a paradigm of violence. More grandly, the experiment in female-only living is a means of attacking the 'whole system' of patriarchy, with the often-voiced sentiment that cruise missiles simply represented one element of a much larger system produced by men. For example, 'Deborah', quoted in the *Irish Times*:

> there's no point in getting rid of cruise without changing the whole system that produced it – attitudes, the way we live, the way we treat each other, patriarchy. But that's not easy to say to people. It's much more difficult to get people to agree to that than banning cruise missiles. Greenham has a negative purpose, to get rid of cruise, and a positive one, the creation of a supportive way of life for many women.[39]

Precisely how protest might be manifest in specifically female ways is indicated by the following announcement, also from 1983, advertising an action:

> Bring Mirrors – to turn the base inside out, trees to plant, candles for silent vigil, instruments for songs . . . What men can do to support: this is the first time for a big gathering that

we are asking that ONLY WOMEN come to the base. Please show your support by respecting this and by supporting the concept of women only space. Men and older boys can help by organising children's Fire Dragon Feasts and crèches *in local areas* leaving mothers free to come on their own if they want to. Your financial help is also welcome.[40]

Here (as at 'Embrace the Base' the previous year) an action is envisaged from the start as non-aggressive, countering the violence of the missile base with games and gardening. Men's assistance is kept at arm's length – in a funny inversion of normative childcare arrangements, they are encouraged to help by staying away, keeping children busy, leaving their female partners free to do the real protest work. As news media reports made clear – often in profoundly negative ways – the camp was motivated to create a male-free environment in which a distinctly female political voice could be heard. There were extensions of this into sexual politics too, and sexual experimentation, which angered and fascinated the news media in equal measure. Given the relative lack of openness about sex in the UK news media of 1981, there were few detailed accounts of lesbianism, if plenty of insinuation. Later stories about the base tell of Greenham as a highly developed queer space, one where perhaps for the first time it was possible to have an openly lesbian identity. In these accounts, sexual identities become fluid, and new identities (sometimes rather unlikely) became possible at Greenham. The camp therefore had a secondary, less public role, as a kind of research and development project for new forms of female sexuality.

In one version sexuality was one of the camp's major fault lines, with 'dyke' Greenham and 'respectable' Greenham continually pitted against each other. 'Respectable' – represented by Yellow Gate, a largely middle-class community – was respected by the mainstream media and wished to control the camp's media representation. CND more than once stated that a 'popular' cause, namely the removal of cruise missiles, was made unpopular by the presence of separatist feminists at the camp. More generally, as Sasha Roseneil notes, 'there were sometimes open clashes between queer Greenham and respectable Greenham as vociferous women of the queer tendency defended their rights to kiss their girlfriends, smoke dope, drink alcohol, and behave as they wished.' For queer Greenham, the camp as a site of sexual experimentation was at least as important as the camp as site of protest. So there was a lot of rather theatrical touching. Jinny List:

'we touched each other all the time. You couldn't go anywhere without kissing everyone. It would have been rude not to.' Members of the Green Gate camp delighted in provoking drinkers in local Newbury pubs, 'talking loudly about lesbian sex . . . making jokes about heterosexuality . . . kissing their lovers passionately.'

> Lesbian sexual desire was an important part of life at Greenham . . . the atmosphere was often experienced as highly sexually charged; and the value placed on pleasure and fun extended to making Greenham's culture a pro-sex one. There were few opportunities for privacy and secrecy, and a keen interest was taken in the unfolding of affairs and relationships.[41]

The 'pro-sex' culture reported here had a number of neo-architectural forms, such as at Green, Blue and Yellow gates a tendency for groups of women to 'make big beds together', under tarpaulins, in vans or sometimes in the open air. 'On occasions the women would have sex with each other, on others they would just talk and cuddle.' Elsewhere, there was apparently a 'passion bender' at Blue Gate, where residents had 'a hell of a lot of fun'.[42] At the same time, an area of Yellow Gate was known derisively as 'monogamy mountain' for its establishment of quasi-normative patterns of behaviour, albeit still in the context of homosexuality. Both modes of behaviour, the queer and the quasi-normative, were represented spatially: 'monogamy mountain' was derided precisely because it started to acquire some of the accoutrements and structural permanence of suburban life. The 'passion bender' and the communal bed were temporary structures, much better adapted to the urgencies of desire; the 'bender' itself not only had a funny name connotative of sexual deviance, but already had a festival-proven pedigree as a radical structure, connotative of opposition to normality. Resembling an organic version of a Drop City dome, it had an erotic charge all of its own.

The sexual experimentation at Greenham even extended beyond the wire fence. One of the long-term lesbian camp members, Rowan Gwedhen, left Violet Gate temporarily to visit Australia in the mid-1980s, finding to her abject horror on her return what seemed to her a 'heterosexual revolution' that mainly consisted in flirting with male soldiers.[43] Something like this had already occurred in 1982, when a small group of protestors took advantage of the base nightclub, then free to Newbury residents on a Saturday as a friendly gesture towards the local community. Changed into dance gear, they had themselves smuggled into the base by a sympathetic taxi driver. Once there, as a *Guardian* correspondent described, they set about converting the soldiers to their cause. The soldiers were friendly enough 'but seemed scared the officers would discover who we were . . . we insisted on staying and dancing and having a drink with them. Now at least they know we are human beings.'[44]

It's a funny story, in line with the newspaper's largely positive treatment of the camp. It is also a story of eroticism as transgression. The creation of the women-only camp in 1982 meant the creation of a space in which lesbian sex could openly flourish. It also meant a lot of sexual regulation, with men allowed to visit in some ways, and not others. On a more tiresome everyday level, it meant the constant defence of the women-only position to media visitors determined to wear them down. Now *that* is not erotic – and it is significant that the playing out of lesbian fantasies, at least as described by Roseneil and others, occurs in liminal zones away from the main camp, in 'passion benders' or beds under the stars. Once Greenham had been established as *normatively* queer, what could be more transgressive than to flirt with the enemy? There is also implicit in this and other similar stories an undercurrent of subversion in the relationship between the protestors and soldiers per se, in that the former were in many cases older and more sexually experienced (the soldiers' reaction to being discovered by their superiors suggests as much) and the entry into the base suggests a subversion of normative sexual power relations. The soldiers *ought* to be in charge, but they're left helpless. It reiterates, deliciously, the cruel joke of puberty when girls leave boys temporarily in the dust.

The most famous of all Greenham's actions was 'Embrace the Base', which took place on 12 December 1982, a little over a year after the original camp had been set up. The date was significant: it marked the date the original decision had been made to site cruise missiles at the site. The action was straightforward, but rich in symbolism: a gathering of as many women as possible to link arms around the 9-mile perimeter fence of the base, with the basic idea imported by one of the protestors, Barbara Doris, from an encircling of the Pentagon in Washington, DC, the previous year.[45] The fence was also to be decorated with a range of artefacts, connoting as clearly as possible the female nature of the protest against the maleness of the base – photographs of children, children's toys, flowers, nappies, tampons, wool, anything, in fact, however unlikely, that stressed the female origins of the protest.

Greenham Common, Embrace the Base action, 12 December 1982, photograph by Raissa Page. The best-known image of the Greenham campaign.

Other publicity used more obviously sexualized images; one widely circulated had a bare-breasted earth mother with halo emerge from a web.[46] The event itself was a tremendous success, exceeding the ambitions of the organizers (such as they were). It was also a colossal media event in the UK, reported on the front page of every national newspaper on the following day. Between 30,000 and 35,000 protestors showed up, from every part of the UK, the 'zenith, the high spot of the whole Greenham story' according to one of the key figures, Ann Pettitt, because 'that was when the original message went thumping round the world'. Pettitt's account makes clear the importance of the decorating of the fence, what might in art terms be called an intervention:

> You brought a gift which symbolised the life, how important
> life was to you. You brought a gift that was important to you

and it was a gift to the base to symbolise life. So the whole of
the fence was just covered with these, absolutely extraordinary,
the whole of the fence covered with things . . . One woman had
hung her wedding dress on the fence and left it there. She hung
her wedding on the fence and walked away and left it. To me,
I just sort of walked around with tears streaming down my face
looking at these things, you know laughing and crying at the
same time. I remember Carmen (a fellow protestor) telling
me that she saw a whole beautiful dinner service clipped to
the fence. A lot of things were just left, they were sacrificed,
they were left you know. It was a marvellous day. The whole
of that nine-mile fence covered with these things, or with
flowers, obviously a lot of paintings, a lot of pictures of babies,
a lot of embroidery.[47]

Pettitt's recollections are well supported by the photographs of the
day, in which a powerful incongruity is set up between the intimacy
(and domestication) of the decoration and the harshness of the base
environment. Many women brought banners and left them attached
to the fence, reviving and relocating a domestic tradition, and in
effect turning the base inside out.

In November 1983, a USAF C5A transport plane arrived at
Greenham Common with the first of the consignment of 96 Toma-
hawks. What was potentially a failure for the camp quickly became
a focus for another kind of protest, 'Cruisewatch'. Here, protestors
set out to disrupt the exercises in which missiles were taken out in
convoy from the base. Using internal information on the timing
of convoys, protestors ambushed them, spraying windscreens with
paint, peace signs and other graffiti, and in some cases rendering the
vehicles immobile. Other images show protestors physically engaged
with the vehicles and military personnel – lying down in front of
vehicles was a common tactic, as was climbing on top of vehicles.
Associated with this activity was some gentler subversion of local
road signs. Cruisewatch was well publicized and resulted in some
spectacular photographs. In one, a personnel truck illuminated by
flash is shown almost completely covered in paint, peace signs and
the exhortation 'GO HOME'. In another, a missile transporter emerges
from pitch darkness, showing only too clearly its windscreen
painted out on one side, a peace sign on the other. That action
was in many ways an exaggerated and bizarre cock-tease, in which
women protestors lay in wait, in darkness, for a ludicrously phallic

object to appear – on which they then pounced, literally, rendering it immobile by covering it in white fluid. This and all the other actions engaged in by the camp involved a high degree of untheorized but real sexual transgression.

One of the most suggestive summaries of the Greenham camp comes from Jarrett McGehee, USAF Commander of the base from 1983–6. Conceding that they were in fact extremely well organized, he says of the camp:

> Try to imagine something so primitive, a state so primitive, that has none of the conveniences that you or I live with day to day, running water, shelter, warmth, clothing. The things that would never enter our mind not to have. If you have no shelter, if you have no proper clothing, if you have none of the conveniences, like running water or things of that nature, it would be very easy to become animal, like an animal, and live like an animal, like a wild animal in the virgin forest. That was the first impression I had, that these people had reverted to a former time. Women, filthy, absolutely filthy, in rags, carrying shopping carts full of their belongings, wandering around this hotchpotch of a camp site made with old discarded pieces of plastic and wood and barrels and whatever else they could find. It was almost ghost like. Women always seemed to be on the move, always seemed to be wandering aimlessly throughout the squalor.[48]

Jarrett's account of the protest both here and in a much longer set of interviews for the Imperial War Museum is poetic, but strangely sympathetic. The camp was an adversary, but one whose collective discipline, denial of self, and tactical originality drew repeated admiration from McGehee. His version also has a powerful, if unwitting, psychosexual dimension, in its imagination of Woman returned to – or more correctly, as – a state of nature. This identification of woman with nature is of course one of the most ancient archetypes, from the Medusa, to the implacable Lilith of Hebrew myth, to Lady Macbeth, to any number of Hitchcock anti-heroines. However regressive and unhelpful a myth it might be, it was an object of enduring fascination for feminist academics in the 1980s, from Julia Kristeva to Camille Paglia. Paglia, most controversially, chose to reclaim the archetype, rather than try to deny it: in *Sexual Personae* (1992) she celebrated – to the horror of feminists – woman as the embodiment of 'chthonic' nature. In her world view, disgust of the female was 'rational' because procreative processes were of themselves disgusting: 'Disgust is reason's proper response to the grossness of procreative nature.' The West's primary image of woman, she continued, is

> the *femme fatale*, the woman fatal to man. The more nature is beaten back, the more the *femme fatale* reappears, as a return of the repressed. She is the spectre of the west's bad conscience about nature . . . a malevolent moon that keeps breaking through our fog of hopeful sentiment.

And on she went, contrasting woman's chthonic identification with nature with a 'natural' male nature driven to make order out of the world by making 'things', a word in which she luxuriates. But these things – 'paved roads, indoor plumbing, washing machines, to eye-glasses, antibiotics, and disposable diapers . . . the George Washington Bridge' were fragile and fleeting against the eternal forces of nature.[49] I hardly need to spell out why this mythical idea of woman should so infuriate the feminist mainstream, reiterating for modern approval a set of the most reactionary archetypes. And yet reading Paglia up against the accounts of Greenham – from both sides – you have the sense that the protest not only consciously activated these ancient archetypes, but found success through them. They didn't succeed by being rational, but by being the opposite – crazy, libidinous, howling, filthy, devolving back to a state of nature against which even the mighty USAF were in many ways powerless. Their 'architecture' could never be anything other than the foul mess it was; to do anything more formal would have been to accede to the rational. And perhaps thinking about feminist space in this most radical and devolved form has lessons for thinking about the erotic in any architectural context. Perhaps *all* buildings are meant to contain the libido?

eight

Queer and Other Spaces

IT HAS BECOME a commonplace to describe certain architectural and urban spaces as queer. Since the early 1970s, areas of American cities (particularly New York and San Francisco) developed specifically gay identities, explored in the case of San Francisco in the popular fiction of the novelist Armistead Maupin. The UK in particular followed suit, developing identifiably male gay zones in London, Manchester and Brighton, and novels and TV representation to match. The American sociologist Richard Florida argued repeatedly that gay 'villages' were positive urban assets: gay men were typically affluent, design-conscious, high-spending urbanites with time on their hands.[1] Who better to lead the regeneration of rundown urban neighbourhoods? Via Florida or Foucault, in popular culture or the novels of Edmund White or Alan Hollinghurst, a notion of queer space was widely disseminated. Its typologies became urban clichés: parks appropriated for cruising, beaches for weightlifting, private sex clubs, excessively 'designed' bars, saunas, bathhouses and gyms. To post-feminist writers such as Camille Paglia and Catherine Hakim, gay culture seemed to be uniquely sexed; gay men seemed to have vastly more sex, and in more varieties, than any other social group.[2] For academics in the humanities it became clear how much of existing Western culture was really queer culture, once you started looking. Iconic cultural objects such as Michelangelo's *David* or *The Wizard of Oz* became unreadable *except* in queer terms.[3] Queer does not equate to the gay male experience, but I concentrate on that experience here as it had the most visible impact on the built environment.

I was curious about the new visibility of gay culture, having returned to live in Manchester, England, in 1993 after a decade elsewhere. Suddenly, Canal Street ('Anal Treet') was where it was all

David Hockney, *Peter Getting Out of Nick's Pool*, 1966, acrylic on canvas. Winner in 1967 of first prize in the John Moores Painting Prize competition, held every two years at the Walker Art Gallery, Liverpool. One of a long series of images of Californian swimming pools painted after the artist's arrival in Los Angeles, where he was to remain resident for over 40 years. It depicts the 19-year-old Peter Schlesinger, Hockney's then boyfriend. The setting is a small apartment complex built in 1956 at 1145 Larrabee St, just north of Sunset Boulevard in Los Angeles, in which the art dealer Nick Wilder had a property. It is not a case study house but has elements of those designs – a flat roof, low ceiling height, a pool, large windows. Angeleno realtors describe it as 'hip'.

happening, with an explosion of bars and clubs, and visible gay clientele of a kind I'd only ever seen in Provincetown on Cape Cod. Canal Street not only had money and property development, but a look, consisting of outrageous pink and purple interventions in otherwise dour ex-industrial buildings. Once Russell T. Ward had made the remarkable mainstream television series *Queer as Folk* (1999), Canal Street became fashionable, for straight men too. I frequently saw straight, working-class youths insist to nightclub doormen that they were gay ('I'm a poof! Honest!') to be admitted. Finding myself between long-term relationships at one point, a straight friend suggested, quite seriously, that I 'go gay' for a while, arguing that it might be 'interesting'. I didn't take him up on that suggestion, feeling (among other things) that the plan was for his own vicarious sexual pleasure. But for three years, Canal Street was largely where I ate and drank, and I observed with fascination how the built environment developed to facilitate a voracious sexual market. The bar Manto was the classic example: a conversion of an early century working-man's reading room, it was opened up to the street, and internally to provide both a dance floor, and the maximum number of vantage points for clients to observe each other.[4] A world away from the furtive and secret clubs that used to define Canal Street, it was in effect a sexual trading floor. The contacts made in this and other public markets (that is, bars) then led either to sex in more private clubs and saunas in the so-called Village, or to a good deal of alfresco sex under the canal bridges or the park. It looked like a huge amount of fun.

Canal Street had some unexpected architectural consequences. As well as the high-end conversions of the central area, it produced a demand for cheaper housing close to the central city. This was satisfied, unintentionally, by a mass-market developer, Bellway, in concert with the city council in their redevelopment of Hulme, a mile to the south of the city centre. Begun in the early 1990s after the demolition of all remaining public housing mega-structures, the new Hulme was suburban in scale and form, and adapted elements from then prevalent New Urbanist theories: clearly defined public and private realms, defensible space, conventional streets, squares and parks, and a majority of traditional cottage-style homes, vaguely reminiscent of the area as it had been in its heyday at the start of the twentieth century. The form of the development supposed nuclear families in single-family homes. The reality, as far as I could tell as an early resident, was a development inhabited almost entirely by gay

Canal St, Manchester. A greatly abused sign. Bridge over the Rochdale Canal visible in the background.

men. It was known locally as 'Fairy Villas', a marvellously arch phrase that alluded both to the developer's bucolic fantasy and the sexually libertarian one of the residents.[5]

What was happening on Canal Street in the early 1990s was of course intensely connected with other contemporary efflorescences of queer culture, regardless of whether they were found in San Francisco or Sydney. As a topic for architectural history and theory, it had huge potential, not least because so many of the metaphors used to describe queer culture are architectural in nature (closets, cottages, bathhouses, saunas – it was a culture that had evolved precisely in relation to the architectural spaces that had allowed it to exist or not). A small number of writers took it on as a topic, notably Joel Sanders, who assembled an important anthology, *Stud*, in 1996, and Aaron Betsky, who curated a decidedly queer Venice architecture biennale in 2008, titled, with one eyebrow arched, *Out There*.[6]

However, in spite of the increasing visibility of queer culture in general, it was still at the time of writing this book marginal to architectural culture in a way that it was not to the theatre, the literary world or the art museum. Part of the problem was perhaps architecture's continued attachment to the historic avant-garde, which may have been interested in sex, but invariably in terms of men having sex with women. Queers had a rough time of it in New York's mid-century avant-garde. Or as Daniel Hurewitz has argued in respect of California,

Canal St, Manchester. 'Origin' development by West Properties, targeting gay buyers. The scheme, in two blocks by Ian Simpson, stalled in 2009.

LA's bohemia had a tortured relationship with homosexuality; it formed no part of the socially progressive, health-focused sexuality framed by Californian modernism.[7]

Until recently, queer culture was to all intents and purposes invisible, hence the need to investigate it through gossip and inference as much as by more formal methods. It is a problem well described by Gavin Butt in his book *Between You and Me*, which catalogues the difficulty in analysing queer artists in a world that could not until recently accept they existed – Andy Warhol, now so firmly in the queer artistic canon, could only be identified in that way after his death.[8] For Sanders, dealing with the specific problem of architecture, the solution was a re-reading of spaces normally understood as heterosexual for homosexual inference. The most striking of these re-readings is perhaps that of Skidmore Owings & Merrill's 1958 Cadet Quarters for the USAF. Here Sanders and his co-author John Lindell use the USAF's own words and images to produce a strikingly queer reading of the complex. 'Bring Me Men', they exhort at the beginning of the chapter, an apparently lustful demand that turns out to be the Academy's own motto. The chapter's signal image, published opposite the opening text, is SOM's neat closet design for the shared cadet rooms; photographed with the sliding doors in the open position, it shows off well the Cecil B. de Mille-designed ceremonial uniform, as well as a remarkable range of highly polished footwear. The closet is a literal closet on one level but also – it hardly needs to be said – a figurative one, descriptive of the condition of repressed homosexual feelings. So the image of the closet, with its shiny boots, its twin uniforms displayed as a pair, its anthropomorphism, and its location next to a headline reading 'Bring Me Men' is only legible in queer terms. Having declared the Academy is a fundamentally queer space in this way, Lindell and Sanders find a whole range of circumstantial pieces of evidence to prove the case. It has to be said that queerness, like irony, once it is out, is almost impossible to suppress: almost everything is legible as queer. The once no doubt innocuous image of two cadets on page 77 now reads only as a prelude to seduction: instead of focusing on the design of the interior (the clever organization of the cabinets, the practical design of seating), the reader looks in wonder at the cadets' apparent lust for each other. Lips perfectly aligned, gazing deeply into each other's eyes . . . surely they can't be . . . Are they *really*? It is a seductive image, and a seductive argument. But it is based on the sketchiest of evidence, inference and assertion rather than data. This is not the Kinsey Report.

Broadly speaking, queer theory's success has been to establish a more complex and nuanced understanding of our sexual lives. We no longer expect things to be straightforward; in many ways, whatever our political persuasion, we now expect complexity and difference. One of queer theory's problems, however, is that its desire to 'out' leads to advocacy research, and (sometimes) errors of fact. In the case of som's usaf Academy, Sanders and company offer a mischievous (mis)reading of space that implies that the entire facility was a queer space – even in the most fevered queer imagination, we know this cannot be the case, and with time could probably substantiate it. More seriously, it leads to errors of fact – the architect Charles Moore, for example, has been repeatedly described as gay when he was not. That is a problem we will return to later.[9] Moore's alleged homosexuality exists in the realm of what Butt calls 'gossip'.[10] The gossip question is one difficulty; another, perhaps more serious question is whether an architect's sexuality might have any impact on the results of their building. That second question is harder to prove – but it *is* worth investigating space that seems to declare itself queer, regardless of what its authors do in bed. Sexuality here is much more than the question of what individuals do, but a whole attitude to the world, with implications for the way it looks.

Queer Space

For Aaron Betsky, queer space is straightforward. It is space in which the goal is, simply, orgasm. Queer space arose in response to the institutions and spaces created by modernity, which, as Aaron Betsky has described, didn't work too well for gay men:

> They did not have families at the core of their lives, so the disciplining of the body turned into its reverse, i.e. the satisfaction of desire, and the public space was where the queer man had to hide his desire.[11]

The result was the appropriation of a range of existing spaces for queer purposes, very typically, he writes, those away from public gaze, often furtive, dark or private; queer space, according to Betsky, 'creates itself in darkness, in the obscene, in the hidden'.[12] Hence the metaphor of the closet, a dark, private space not meant for human habitation. In the real world, the closet materialized in specific spaces. In Britain, the public toilet became indelibly associated with gay sex through the practice of cottaging, often involving periodic stays in the stalls of particular venues, and their impromptu modification – holes might be bored between stalls through which a penis might be inserted, or at which an eye placed. The expression itself, 'cottaging' carried with it a marvellous range of architectural associations, ironically alluding to a cosy and feminized world, when the reality was usually a stinking, Victorian ruin. The unconscious brilliance of the term is that it speaks of both worlds simultaneously, and gay men could identify with both. Other spaces came to be normatively gay: boarding schools, prisons, ships, in other words institutions with a captive and sexually frustrated male population. Or, as the British art historian Adrian Rifkin has noted poetically in relation to the gay underworld of Paris, a gay space might be almost nothing at all, 'the twisting of a stairwell, the shelter of a lean-to, an industrial courtyard'.[13]

The kind of architecture described here is by necessity temporary, provisional and furtive, and it is precisely these qualities, Rifkin implies, that allow a sexually libertarian culture to exist. The corollary of this argument is hostility to any processes that might threaten this culture. Regeneration, or as Rifkin calls it in the article, 'gentrification', produces spaces that actively reduce the potential for sexual encounters.[14] Rifkin gives the signal example of the 'digicode', or the widespread introduction of electronically secured doorways to

Paris tenements, preventing the temporary use of the doorway
or stair for sex. What Rifkin describes is an extreme form of the
sexualization of space in which almost any architectural space,
however unlikely or provisional, can be erotically charged. And
so to perhaps the most clichéd queer space, the bathhouse, made
notorious in San Francisco in the 1970s. Here was 'a new kind of
nature' of fleeting and often anonymous sexual contacts facilitated
by codes in which the internal architecture was crucial; a stall, perhaps, with a door that could be rented by the hour, and which could
be made relatively private or public depending on inclination and
the position of the door. The architecture and the activity inside
might condition each other. 'Rubbing, piercing, probing: these
activities are enacted at once spatially and sexually, with walls as
with flesh.'[15] This collision of the spatial and sexual may not be
exclusively queer, but it has certainly been more thoroughly explored
in the queer context than anywhere else. The need for opportunism
and the male capacity for rapid arousal produced the most inventive
use of space.[16] Queer space is perhaps best exemplified not in buildings, however, but in the fantastic imagination of Touko Laaksonen,
better known as Tom of Finland (1920–1991). Laaksonen drew on
an amateur basis for American muscle magazines from 1957, but it
was 1973 by the time he was drawing full-time professionally, and
1978 by the time he had achieved celebrity status through the friendship of the photographer Robert Mapplethorpe and others. Where
Mapplethorpe aestheticized the (primarily male) queer body, to the
point at which it became an abstraction, Laaksonen kept it real. His
reality had no pretence to beauty at all: grotesquely filthy for the
most part, all gaping arseholes and bulging cocks, it depicts a world
of relentless fucking in any and every combination. And unlike
Mapplethorpe it also depicts it in space, showing (as Betsky and
Rifkin put in words) sex *in relation* to spatial surroundings, using
whatever space comes to hand as leverage, or cover or an impromptu
sex aid. Space defines and narrates the sexual scenarios described, but
also makes clear how (in this peculiarly obsessive world) attenuated
space tends to be: a sauna or bar at most, but more often just a wall
or a boot. No one else describes so well the provisional character of a
space in which the slightest thing can trigger arousal. It's also a set of
clichés that are only really manifest in a few select parts of the world,
and Tom of Finland's fevered imagination. Gay men in this world

Tom of Finland (1920–1991), 'Untitled' (No. 1 from the series *Motorcycle Thief*), 1964.

view are always ready for sex, and the architecture (such as it is) is subservient to that purpose.

Queer Architecture

Precisely where architecture is in all this is a matter of debate. For the most part, modern architecture (like other modernist cultures) was a determinedly male and heterosexual one, and that identity persisted longer than in other modernist cultures. Openly gay architects are rarer than one might think in a seemingly liberal profession. One of the few contemporary architects to make something of his sexuality is the London-based Nigel Coates, whose work has repeatedly incorporated structures resembling supine human bodies. For the 2008 Venice Biennale (curated by Betsky), he produced *Hypnerotosphere*, a collection of sculptural furniture pieces, lit by hanging chandeliers and animated by a film of male dancers projected on a circular screen. The installation had a certain abstract quality – but the queer references were clear enough for anyone who cared to look. The strongly homoerotic film provided the atmosphere, and in that context under the glamour of the chandeliers, the furniture pieces read not only as bodies or body parts, but seemed to invite sexual engagement themselves (when I saw the show in the Venice Arsenale in November 2008, I didn't see anyone attempt a sexual act with the installation, but it seemed to be only a matter of time). *Hypnerotosphere*, in other words, referenced precisely the highly sexual, but highly provisional, quality of queer space found in anyone from Rifkin to Tom of Finland.

Coates's bodily references are possible, arguably, because of the kind of architectural world he inhabits. He isn't chasing contracts for housing or schools, but museums, pavilions and cultural events – projects, in other words, which positively invite experimentation. In that context, queer architecture is both feasible and desirable. It connects to the world of surfaces and play that Susan Sontag called, in a famous essay, camp. Camp was, she wrote, concerned with artifice, exaggeration, extravagance, style over content and aesthetics over morality.[17] The association with homosexuality – in fact the definition of camp in large part by homosexuals – she ascribed to the 'situation' of homosexuality, such as its legal status. She left the reader to infer what she meant by that, but we can probably surmise that a publicly suppressed culture might be unusually alert to the meanings residing on surfaces.

Nigel Coates, *Hypnerotosphere*, Venice Biennale installation, 2008.

But all this far exceeds what might be found in the workaday *practice* of architecture, the world of regulations, clients and commissions. Is there any relation at all? There have been attempts, of course, to make queer claims on architects. This involves more than the declaration that (say) Paul Rudolph was homosexual, but that architects' sexuality had some direct bearing on their work. This argument has been most clearly made in relation to Philip Johnson (1906–2005). Like his artist contemporary, Andy Warhol, Johnson was coy about his sexuality during much of his lifetime. There is a notorious remark made in 1943 about Nazi soldiers – 'all those blond boys in black leather' – but for the most part the topic was not discussed.[18] Also as with Warhol, no serious attempt was made to link the architect's sexuality with his output until towards the end of his life. At that point, the 1949 Glass House, built for the architect himself in New Canaan, Connecticut, is transformed from an unusually pure example of Miesian modernism to the way modernism itself has been 'queered'. Academic interest now tends to focus on the way the private functions of the house are eroticized and made spectacular. It is (according to Betsky) the 'ultimate Sadean pleasure palace . . . probably the most succinct statement of queer space built in this country in the last fifty years.'[19]

Betsky's other key Johnson case is the AT&T skyscraper in Manhattan, now known as the Sony building. At the time of its building, it was merely an incomprehensible formal move for an architect long associated with modernism. In Betsky's reading, AT&T represents the queering of modernism. Perhaps his queerest building, it exacted a 'queer revenge' on Sony's executives by placing the ample buttocks of Mercury in their full view as they exited the ground-floor elevators.[20] Some caution is needed here. The queering of architectural theory can result in advocacy research, as already mentioned. Johnson's architecture is queer, in other words, because Betsky and others say it is, rather than because it is based on much evidence. And while we know Johnson was homosexual, there is little that is concrete to suggest that his sexuality directly informed his architecture. There is in fact no reason why the prominent display of male buttocks should be regarded as essentially gay behaviour when (for example) the practice of 'mooning' is so endemic in heterosexual male culture, but understood as a bathetic, de-sublimatory act rather than anything sexual. There is also something of a disjunction between the spaces objectively used for sex – the bathhouses, sex clubs and so on – and the interiors otherwise *read* as queer. Betsky, for example, describes the bedroom of the Glass House as a particularly queer space, but the queerness constitutes itself in modes of interior decoration rather than sexual acts; indeed, not much seems to happen at the Glass House, despite its theoretical status.

That said, these queer architectural readings do nonetheless show how buildings might be thought of in ways that depart from the rational and normative, and how they might properly take account of lived experience. The introduction of subjective experience, in other words how we feel about architectural space, is one area in which queer architectural history makes a significant contribution. It may be not much more than speculation, but it does at least ask questions which professional architectural discourses tend to suppress. Queer space may not therefore be about sexual acts – with the specific exception of the bathhouse – but it may provide a way to talk about alternative ways of inhabiting architectural space, and indeed of imagining space altogether.[21] It's a sense of building quite distinct from the other modes cited in earlier chapters. Modernism might have sublimated the body, but in a wholly rational way, subordinated to newly formulated, rational regimes of health. It's distinct too from the feminist proposal cited in the previous chapter, with its wholly rational concern for the problems of single parenthood.[22] Queer space by contrast has nothing rational about it. It is by nature profligate and wasteful, superficial and irrational, an architecture of play.[23]

Moore and Mistaken Identity

For architectural theorists, it is a measure of the success of the project of queer theory that Johnson's work has so quickly come to stand for queer architecture when for most of its existence it did not. (More generally, it's a measure of the project's success that these readings proliferate so quickly – sometimes it seems almost everything and everyone is legible as gay.) It is also a problem when it produces misreadings. At this point I wanted to discuss the architecture of Charles Moore (1925–1993), whose writings I knew well and whose staff club for the University of California, Santa Barbara, I much admired. I had understood from various architectural historians that he was homosexual, and had seen this asserted in print several times, most recently in a book by Jorge Otero-Pailos that described an incident early in Moore's career when he was refused tenure at Princeton for his alleged sexual orientation. The question is only discussed in code; a letter of 1959, which is quoted, refers only to Moore as an 'uncertain quantity personally', and an anxiety among senior staff to 'avoid a climate too often associated with art centers'.[24] Moore went directly to the College of Environmental Design at Berkeley after that, the implication being that like countless others in the 1950s and 1960s, he went west in search of a more liberal climate. There is plenty of clichéd circumstantial evidence that seems to confirm this view. Moore owned a 'fabulous banana yellow mustang', a most unlikely car for a respectable 50-something academic; he was 'under spell of his mother' and 'steadfastly devoted to her'; he 'admired vulnerability' as if (implicitly) responding to something in himself; he wore a splendid moustache, waxed *up* at the ends in defiance of contemporary fashion; his birthday parties were always huge costume affairs at which no expense was spared; his fiftieth involved tap dancers, a procession involving all the guests and a gold cake.[25]

But I got Moore wrong. The Moore Foundation in Austin insisted, at considerable length, that the 'queer' Moore was a fabrication, based on inference and assertion rather than fact. Moore's work schedule was so ferocious, his life was in effect his work, and it left no time for a sexual life of any kind, and there is no record of one. I am happy to accept that, and in particular the view – firmly put by the Foundation – that Moore would neither have recognized nor understood the term gay in relation to himself. It does seem a clear case where an imperializing queer theory wishes to capture things, and people, which, strictly speaking, it should not.[26]

I have no interest in Moore's private life per se. I am however interested in the way that his buildings, and architectural theory, might be thought of in terms of sex. Moore was certainly interested in human bodies, more so than almost any artist of his generation. He argued consistently for the consideration of the way architectural space might be lived; space was no abstraction, but something inhabited, corporeally. He was fixated on the relationship between the body and architecture, or more accurately, the *experience* of the body in architecture. This was the subject of a book-length study, *Body, Memory and Architecture* (1977) with architecture students in mind, co-authored with Kent Bloomer. It says nothing about sex of itself, but its fixation on bodily experience arguably makes the building itself something like an extended erogenous zone, as if every part of every building were considered capable of bodily affect. It is worth quoting at length from the preface. Identifying a lack in conventional architectural teaching, the authors stated:

> We observed that reference was seldom made to the unique perceptual and emotional capacities of the human being; even historians concentrated on the more general influence of culture on the form of buildings and landscapes. Issues of joy and beauty were often regarded as quaint and arbitrary ... It became apparent to us that behind this conflict was the general assumption, seldom debated, that architecture is a highly specialized system with a set of prescribed technical goals rather than a sensual social art responsive to real human desires and feelings. This limitation is most frighteningly manifested in the reliance on two-dimensional diagrams that lay more stress on the quantifiable features of building organization than on the polychromatic and three-dimensional qualities of the whole architectural experience. At the same

time we have been observing that the human body, which is
our most fundamental three-dimensional possession, has not
itself been a central concern in the understanding of architectural form; that architecture, to the extent that it is considered
an art, is characterized in its design stages as an abstract visual
art and not as a body centred art.[27]

Now the key words here in this introductory statement are *joy*
and *beauty* (which lead the authors, heretically, into the territory
of pleasure), *desires*, *body* and *experience*. These terms are central to
a psychoanalytically informed view of the world, but as the authors
correctly point out, have been suppressed in architectural discourse.
That modernist practice might have sometimes – in Mies, for example
– produced the sensuous use of materials is correct too, but there is
no question about the impoverishment of the discourse. This opening gambit led the authors to wide-ranging discussion of the haptic
perception of architectural space, illustrated with their own sketches
and cartoons. Like Kevin Lynch's *Image of the City* (1962), they drew
on common-sense knowledge of the existing built environment –
their prose resembles Lynch a good deal in its breezy tone and lack
of pretension. But unlike Lynch, their language (*desires, joy, body*)
speaks of a familiarity with psychoanalytical discourse, and of a
world made complex by the erotic.

Moore and two colleagues had already explored these themes
in the book *The Place of Houses* (1974). Less a manifesto, it was a
detailed exploration of design principles legible in Western building
over several centuries, much of it vernacular. They extracted principles
from buildings as they existed in the world, rather than plans, and
there was robust historicism, not to say conservatism, throughout
with the American neoclassical vernacular singled out as particularly
worthy. The final part of the book was an ostensibly straightforward
set of design questions an architect might ask of a client. However,
its lengthy exploration of bodily habits and functions took it into
neo-therapeutic territory that recalls Neutra. Here, however, there
is an erotic dimension to the discussion that Neutra's rather lacks.
Here, for example, are Moore's thoughts on bathroom design, which
draw on several long-standing obsessions. Complaining of the mass-
produced package bathroom common to most modern houses ('one
of the more evident stereotypes we live with'), he damned American
assumptions that

washing is best achieved on the slippery bottom of a bathtub in
a room used chiefly for defecation, your lower limbs entangled
in a slimy curtain pulled toward you by the rush of cold air
occasioned by the squirt of hot water onto a small portion of
your back.

By contrast with this modern view, he writes, washing and bathing
were activities traditionally 'shared without shame', and 'excuses for
relaxed social interaction'. 'The whole act of taking off one's clothes,
so as to be especially unconscious of one's body, and its unencumbered
movement and then relaxing, soothed in a series of monumental
spaces – [is] all heightened by that sense of being somewhere.'[28]

That explicit connection of bodily pleasure with architecture
has its clearest expression in the small house he built for himself at
Orinda, California (the house has sadly not survived in its original
form).[29] Orinda put bodily pleasure at the heart of the design, alluding to cultures and histories in which bathing was a public, sociable
activity.[30] A single-storey pavilion of 1,545 square feet, it is open-plan,
built around a giant bathing aedicule in what is, in effect, the living
room. The great serpentine shower head, like a Parisian streetlamp,
is clearly visible in Morley Baer's classic photograph above the grand
piano. Right at the centre of the house, it makes the act of showering
into a public act, exposing it not only to whoever else might be in the
house, but to the exterior world too (admittedly, it's a private lot, but
the principle remains). It is nothing less than a temple to bathing.[31]

For Moore himself, his houses may have had no sexual meaning.
But for others, they genuinely did, and this perception of eroticism
arguably needs taking seriously. Moore's New Haven house, for
example, received a five-page, all-colour treatment in the October
1969 *Playboy*, for example, in which it inevitably carried a weight
of erotic expectation. The house itself was a conversion rather than
a new build, a 1,400-square-foot timber-frame house built in the
1860s. Rather than extend, Moore chose to alter the house by
punching three holes through it – vertical tunnels made of thin
plywood, bringing light into the building and opening up different
parts of the interior space to each other. Moore gave the tunnels
names, each one personifying and anthropomorphizing a different
part of the house. 'The first shaft, named Howard', wrote Moore,

Charles Moore, Orinda House, interior (1962). The bathing aedicule was clearly visible
from outside the house.

'starts by the entry door and drops to the reclaimed basement; a second, called Berengaria, rises midway through the house, reaching from the first floor through the second and the attic to a skylight at the roof; a third, Ethel, drops from a lower skylit shed at the rear to the kitchen in the basement below.' Here the house becomes literally a huddle of bodies. It was no doubt mainly a joke, but underlying it was also a serious statement about the bodily imagination of architecture. The anthropomorphism is made more explicit in Moore's 1974 book *The Place of Houses*, where he writes of 'twisting around Berengaria to the second floor bedroom, bath and sauna'.[32]

The shafts bring light into what might well be described as a high camp interior, full of theatrical clashes of form, materials and taste.[33] The third-floor bedroom is covered with a giant, abstracted, star-spangled banner and a *trompe l'oeil* print of a cathedral dome set into the ceiling. On a lower floor were two portraits – eighteenth century from their appearance – hanging directly above a Wurlitzer jukebox, stacked with old 78s. On the third floor there was a secluded sauna. There's a neon sculpture in pink. It could easily be a Dan Flavin light sculpture, but removed from the austere context of New York minimalism simply to provide some jolly illumination. Every other part of the house is stuffed with incident and detail; there are little nooks everywhere in which one might hide and observe the world. Leftover spaces were stuffed with bottles of spirits, or books. Outsize Pop Art graphics blared from walls. It is relentlessly vertiginous, playful with space, colour and material, a kind of benign Piranesi (the allusion to Piranesi is real enough, but unlike his spaces, which imprison their inhabitants in stone, this one is so flimsy, anyone could punch their way out).

For *Playboy*, the house signified sexual hedonism. Moore was described, correctly, although misleadingly, as a 'bachelor architect' to signal availability; a beautiful young woman is photographed nude, in a state of rapture in the sauna. Guests were described 'usually headed for the bar', matching the expectations of the magazine's readers who when not entertaining young women were invariably mixing cocktails. Formally it was rich in contrasting and sometimes unlikely materials (corduroy, antique brick, silver, vinyl); it is whimsical (large wooden panels representing the numbers one to five can be arranged in any order according to whim); it makes allusions to

Charles Moore, New Haven House, view of main bedroom (1965). The predominant colours are red and white; note the *trompe l'oeil* ceiling.

theatre (the bathroom is dominated by a large theatrical mirror); there are any number of spaces to which guests can retire from the main scene. *Playboy*, of course, appreciated the 'guest cove', an intimate, low space with a bed overlooking the main part of the house, a private space from which the public realm could be observed and, implicitly, used to fuel fantasy – it recalls the pool observation bar that Hefner built into both his Playboy Mansions. The photography celebrated the 'flipped out domain' referred to in the text. Nowhere was there a straight perspective shot of the exterior (and of course none of the axonometric sketches that would have appeared in the architectural press); instead there was a set of psychedelic interiors populated by male–female couples in intimate poses. Edited in classic *Playboy* style, everything in the article seemed to lead to bed: a big, white, empty space, pregnant with possibilities.

To readers now, *Playboy*'s version of Moore's New Haven house is strangely off-key. It does read in erotic terms, but not the straight-forwardly heterosexual terms of the magazine. This has little to do with Moore himself but with the intervening four decades of cultural history in which American Pop Art has become unquestionably queer. It's a family house, repurposed as the opposite, a space for distinctly adult socialization. Whether this in reality meant sex, I don't know – but sex is abundantly present in the design, which is why *Playboy* featured it in the first place. The erotics of the space are one key problem. The other is the fact that Moore, an architect with a notoriously full academic and professional life, chose to devote so much effort to the creation of a space so oriented to pleasure. The same body-pleasure oriented tendency can be found throughout Moore's work, from the 1966 Sea Ranch with its playful sublimation of the changing rooms (supergraphics by Barbara Stauffacher, standard issue u.s. mailboxes for lockers) to the building I know best, the ucsb Faculty Club, and its open-air swimming pools. And this extravagant, generous, bodily quality runs all the way through Moore's output from the individual houses he built for himself in the 1960s to the most public projects such as the Piazza d'Italia in New Orleans, for which he created an entire new classical mode for the columns, the 'Deli Order', incorporating neon highlights and Milano salami sculpted in relief.

A Queer Conclusion

Charles Moore's own life was of no consequence to me in the end. It is not surprising that some might have wanted to claim him for queer theory, however mistaken that might be. His work represents a world in which bodily pleasure is (at the very least) better integrated to everyday life than it ordinarily is. This emphasis on pleasure has been something queer culture has emphasized. If there are – mostly – no children, there is an extraordinary amount of time, energy and money freed up for other things. So queer culture becomes at its extremes a kind of research and development arm for a culture organized around erotic satisfaction. If sex becomes the driver of an adult life, then it leads to a different set of spatial priorities: bathrooms and bedrooms sublimated, public and private blurred. In the real estate market, this is precisely what has happened, with queer zones of cities effectively functioning as avant-gardes, spaces where new tastes can be tested in extreme conditions.

By way of a conclusion, I thought of my own experience in mid-1990s Manchester when I first started to think about these things. I have no idea about the sexuality of the architects and designers who produced the extraordinary phenomenon of Canal Street. Some were gay, I imagine, but many were not; in any case, I doubt there was any meaningful connection between a designer's sexuality and the nature of their work. (I never wrote, for example, of the 'gay' or 'straight' designer of a particular bar – it made no sense.) I was far more alert to the collective nature of the street, and how the built environment might be used, or understood, in ways that often far exceed what their designers imagined. I was simply grateful, as a straight man, that so many people at that time, of whatever sexual persuasion, were willing to commit so much energy to exploring pleasure. That principle will, I suspect, outlive any sexual categorizations we have now.

Epilogue

This book's origins lie in a peculiar historical moment for residents of the rich countries of the northern hemisphere. For these ostensibly fortunate people, the moment was defined by two contradictory impulses. On the one hand, it was a moment of quite unprecedented freedom. Never in human history were so many sexual images available, so easily and cheaply. Any lingering anxieties about the sexual content of advertising or television paled into insignificance against the unstoppable wave of pornography available on the internet. It was claimed as the result of an article of 1995 in *Time* that as much as 80 per cent of internet traffic was porn, a figure (anecdotally) still much believed. This is wrong, but the true figure may be a still very substantial 12 per cent.[1] Along with an unprecedented number of images of sexual acts, it was possible suddenly to know about any and every conceivable sexual predilection. On top of that, the medical knowledge of sexual behaviour and sexual disease was unprecedented. General knowledge about sex was arguably higher than at any previous time, along with the ability to control both disease and fertility in ways that would have been inconceivable less than a century previously. For Americans, the people who had experienced these changes before anyone else, and more thoroughly, it was a time of extraordinary enlightenment – or extraordinary moral decay depending on one's point of view.

On the other hand, it was a period marked by considerable anxieties about sex. When sex, post-Kinsey and post-Hite, became something like a right to pleasure, it was not accompanied by a sense of freedom, rather the reverse. Having solved or assuaged long-standing anxieties about disease, and more or less banished other ones about fertility, sex was defined by a whole new set of

Bikini Land of Venice, Venice, California.

troubles to do with performance (first female, then male, now both) and more recently anxieties about sex in relation to responsibilities of work and childcare. The contemporary literature around sex expresses this very clearly. There's always something *wrong* that can be fixed. The academic works published around the time of writing included several nostalgic for an early modern sense of liberation. The 1920s were no time to be a sexual libertarian, certainly not in Europe, but it was a fertile period to be thinking of such things, via Freud, or more radically via Reich. Some of the recent literature is imbued with nostalgia for such liberatory thinking, even if ultimately critical of it. Christopher Turner's biography of Reich, published in 2011, was a good case. An account of Reich's sexual revolution, including a very detailed description of the orgone accumulator, it was sceptical of the possibility of that revolution while being simultaneously drawn to it. There is something melancholy about the project, a mourning for lost possibilities.[2] His book was attacked by Reich's remaining devotees, which although entirely predictable, was also unfair given the author's evident enthusiasm for the topic and its continued imaginative power.[3] Far more critical of Reich was Jonathan Engel's *American Therapy*, which in its intellectual and historical scope provides some inspiration for this book. Engel's conclusions were pragmatic and conservative: therapy was good, but one should choose one's shrink with care. Even he, however, was clearly drawn to the notion of a large-scale rethinking of sex.[4] These two books were widely read, and seemed to point to a post-Foucauldian assessment of the possibility of liberation. Foucault's *History of Sexuality* famously challenged the whole 'repressive hypothesis', arguing (among other things) that the alleged suppression of sex in the Victorian world was in fact a representation of its perceived power.[5] These books also seemed to mark something of a reaction to feminist conversation of the 1980s, which at its most radical had argued for a form of sexual apartheid in order to remake relations between men and women. Andrea Dworkin's *Intercourse* was widely misrepresented, but it had no time at all for twentieth-century notions of sexual liberation if they emerged from a patriarchal context.[6]

The publishing of two books can hardly be termed a reassessment of sexual liberation, but there were other, related phenomena, including a serious cinematic treatment of Alfred Kinsey, and several well-reviewed accounts of *Playboy* in which Hefner emerged as both more complex and more liberal than normally thought possible. Elizabeth Fraterrigo's work, very helpful in chapter Five, is a good example.[7] The publishing house Taschen, always quick to spot a trend, especially an erotic one, republished the entire early run of *Playboy* in 2010, as mentioned earlier.[8] Alongside all this has been the continued flowering of queer literature, which continued ever more fervently to make the case for sexual pleasure. An important writer throughout this book has been Leo Bersani, who at the height of the AIDS crisis in 1987 made the case for a continued sex-positive approach to the world, refusing to be beaten back by the threat of disease, or conservative morality.[9] Bersani was writing then in the most refined of academic contexts, the New York journal of aesthetics, *October*; his readers would have largely agreed, even if some of the practices he described might have made them wince. But since 1987, Bersani's academic view has flourished in a literary context. Edmund White's memoirs

'History is Myth', Venice, California. Mural by Rip Cronk on corner of Speedway and Windward avenues, painted July 1989.

of New York, published in 2009, described for a broad readership a life in which sex is at least as frequent as eating, perhaps more so, and in which almost every meeting was punctuated by orgasm.[10] The appeal of this is undoubtedly wide, regardless of the sexual orientation of the reader. From the present perspective, it is striking that such a radically promiscuous position should be so widely disseminated, if not emulated. Bersani was correct in 1987 to identify promiscuity as the problem – it was that, and not homosexuality per se that was so unsettling for authority.[11] A quarter-century later, and promiscuity, at least as an idea, is thoroughly mainstream. So much so that for the self-appointed high priests of taste at the *New York Observer*, for youngsters, sex was frankly a bore.[12]

Queer theory has done a splendid job of keeping the erotic going. Nowhere else has there been such a sustained discussion of the vagaries and intricacies of sex, its meanings and the intricacies of its practice. It has been great too for the reconsideration of spatial questions, the rethinking of architecture out of necessity, or sheer boredom, as a sexual playground. The queer imagination has also powerfully impacted on the straight world. Two recent books on (mostly) heterosexual sex threw this into relief: Esther Perel's *Mating in Captivity* and Catherine Hakim's *Honey Money*, both highly controversial on publication.[13] For Perel, a psychotherapist specializing in sexual questions, sex naturally meant promiscuity, danger, competition, difference. Without these things it couldn't function at all, hence the difficulty so many millions of couples seemed to be having with monogamy. For Hakim, a sociologist, sex was destructively constrained by social norms, and women in particular were losers. What was required was a proper, open free-market in sex, in which there would be winners and losers, but from which society overall would ultimately profit. Both Perel and Hakim imagined worlds in which the erotic was properly liberated, occupying a more central and more public part of everyday life. The criticism of Hakim in particular was ferocious, but what she described was a scenario that had many of the elements of queer culture as it already existed.[14]

Revolution or not, many of the same basic questions that so exercised Freud and his followers at the beginning of the twentieth century still remain at the start of the twenty-first. How could, or indeed would, a 'healthy' sexual life be maintained within the bound-aries permitted for it in bourgeois society? It is in some ways surprising therefore that architecture has remained so coy on the topic. My case studies have been largely states of exception, buildings by those either with the money to experiment or so far outside the norm to be unaffected by social mores. Or they have been simply left unbuilt. Architecture's inherent caution is perhaps one reason, as well as the reality – well described by Göran Therborn – that the family has proved a remarkably durable institution, far more than Western liberals often like to recognize. That said, the openness about sex generated by queer and feminist discourses has produced a space in which we might try to imagine again different ways of living.

My (figurative) return to Morningside was salutary. My temporary horror of it was in large part a projection of my own anxieties on to the architecture. When I thought harder about my immediate environment, an 1878 tenement block, during the writing of the book it became clear not only how much I knew about my neighbours' lives, but how few of them were exactly normative: a man who sustained two lovers simultaneously, until one (noisy) night they found out about each other; a couple who chose to keep their lives divided between Edinburgh and Sweden so they could avoid each other's presence as much as possible. There were two young families whose appearance of normality had been achieved at considerable cost. In its recent history, virtually no part of my immediate block could be described as normative. Slightly further afield – which is to say 50 yards or so – there was an outwardly respectable street, described by a friend as a veritable Sodom, the epicentre of a series of catastrophic family break-ups in the 1980s. Round the corner there were plenty of gay men and women, a colony of apparent nudists living opposite, and to the rear, a house being renovated by a successful shrink whose long-standing practice had specialized in the sheer variety and complexity of local sexual relationships. In short, the outward propriety of my street concealed a remarkable variety of sexual lives, virtually none of which matched the standards claimed by the buildings themselves. Another approach to the same question: as much as I had projected a negative fantasy on to Morning-side, I had projected positive ones on to two much sunnier beach cities, Los Angeles and Rio de Janeiro, both of which I had visited often and knew well. Yet in spite of the outward form of these places and their reputation for body-centric cultures, categorically nothing of any sexual nature had ever happened to me in either place in years of visits. For sure I had not been looking for it – but equally, the middle-class academics I knew in those places seemed, if anything, more buttoned-up than their equivalents at home, struggling with family (Brazil) or work (LA); there seemed even less time to play than in superficially Calvinist Edinburgh. This comparison was deeply unscientific – it is a task for someone else to do a proper comparative study. What it did suggest, however, was that the out-ward form of a place had nothing whatever to do with the sexual lives it framed. Human beings will not radically change their sexual habits because of the way their surroundings are organized: they simply adapt.

That would seem to point to an anti-deterministic conclusion, and a safe return home to Morningside. That is not quite right, however. Whatever happens in my neighbourhood it remains as closed to public scrutiny as the architecture, and I remain enough of an old modernist to wish for different images of how our lives might be. In that sentiment I would invoke the philosopher Fredric Jameson on the continual need for utopian thought. Architecture can't coerce people into different lives, but it can provide images of what those lives might be like. If nothing else, I hope this book has reminded readers of the different ways architecture has engaged with the question of sex and how it might again in the future.

References

Introduction

1 E. Perel, *Mating in Captivity: Sex, Lies and Domestic Bliss* (London, 2007).

2 You have to imagine the word 'sex' spoken by an upper-class Scot.

3 S. Freud, *The Penguin Freud Library*, vol. VII: *On Sexuality*, trans. J. Strachey (London, 1991), pp. 101–11.

4 Richard J. Williams, *The Anxious City: English Urbanism at the End of the Twentieth Century* (London, 2004).

5 M. Foucault, *The History of Sexuality*, trans. R. Hurley (New York, 1990), vol. I.

6 J. Butler, *Gender Trouble: Feminism and the Subversion of Identity* (New York, 1990); C. Paglia, *Sexual Personae* (New York, 1992); R. Scruton, *Sexual Desire, A Philosophical Investigation* (London, 1994). There is unexpected commonality between Scruton and Foucault: both understand sex as primarily a social product, not a biological one.

7 H. Havelock Ellis, *Studies in the Psychology of Sex*, 6 vols (Salt Lake City, UT, 2004).

8 Ibid., vol. VI, p. 3.

9 H. Havelock Ellis, *The Task of Social Hygiene* (Boston and New York, 1916).

10 A. Forel, *The Sexual Question: A Scientific, Psychological, Hygienic and Sociological Study* (New York, 1931), p. 13.

11 Ibid., p. 443: 'sexual excesses in the country are more conformable to nature. Apart from marriage, we meet with concubinage, infidelity and sometimes prostitution, but these excesses are never widely spread in small places where everyone knows each other . . .'.

12 S. Zweig, *The World of Yesterday* (London, 1943), p. 77.

13 See account of Sitte and agoraphobia in A. Vidler, *Warped Space: Art, Architecture and Anxiety in Modern Culture* (Cambridge, MA, and London, 2000), pp. 25–50.

14 M. Mead, *Male and Female: A Study of the Sexes in a Changing World* (London, 1949), pp. 325–41.

15 Ibid., p. 329.

16 A. C. Kinsey, *Sexual Behavior in the Human Male* (Philadelphia, 1948).

17 J. Gathorne-Hardy, *Alfred Kinsey: Sex, The Measure of All Things* (London, 1999); *Kinsey*, dir. B. Condon (American Zoetrope/Myriad Pictures, 2004).

18 Kinsey, *Sexual Behavior*, p. 607.

19 Foucault, *History of Sexuality*, vol. I.

20 Ibid., vol. I, p. 3.

21 Ibid., vol. I, p. 28.

22 Le Corbusier, *Towards a New Architecture* (London, 1927), pp. 122–7.

23 Le Corbusier, *The Modulor: A Harmonious Measure to the Human Scale, Universally Applicable to Architecture and Mechanics* (Cambridge, MA, 1954).

24 This argument is developed in more detail in Williams, R. J., *Brazil: Modern Architectures in History* (London, 2009), pp. 63–94.

25 O. Niemeyer, *As curvas do tempo* (Rio de Janeiro, 1999).

26 R. Bofill, *L'Architecture d'un Homme: Entretiens avec François Hébert-Stevens* (Paris, 1978), p. 54.

27 Ibid.

28 R. Bofill and J.-L. André, *Espaces d'une vie* (Paris, 1989), p. 190.

29 'Walden 7 by Taller de Arquitectura, Ricardo Bofill', GA *Houses*, 1 (1976), pp. 18–35.

30 Forel, *Sexual Question*, p. 448.

31 J. Engel, *American Therapy: The Rise of Psychotherapy in the United States* (New York, 2008).

32 *Frasier* (Grub Street Productions/Gramnet Productions/Paramount Network TV, 1993–2004).

33 W. H. Masters and V. E. Johnson, *Human Sexual Response* (Toronto and New York, 1966); S. Hite, *The Hite Report: A National Study of Female Sexuality* (New York, 1976).

34 L. V. Marks, *Sexual Chemistry: A History of the Contraceptive Pill* (New Haven, CT, and London, 2001), p. 193: 'One woman, for instance, put the drug in her vagina, and another confused the term "oral" with "aural" and placed the pill in her ear.'

35 H. Gurley Brown, *Sex and the Single Girl* (New York, 1962); H. Gurley Brown, *Sex and the Office* (London, 1965).

36 *Cosmopolitan*, CLXXII/4 (April 1972), centrefold.

37 See E. Fraterrigo, *Playboy and the Making of the Good Life in Modern America* (New York, 2009); also C. Pitzulo, *Bachelors and Bunnies: The Sexual Politics of Playboy* (Chicago, 2011).

38 *The People vs. Larry Flynt*, dir. M. Forman (Phoenix Pictures, 1996).

39 L. Flynt, *An Unseemly Man: My Life as a Pornographer, Pundit and Social Outcast* (London, 1996).

40 C. Hakim, *Honey Money: The Power of Erotic Capital* (London, 2011).

one The Care of the Body

1 Gebhard in K. Frampton, *Modern Architecture: A Critical History* (London and New York, 1992), p. 249.

2 G. Marmostein, 'Steel and Slurry: Dr Philip M. Lovell, Architectural Patron', *Southern California Quarterly*, LXXXIV/3–4, p. 244.

3 P. Lovell, *Health of the Child* (Los Angeles, 1926), title page.

4 Marmostein, 'Steel and Slurry', pp. 241–70.

5 Neutra, letter to Philip Lovell, Newport Beach, 28 January 1969, UCLA archives, 1974, box 75, f5. Neutra is desperate for Lovell to confirm his integrity as an architect here, against slurs that he 'stole' the Health House commission from Schindler.

6 Lovell, *Health of the Child*, p. vii.

7 T. S. Hines, *Richard Neutra and the Search for Modern Architecture* (New York and Oxford, 1982), pp. 75–6.

8 Lovell, *Health of the Child*, pp. 3–4.

9   See A. M. Stern, *Eugenic Nation: Faults and Frontiers of Better Breeding in Modern America* (Berkeley, CA, and London, 2005).
10 Hines, *Richard Neutra*, pp. 75–6.
11 Quoted in Marmostein, 'Steel and Slurry', p. 252. The book is now extremely rare, unlike Lovell's *Health of the Child*.
12 Lovell, *Health of the Child*, pp. 155–6.
13 Quoted in Marmostein, 'Steel and Slurry', p. 252.
14 R. Schindler, 'A Co-operative Dwelling', *T-Square*, II/2 (February 1932), pp. 20–21.
15 J. Steele, *R. M. Schindler, 1887–1953, An Exploration of Space* (Cologne, 2005).
16 Reported in Hines, *Richard Neutra*, p. 60.
17 Marmostein, 'Steel and Slurry', p. 248.
18 R. M. Schindler, 'Care of the Body: Shelter or Playground', *LA Times* (21 April 1926), pp. 26–7.
19 R. M. Schindler, 'Care of the Body: Plumbing and Health', *LA Times* (21 March 1926), pp. 25–6.
20 Neutra, account of conversation between R.J.N. and Dr Philip M. Lovell, 27 May 1962, UCLA archives, box 75, f9.
21 Marmostein, 'Steel and Slurry', p. 254. See also Hines, *Richard Neutra*, pp. 76–7.
22 Steele, *R. M. Schindler.*
23 Interview with Dionne Neutra quoted in Marmostein, 'Steel and Slurry', p. 257.
24 Hines, *Richard Neutra.*
25 Ibid.
26 Ibid., p. 81. Lovell's recipes were indeed complex and labour-intensive. See the appendix to *Health of the Child*.
27 R. M. Schindler, 'Care of the Body', *LA Times.*
28 P. M. Lovell, undated text on Neutra, 1929, from opening of the house, UCLA archives, box 75, f10.
29 Hines, *Richard Neutra.*
30 P. M. Lovell, undated text on Neutra, 1929.
31 Reported by Marmostein, 'Steel and Slurry', p. 255.
32 S. Lavin, *Form Follows Libido: Architecture and Richard Neutra in a Psychoanalytical Culture* (Cambridge, MA, and London, 2004).
33 Good definition by Neutra's son, Dion, quoted in in B. M. Lamprecht, *Neutra: Complete Works* (Cologne and London, 2000), p. 7.
34 R. Neutra, *Life and Human Habitat* (Stuttgart, 1956).
35 Hence the title of Susie Orbach's semi-fictional account of her experience as an analyst, *The Impossibility of Sex* (New York, 2000). Wilhelm Reich was, notoriously, one psychoanalyst who *did* cross the threshold between analysis and sex, and his reputation suffered as a result.
36 E. Perel, *Mating in Captivity: Sex, Lies and Domestic Bliss* (London, 2007).
37 Lamprecht, *Neutra*, p. 42.
38 Lavin, *Form Follows Libido.*
39 R. Neutra, letter to Mr and Mrs Chueys (8 July 1955), UCLA archives, box 36, f1.
40 Ibid.
41 The changes had mainly to do with increasing the extent of glazing, to make use of improved glass technology; the overall design principles of the original house remained the same.
42 Hines, *Richard Neutra.*
43 Ibid.

44　Perel, *Mating in Captivity*.

45　Lovell, *Health of the Child*, p. 156.

46　Neutra, *Life and Human Habitat*, p. 251.

47　Marmostein, 'Steel and Slurry', p. 257.

two **Inside the Orgone Accumulator**

1　S. Lavin, *Form Follows Libido: Architecture and Richard Neutra in a Psychoanalytical Culture* (Cambridge, MA, and London, 2004). This is, crudely summarized, Lavin's argument.

2　Hawkwind, *Space Ritual: Alive in Liverpool and London* (United Artists, 1973).

3　J. Kerouac, *On the Road* (London, 1958), p. 144.

4　R. Morris, 'Three Extra-Visual Artists', in *Continuous Project Altered Daily: The Writings of Robert Morris* (Cambridge, MA, and London, 1994).

5　Lavin, *Form Follows Libido*. For the argument about Moore and Reich, see J. Otero-Pailos, *Architecture's Historical Turn: Phenomenology and the Rise of the Postmodern* (Minneapolis and London, 2010), pp. 108–12.

6　The most informed account of the case can be found in M. Sharaf, *Fury on Earth: A Biography of Wilhelm Reich* (New York, 1994).

7　W. Reich, *The Sexual Revolution* (New York, 1969); W. Reich, *The Invasion of Compulsory Sex-Morality* (New York, 1971). It is not always easy to ascertain the sequence of Reich's publications, nor their original form. The best guide in English is Sharaf, *Fury on Earth*, pp. 521–4.

8　Brief account in O. Hatherley, *Militant Modernism* (Winchester, 2008), pp. 74–5.

9　Reich, *Sexual Revolution*, p. 157.

10　Reich, *Invasion*, pp. xxiii–xxiv.

11　See Stefan Zweig's remarks about the extent of prostitution in early twentieth-century Vienna in his *The World of Yesterday* (London, 1943), p. 77. Good commentary on this is in J. Mitchell, *Psychoanalysis and Feminism* (London, 1974), p. 426. See also the Introduction of the present volume.

12　Reich, *Invasion*, p. xxiv.

13　The edition Reich used is B. Malinowski, *The Sexual Life of Savages in North-western Melanesia* (London, 1929).

14　Reich, *Invasion*, p. 21.

15　Malinowski, quoted in Reich, *Invasion*, pp. 10–11.

16　Reich, *Invasion*, p. 22. There is no evidential basis for this assertion. Reich's remarks are based entirely on Malinowski, whom he interprets in his own way.

17　Sharaf, *Fury on Earth*, p. 522.

18　Reich, *Sexual Revolution*, pp. 154, 183.

19　Lenin quoted in Reich, *Sexual Revolution*, p. 187.

20　Ibid., p. 190.

21　W. Reich, *The Mass Psychology of Fascism* (London, 1975).

22　P. Reich, *A Book of Dreams* (London, 1974), p. 43.

23　See www.orgonics.com, accessed 8 June 2010.

24　W. Reich and A. S. Neill, *Record of a Friendship: The Correspondence Between Wilhelm Reich and A. S. Neill, 1936–1957*, ed. Beverley R. Placzek (London, 1982).

25　J. Greenfield, *Wilhelm Reich vs. the USA* (New York, 1974), pp. 368–74.

26　W. Reich, *People in Trouble* (New York, 1953), appendix. See also Sharaf, *Fury on Earth*, p. 221.

27 The sky's blue colour is indisputably the result of the scattering of light in the earth's atmosphere; blue predominates over other colours in the spectrum because of its short wavelength.

28 Greenfield, *Wilhelm Reich*.

29 The accumulator was claimed to be of use in the following: 'anemia, headaches, acute and chronic colds, hay fever, rheumatism, arthritis, varicose ulcers, chronic illnesses, bruises, cuts, lesions, abrasions, wounds, burns, sinusitis, migraine, vascular hypertension, high blood pressure, decompensated heart disease, brain tumors, arteriosclerosis, apoplectic attacks, skin inflammation, conjunctivitis, immobilization of vaginal bacteria, chronic fatigue, undernourishment, diabetes.' USA vs Wilhelm Reich 1954–7, Complaint for Injunction (10 February 1954), p. 18, www.wilhelmreichtrust.org/complaint_for_injunction.pdf.

30 W. Burroughs, 'My Experiences with Wilhelm Reich's Orgone Box', in *The Adding Machine: Collected Essays* (London, 1985).

31 M. E. Brady, 'The Strange Case of Wilhelm Reich', *New Republic* (26 May 1947).

32 M. E. Brady, 'The New Cult of Sex and Anarchy', *Harper's Magazine* (April 1947).

33 *WR: Mysteries of the Organism*, dir. D. Makavejev (Neoplanta/Telepol, 1971).

34 Hatherley, *Militant Modernism*.

35 Ibid., p. 93.

36 Kupferberg was the leader of the avant-garde pop group The Fugs. In the scene, he appears in an orange jumpsuit and tin helmet, caressing a rifle.

37 D. Malcolm, 'Dusan Makavejev: *WR: Mysteries of the Organism*', *Guardian* (3 June 1999).

38 'On the Fiftieth Anniversary of Reich's Death, Distortion and Slander at the Reich Exhibit in Vienna', Wilhelm Reich Museum Newsletter, www.wilhelmreichmuseum .org, 2008.

39 Ibid.

three **Communal Living**

1 R. D. Laing, *Sanity, Madness and the Family: Families of Schizophrenics* (London, 1970), p. 179. The case study I allude to here is 'Jean Head'.

2 A. Laing, *R. D. Laing: A Life* (Stroud, 2006), pp. 8–9.

3 Ibid.

4 A. Huxley, *Brave New World* (London, 1932).

5 See www.twinoaks.org, accessed 13 May 2011. 'Intentional community' is the contemporary expression for 'commune'.

6 B. F. Skinner, *Walden Two* (Englewood Cliffs, NJ, 1976), p. 74.

7 Ibid., p. 129.

8 Ibid., p. 122.

9 Ibid.

10 Ibid., p. 130.

11 Ibid., p. 202.

12 See www.twinoaks.org, accessed 16 May 2011. See also the account of Twin Oaks's early years by its founder: K. Kinkade, *A Walden Two Experiment: The First Five Years of Twin Oaks Community* (New York, 1974).

13 O. Figes, *A People's Tragedy: The Russian Revolution, 1891–1924* (London, 1997), p. 740.

14 Ibid., p. 740.

15 M. Sharaf, *Fury on Earth: A Biography of Wilhelm Reich* (New York, 1994), pp. 142–3.

16 W. Reich, *The Mass Psychology of Fascism* (London, 1975).

17 W. Reich, *The Sexual Revolution* (New York, 1969), pp. 219, 226, 228, 231.

18 The kibbutz was an important idea in Laing's circle too. Laing's early collaborator Aaron Esterson had experienced life on a kibbutz, and liked it; his positive experience of intentional community partly informs the critique of schizophrenia, *Sanity, Madness and the Family*. On Esterson, see Laing, *R. D. Laing*, p. 70.

19 M. Spiro, *Kibbutz: Venture in Utopia* (Cambridge, MA, 1956), p. 59.

20 J. Peres, 'In 50 Years the Kibbutz Movement has Undergone Many Changes', *Chicago Tribune* (9 May 1998).

21 Spiro, *Kibbutz*, p. 112.

22 In E. Krausz and D. Glanz, eds, *The Sociology of the Kibbutz: Studies of Israeli Society* (New Brunswick, NJ, and London, 1983), vol. II, pp. 256–7.

23 Ibid.

24 Spiro, *Kibbutz*, pp. 111–12.

25 Krausz and Glanz, *Sociology of the Kibbutz*, p. 258.

26 M. Spiro, *Children of the Kibbutz* (Cambridge, MA, 1965).

27 Spiro, *Kibbutz*, pp. 129, 232.

28 In series 11 of the UK version of the popular reality TV show *Big Brother*, a communal shower was instigated in order to try to provoke the contestants into televised sexual relations with each other (it failed).

29 In Krausz and Glanz, *Sociology of the Kibbutz*, pp. 233, 255, 264.

30 A. M. Bowes, *Kibbutz Goshen: An Israeli Commune* (Prospect Heights, IL, 1989), p. 90.

31 D. McNally, *A Long Strange Trip: The Inside History of the Grateful Dead and the Making of Modern America* (London, 2002), p. 208.

32 Grateful Dead, *Aoxomoxoa* (Warner Bros, 1969).

33 'The Hippies: Philosophy of a Subculture', *Time*, XC/1 (7 July 1967), p. 22.

34 P. Read, 'Infinite Points of Time: Morningstar Chronicles, Part 1 (California)', *The Digger Archives*, www.diggers.org/archives.htm, accessed 1 November 2012.

35 Ibid.

36 B. Wheeler, 'Home Free Home: Introduction', *The Digger Archives*, www.diggers.org/archives.htm, accessed 1 November 2012.

37 'Friar Tuck', in 'Home Free Home: Chapter 8, More Arrests and Bill Wheeler's Offer', *The Digger Archives*, www.diggers.org/archives.htm, accessed 1 November 2012.

38 M. Matthews, *Droppers: America's First Hippie Commune, Drop City* (Norman, OK, 2010), p. 190.

39 'Gwen', in 'Home Free Home: Chapter 10, First Ridge Settlers', *The Digger Archives*, www.diggers.org/archives.htm, accessed 1 November 2012.

40 'Home Free Home: Chapter 8', *The Digger Archives*, www.diggers.org/archives.htm, accessed 1 November 2012.

41 T. C. Boyle, *Drop City* (London, 2003).

42 J. Curl, *Memories of Drop City, The First Hippie Commune of the 1960s and the Summer of Love* (Lincoln, NE, 2007).

43 F. D. Scott, *Architecture or Techno-Utopia: Politics After Modernism* (Cambridge, MA, 2007), pp. 172–4.

44 S. Sadler, 'Drop City Revisited', *Journal of Architectural Education*, LVIII/1 (2006), pp. 7–8.

45 Curl, *Memories of Drop City*, p. 34.

46 Ibid. Curl describes Drop City as the place he in fact stopped taking drugs; BBC2, *Towards Tomorrow, c.* 1968, available as 'Drop City' at www.youtube.com, accessed 16 May 2011.

47 Curl, *Memories of Drop City*, pp. 93–4.

48 Matthews, *Droppers*, p. 164.

49 Curl, *Memories of Drop City*, p. 44.

50 Matthews, *Droppers*, p. 190.

51 F. D. Scott, *Architecture or Techno-Utopia: Politics After Modernism* (Cambridge, MA, 2007), p. 160.

52 Matthews, *Droppers*, p. 163.

53 Curl, *Memories of Drop City*.

54 L. Cumming, 'Alex Hartley, The World is Still Big', www.guardian.co.uk, 27 November 2011.

55 Conversation with Alex Hartley (15 June 2012).

56 Colonial Williamsburg, Virginia – a reconstructed eighteeenth-century city, staffed by volunteers in historic dress.

57 Matthews, *Droppers*, p. 165.

four **Phallic Towers and *Mad Men***

1 See 'The Most Phallic Building in the World: The Winner!', www.cabinetmagazine .org, accessed 20 March 2013.

2 A. Forty, *Words and Buildings: A Vocabulary of Modern Architecture* (London, 2000), p. 51.

3 A. Rand, *The Fountainhead* (London, 1994), p. 8.

4 Charles Moore's view is telling. He called Roark a 'dangerous baboon', declaring his sympathies instead with the supercilious, vacillating Peter Keating. C. Moore, *Charles Moore: Buildings and Projects, 1949–1986*, ed. E. J. Johnson (New York, 1986), p. 16.

5 The film version of *The Fountainhead* clearly invokes Mies too: the curtain-walled skyscrapers by Roark are essentially Mies designs.

6 The commissioning process is well covered in R.A.M. Stern, T. Mellins and D. Fishman, *New York 1960: Architecture and Urbanism Between the Second World War and the Bicentennial* (Cologne, 1997), pp. 343–5.

7 W. H. Jordy, 'Seagram Assessed', *Architectural Review*, CXXIV/743 (December 1958), pp. 374–82.

8 A. Whitman, 'Obituary: Mies van der Rohe Dies at 83; Leader of Modern Architecture', *New York Times* (19 August 1969).

9 Quoted by Beatriz Colomina in D. Mertens, ed., *The Presence of Mies* (Princeton, NJ, 1994), p. 197.

10 Whitman, 'Obituary'.

11 'Art: Less is More', *Time* (14 June 1954), available at www.time.com.

12 Friedman, A. T., *Women and the Making of the Modern House* (New York, 1998), p. 133; quoted, p. 131.

13 Stern et al., *New York 1960*, pp. 420–21.

14 *Life*, 42 (11 February 1957), pp. 89–96.

15 Ibid., p. 90

16 Veto advertisement, *Life* (11 February 1957), p. 72.

17 A. Chave, 'Minimalism and the Rhetoric of Power', *Arts*, 64 (January 1990), pp. 44–63.

18 *Mad Men*, prod. M. Wiener (Lionsgate/AMC, 2007–).

19 For an account of how 'gossip' might be used as an interrogative method, see G. Butt, *Between You and Me: Queer Disclosures in the New York Art World, 1948–1963* (Durham, NC, 2005).

20 Like Beatriz Colomina, I tend to think media representations of architecture are as real as any other aspect of architectural production. See Stead, N., 'Interview with Beatriz Colomina', *Architecture Australia*, XCIII/5 (September–October 2004), p. 102.

21 New York here is as usual a fiction: the series was filmed mostly in Los Angeles.

22 According to Mark Grief, the slogan was invented in 1917. See M. Grief, 'You'll Love the Way it Makes you Feel', *London Review of Books*, XXX/20 (23 October 2008), p. 15.

23 S. Freud, 'Civilization and its Discontents', in *The Penguin Freud Library*, vol. XII: *Civilization, Society and Religion*, trans. J. Strachey (London, 1991), pp. 57–145.

24 D. Singmaster, 'A Room With a Loo', *Architect's Journal*, CCVIII/5 (July 1998), pp. 23–36.

five **Pornomodernism**

1 M. Grief, 'You'll Love the Way it Makes you Feel', *London Review of Books*, XXX/20 (23 October 2008), pp. 15–16. Grief's highly critical take on the series centres on the idea of forbidden pleasure.

2 See 'Hugh Hefner's Playboy', 6 vols, at www.taschen.com.

3 L. Kipnis, *Bound and Gagged: Pornography and the Politics of Fantasy in America* (New York, 1996); A. Dworkin, *Pornography: Men Possessing Women* (London, 1981).

4 A. Lee, *Girl With a One Track Mind* (London, 2006); *Porn: A Family Business*, dir. J. Blumenfield and A. Marsh (Maxwell Productions, 2003–6).

5 See www.taschen.com. One of Taschen's main publishing categories, along with architecture, is 'Sexy Books', under the editorship of Dian Hanson. At the time of writing, it had republished its monumental *Big Penis* and *Big Breasts* books in 3-D versions.

6 The title referred to is N. Harris, *Naomi Harris, America Swings* (Cologne and London, 2010).

7 'The Playboy Town House', *Playboy* (May 1962), pp. 83–94. The same issue celebrates the design of the new club for Washington, DC. Like the Town House, the club was self-consciously modern, 'the ultimate in architectural design'. Behind the seven-storey glass facade, the key features were to include a 'floating fireplace' and an indoor garden. The club promised 'comfort and ease amid impressive surroundings'. The facade itself, like that of the Town House, was undemonstrative and Miesian, indistinguishable from the regional HQ of a small bank.

8 'Snazzy Four-Story Home for Gold Coast', *Chicago Daily News* (23 September 1959), p. 42: 'House to cost $150,000. A modern house will add a new note to an old North Side neighbourhood. The building will be 20 feet wide and four stories high at 28 E Bellevue. It will be the first single-family residence to be built in the area in 50 years, said architect R. Donald Jaye. A "LIGHT WELL" with balconies on the two upper floors focuses on a second floor swimming pool. The well divides the third floor living room from the study and the fourth floor master bedroom.

Construction is to start in two months with completion set for early spring of 1960. The building will cost $150,000. It is being built for Hugh M. Hefner, editor and publisher of Playboy magazine. IN ADDITION to the pool, the second floor has a recreation room, kitchen and dining area. The third floor has an 18-by-40-foot living room with a 24-foot entertainment wall for photographs and television. The first floor will contain a carport, mechanical equipment room and servants' quarters. An open stairway connects the second floor with the third and a circular staircase connects the third floor with the fourth. An elevator serves all the floors. LIGHTING will be controlled by individual rheostats. Floors are hollow for radiant heating. The house will be air conditioned. The interior of the five-bath house will be of stone, wood, terrazzo and tile. The exterior will be of exposed concrete colored black, marble panels, plate glass and aluminum.'

9   'The Playboy Town House', *Playboy* (May 1962), p. 84.

10   Ibid., p. 89.

11   Ibid., p. 105.

12   The plot centres on a photographer (played by James Stewart) confined to his apartment after an accident. The plot revolves around what he sees, and imagines, of his neighbours' lives.

13   M. Amis, *The Moronic Inferno and Other Visits to America* (London, 1986), pp. 170, 179.

14   G. Edgren, *Inside the Playboy Mansion* (London, 1998), pp. 8, 82, 111.

15   'Mystery Illness May be Tied to Playboy Mansion's Famed Grotto', http://latimes.com/blogs, 22 April 2011.

16   N. Olsberg, ed., *Between Earth and Heaven: The Architecture of John Lautner* (New York, 2008).

17   B. Wolfe, 'Swimming in Red Ink', *Playboy*, 11 (July 1964), pp. 93, 98, 100, 116; 'A Playboy Pad: Pleasure on the Rocks', review of John Lautner, Elrod House, *Playboy*, XVIII/11 (November 1971), pp. 151–5, 208.

18   Olsberg, *Between Earth and Heaven*.

19   B. A. Campbell-Lange, *John Lautner: Disappearing Space* (Cologne, 2005), p. 8.

20   Olsberg, *Between Earth and Heaven*, p. 42.

21   Ibid., pp. 53, 64.

22   'A Playboy Pad', p. 208; 'House Spectacular: Full of Daring Ideas', *House and Garden* (May 1969), p. 103.

23   Wolfe, 'Swimming in Red Ink', p. 98.

24   See 'Biography', www.helenart.com, accessed 17 October 2010.

25   Campbell-Lange, *John Lautner*, p. 85.

26   Olsberg, *Between Earth and Heaven*, pp. 101–2.

27   D. Blasberg, 'Who the Hell is James Goldstein?', www.interviewmagazine.com, 22 January 2010.

28   'The bathroom from hell', according to one of Goldstein's entourage. Author visit to Sheats-Goldstein house, June 2009.

29   See discussion in A. T. Friedman, *Women and the Making of the Modern House* (New York, 1998), pp. 26–8.

30   Goldstein denies that the house has been used for a porn shoot. Perhaps *Possessions* is too tame to qualify. Blasberg, 'Who the Hell is James Goldstein?'

31   G. Matt, T. Edlinger and F. Waldvogel, *The Porn Identity: Expeditionen in die Dunkelzone*, exh. cat., Kunsthalle Wien, Vienna (2009).

six **The Hotel**

1   Chic & Basic, a boutique hotel on the Herengracht.
2   Hitchcock's fascination with sex is indisputable, but not matched by any desire for it: his marriage was celibate. See J. R. Taylor, *Hitch: The Life and Times of Alfred Hitchcock* (New York, 1976).
3   E. Perel, *Mating in Captivity: Sex, Lies and Domestic Bliss* (London, 2007), p. 55.
4   The long history of Japanese immigration to Brazil may partly account for this, but Brazil's huge Japanese population is really a product of the coffee boom of the late nineteenth century.
5   S. Chaplin, *Japanese Love Hotels: A Cultural History* (London, 2007), pp. 53, 73–80.
6   Ibid., p. 1.
7   Ibid., pp. 58–9.
8   Ibid., p. 93.
9   D. Gimaraens and L. Cavalcanti, *Arquitectura de motéis Cariocas: Espaço e organização social* (Rio de Janeiro, 1982), p. 22.
10 Perel, *Mating in Captivity*.
11 Gimaraens and Cavalcanti, *Arquitectura de motéis Cariocas*, pp. 27, 46, 65.
12 D. Albrecht and E. Johnson, *New Hotels for Global Nomads* (London and New York, 2002), pp. 9, 35.
13 P. Cook, 'The Hotel is Really a Small City', *Architectural Design* (February 1968), pp. 90–93.
14 'John C. Portman', *L'Architecture d'Aujourd'hui*, 193 (October 1977), pp. 48–61.
15 The restaurant closed for 'technical reasons' in 2004. No plans have been announced to reopen it, see www.emporis.com, accessed 13 November 2010.
16 J. Portman, 'An Architecture for People and not for Things', *Architectural Record*, CLXI/1 (January 1977), p. 137.
17 S. Freud, 'Character and Anal Erotism', in *The Penguin Freud Library*, vol. VII: *On Sexuality*, trans. J. Strachey (London, 1991), pp. 169–75; J. Lacan, 'The Mirror Stage as Formative of the Function of the I', in *Écrits: A Selection*, trans. A. Sheridan (London, 2001); L. Mulvey, 'Visual Pleasure and Narrative Cinema', *Screen*, XVI/3 (Autumn 1975).
18 Portman, 'Architecture for People', p. 133.
19 P. Riani, P. Goldberger and J. Portman, *John Portman* (Milan, 1990), pp. 31, 37.
20 At the time of the hotel's inauguration, NASA was, coincidentally or not, experimenting with clusters of rocket boosters and fuel tanks to launch rockets.
21 A. Seidenbaum, 'The Portman Prescription', *Los Angeles Times* (18 June 1976), p. B15; L. Dwan, 'Roundabout', *Los Angeles Times* (31 July 1977), p. 090; P. Goldberger, 'Two Hotels in Los Angeles: Contrasts in Fresh Attempts', *New York Times* (5 March 1977), p. 6.
22 F. Jameson, 'The Cultural Logic of Late Capitalism', in *Rethinking Architecture: A Reader in Cultural Theory*, ed. N. Leach (London, 1996), pp. 238–46.
23 J. Smith, 'A Bonny Adventure', *Los Angeles Times* (16 February 1977), p. A1.
24 Dwan, 'Roundabout', p. 090.
25 Goldberger, 'Two Hotels in Los Angeles', p. 6.
26 Smith, 'A Bonny Adventure'.

seven What Would a Feminist City Look Like?

1 H. G. Wells quoted in R. Williams, *The Country and the City* (London, 1973), p. 5.
2 A. T. Friedman, *Women and the Making of the Modern House* (New York, 1998).
3 Originally in *House Beautiful* (May 1953); quoted in Friedman, *Making of the Modern House*, pp. 141–2.
4 A. Betsky, *Building Sex: Men, Women, Architecture and the Construction of Sexuality* (New York, 1995).
5 A. Rand, *The Fountainhead* (London, 1994).
6 See Bureau of Labor Statistics, www.bls.gov/cps/cpsaat39.pdf, accessed 28 November 2011. In the UK, the equivalent figure is as high as 87 per cent. In both the U.S. and the UK, the proportion of male architecture graduates ranges between 60 and 65 per cent: Garry Stevens, 'Women in Architecture Part 2: Big Swinging Dicks', www.archsoc.com, accessed 28 November 2011.
7 L. Nochlin, 'Why Have There Been No Great Women Artists?', *ARTnews* (January 1971), pp. 22–39, 67–71.
8 J. Jacobs, *The Death and Life of Great American Cities* (New York, 1961); B. Friedan, *The Feminine Mystique* (London, 1965); D. Hayden, 'What Would a Non-Sexist City Be Like?', *Signs: Journal of Women in Culture and Society*, V/3 (1980), pp. s170–87.
9 C. Paglia, *Sexual Personae* (New York, 1992).
10 *The Stepford Wives*, dir. B. Forbes (Columbia Pictures, 1975); *American Beauty*, dir. S. Mendes (DreamWorks, 1999); *Mad Men*, prod. M. Wiener (Lionsgate Television, 2007–).
11 Friedan, *Feminine Mystique*.
12 B. Friedan, *Life So Far* (New York, 2000).
13 Hayden, 'Non-Sexist City', pp. s170–87.
14 Friedan, *Feminine Mystique*, pp. 17–18, 25, 73.
15 Ibid., p. 170. This is a bit tough on Freud. The letters are youthful fantasies. Also a bit tough on Kinsey: he did not, as she suggests, argue that women should not be educated.
16 Ibid., p. 19.
17 Ibid., p. 235.
18 Ibid., p. 245. It is a remarkably strong turn of phrase to use so soon after the Second World War.
19 The tension between suburban normalcy and an emergent feminist consciousness is the subject of A. J. Barkman, 'Mad Women', in '*Mad Men' and Philosophy: Nothing is as it Seems*, ed. R. Carveth and J. B. South (Hoboken, NJ, 2010), pp. 203–16.
20 C. Paglia, *The Birds* (London, 1998); C. Paglia, *Sexual Personae* (New York, 1992), p. 51.
21 *Desperate Housewives*, prod. M. Cherry (ABC/Cherry Productions, 2004–); *American Beauty*.
22 Hayden, 'Non-Sexist City'.
23 Ibid., p. s171.
24 Ibid., p. s175.
25 A. Dworkin, *Pornography: Men Possessing Women* (London, 1981); A. Dworkin, *Intercourse* (New York, 1987).
26 Hayden, 'Non-Sexist City', p. s186.

27 Ibid.

28 K. Frampton, *Modern Architecture: A Critical History* (London and New York, 1992); P. Hall, *Cities of Tomorrow* (Oxford, 1996); C. Jencks, *Modern Movements in Architecture* (London, 1973).

29 N. Leach, ed., *Rethinking Architecture* (London, 1997). See also the author's review of this in R. J. Williams, 'Rethinking Architecture?', *Art History*, XXII/1 (March 1999), pp. 131–6.

30 Friedman, *Making of the Modern House*.

31 For a chronology of key events at Greenham, see 'Chronology', www.yourgreenham .co.uk.

32 P. Stallybrass and A. White, *The Poetics and Politics of Transgression* (Ithaca, NY, 1986), p. 23.

33 Ibid.

34 J. May, 'Sid Rawle Obituary', www.guardian.co.uk, 15 September 2010.

35 S. Roseneil, *Common Women: Uncommon Practices* (London and New York, 2000), p. 148.

36 L. Irigaray, *The Sex Which is Not One* (Ithaca, NY, 1977), p. 33.

37 'Greenham Women Everywhere' (1983), British Library Collection, London.

38 B. Harford and S. Hopkins, eds, *Greenham Common: Women at the Wire* (London, 1984), p. 33.

39 F. O'Connor, 'A Debate about Women and Not Just Missiles', *Irish Times* (23 December 1983), p. 5.

40 'Full Moon in June', festival poster (25 June 1983), British Library Collection, London.

41 Roseneil, *Common Women*, pp. 158, 282, 284, 286.

42 Ibid., p. 78.

43 Ibid., p. 163.

44 J. Stead, 'Greenham Women Gatecrash Base for a Spot of Peace on the Disco Floor', *Guardian* (20 December 1982), p. 4.

45 See 'Greenham Common' at Imperial War Museum, www.iwm.org.uk/upload/ package/22/greenham/peacecamp.htm, accessed 15 June 2011.

46 See University of Bradford Special Collections, specialcollectionsbradford, 'Embrace the Base', at www.flickr.com.

47 See 'Greenham Common' at Imperial War Museum, www.iwm.org.uk/upload/ package/22/greenham/peacecamp.htm, accessed 15 June 2011.

48 Ibid. A much longer account of Greenham by McGehee can be found in the interview conducted with him by the Imperial War Museum. See 'American commander of USAF Greenham Common air base, Berkshire, 1983–1986' (1995), www.iwm.org.uk/collections.

49 C. Paglia, *Sex and Violence or Nature and Art* (London, 1995), pp. 17, 18, 55.

eight **Queer and Other Spaces**

1 R. Florida, *Cities and the Creative Class* (New York, 2005).

2 C. Hakim, *Honey Money: The Power of Erotic Capital* (London, 2011); C. Paglia, *Sex and Violence or Nature and Art* (London, 1995), p. 39: 'the first medical reports on the disease killing male homosexuals indicated men most at risk were those with a thousand partners in their lifetime. Incredulity. Who could such people be? Why, it turned out, everyone one knew. Serious, kind, literate men, not bums or thugs.'

3   For a queer reading of Michelangelo, see G. Butt, *Between You and Me: Queer Disclosures in the New York Art World, 1948–1963* (Durham, NC, and London, 2005), pp. 61–2.

4   See account of Manto, Manchester (UK) in J. Harris and R. J. Williams, eds, *Regenerating Culture and Society* (Liverpool, 2011), pp. 262–4. Here Manto represents gay urban culture as the research and development arm of urban culture more generally.

5   For more on Hulme see R. J. Williams, *The Anxious City* (London, 2004), pp. 214–15.

6   J. Sanders, ed., *Stud: Architectures of Masculinity* (Princeton, NJ, 1996); La Biennale di Venezia, *11 Mostra Internazionale di Architettura: Out There, Architecture Beyond Building* (Venice, 2008).

7   D. Hurewitz, *Bohemian Los Angeles and the Making of Modern Politics* (Berkeley, Los Angeles and London, 2007).

8   Butt, *Between You and Me*.

9   K. Keim, *An Architectural Life: Memoirs and Memories of Charles W. Moore* (Boston, 1996). Written by Moore's colleague and lover, there's a coy allusion to the problem on p. 12: 'Moore's personal life was public, and his public life was personal . . . Like no-one else Charles dedicated his life *entirely* to architecture.'

10 My sources here include Volker Welter and Christopher Long.

11 A. Betsky, *Queer Space: Architecture and Same-sex Desire* (New York, 1997), p. 9.

12 Ibid., p. 21.

13 A. Rifkin, 'Gay Paris: Trace and Ruin', in N. Leach, ed., *The Hieroglyphics of Space* (London, 2002), p. 126.

14 See also B. Tschumi, *Architecture and Disjunction* (Cambridge, MA, and London, 1996).

15 Betsky, *Queer Space*, p. 166.

16 Rifkin, 'Gay Paris', p. 126.

17 Sontag, 'Notes on Camp', in *Against Interpretation* (New York, 1964).

18 E. Petit, ed., *Philip Johnson: The Constancy of Change* (New Haven, CT, 2009), p. 141.

19 Betsky, *Queer Space*, p. 116.

20 Ibid., p. 117.

21 Another way of talking about the experience of architecture invokes phenomenology, as in J. Otero-Pailos, *Architecture's Historical Turn: Phenomenology and the Rise of the Postmodern* (Minneapolis and London, 2010).

22 D. Hayden, 'What Would a Non-Sexist City Be Like?', *Signs: Journal of Women in Culture and Society*, V/3 (1980), pp. S170–87.

23 E. Perel, *Mating in Captivity: Sex, Lies and Domestic Bliss* (London, 2007).

24 Otero-Pailos, *Architecture's Historical Turn*, p. 108.

25 Keim, *An Architectural Life*.

26 Email conversation with Kevin Keim, Director of the Moore Foundation, September 2012.

27 K. C. Bloomer and C. W. Moore, *Body, Memory and Architecture* (New Haven, CT, 1977), p. x.

28 C. Moore, G. Allen and D. Lyndon, *The Place of Houses* (New York, 1974), p. 121.

29 See 'Preservation Nightmare: Charles Moore's Orinda Home Eaten by Oversized Ranch', www.bayregionstyle.wordpress.com (7 March 2011).

30 C. Moore, *Water and Architecture*, unpublished PhD thesis (Princeton University, 1957).

31 G. Allen, *Charles Moore* (New York, 1980), p. 24.

32 Moore et al., *Place of Houses*, pp. 62–3.

33 To be fair, the Moore Foundation would object here to the use of the term 'camp'. To me, Susan Sontag's definition does seem appropriate, however. It is a house unusually preoccupied with surface. Email conversation with Kevin Keim, September 2012.

Epilogue

1 'The Changing Adult Business: At a xxx-roads', www.economist.com, 21 October 2011.

2 C. Turner, *Adventures in the Orgasmatron: How the Sexual Revolution Came to America* (New York, 2011).

3 Newsletter, www.wilhelmreichtrust.org, November 2011. They complain, rightly in my view, about Christopher Hitchens's review of Turner, but wrongly about Turner's sympathetic and well-researched book. Hitchens's review turns Reich into a joke figure. The Hitchens review can be found at www.nytimes.com, 23 September 2011.

4 J. Engel, *American Therapy: The Rise of Psychotherapy in the United States* (New York, 2008).

5 M. Foucault, *The History of Sexuality*, vol. 1, trans. R. Hurley (New York, 1990).

6 A. Dworkin, *Intercourse* (New York, 1987).

7 E. Fraterrigo, *Playboy and the Making of the Good Life in Modern America* (New York, 2009).

8 Useful review by C. Turner, 'Hugh Hefner in Six Volumes', www.guardian.co.uk, 17 July 2010.

9 L. Bersani, 'Is the Rectum a Grave?', *October*, 43 (Winter 1987), pp. 197–222.

10 E. White, *City Boy: My Life in New York during the 1960s and 1970s* (New York, 2009)

11 Bersani', 'Rectum', pp. 211–12.

12 N. Freeman, 'Sexless and the City', www.observer.com, 15 March 2011; B. Hood, 'Everyone's Bored of Sex', www.theatlanticwire.com, 17 April 2011.

13 E. Perel, *Mating in Captivity: Sex, Lies and Domestic Bliss* (London, 2007); C. Hakim, *Honey Money: The Power of Erotic Capital* (London, 2011).

14 See especially Z. Williams, 'Catherine Hakim: Charm School Marm: Interview', www.guardian.co.uk, 19 August 2011.

Bibliography

Books and Catalogues

Adkins, L., and V. Merchant, eds, *Sexualizing the Social: Power and the Organization of Sexuality* (Basingstoke and London, 1996)

Agrest, D., P. Conway and L. K. Weisman, *The Sex of Architecture* (New York, 1996)

Albrecht, D., and E. Johnson, *New Hotels for Global Nomads* (London and New York, 2002)

Allen, G., *Charles Moore (Monographs on Contemporary Architecture)* (New York, 1980)

Amis, M., *The Moronic Inferno and Other Visits to America* (London, 1986)

Bachelard, G., *The Poetics of Space*, trans. M. Jolas (Boston, 1994)

Bader, M., *Arousal: The Secret Logic of Sexual Fantasies* (London, 2003)

Bahr, E., *Weimar on the Pacific: German Exile Culture in Los Angeles and the Crisis of Modernism* (Berkeley, Los Angeles and London, 2007)

Ballard, J. G., *High Rise* (London, 1977)

Bangert, A., and O. Riewoldt, *New Hotel Design* (London, 1993)

Banham, R., *Los Angeles: The Architecture of Four Ecologies* (London, 1971)

Basar, S., and S. Trüby, eds, *The World of Madelon Vriesendorp: Paintings/Postcards/Objects/Games* (London, 2008)

Bayley, S., *Sex, Drink and Fast Cars* (London, 1986)

Beauvoir, S. de, *The Second Sex* (London, 1988)

Betsky, A., *Building Sex: Men, Women, Architecture and the Construction of Sexuality* (New York, 1995)

—, *Queer Space: Architecture and Same-sex Desire* (New York, 1997)

—, ed., La Biennale di Venezia, *11 Mostra Internazionale di Architettura: Out There, Architecture Beyond Building* (Venice, 2008)

Bofill, R., *L'Architecture d'un homme: Entretiens avec François Hébert-Stevens* (Paris, 1978)

—, *Ricardo Bofill: Taller de Arquitectura* (Barcelona, 1984)

—, and J.-L. André, *Espaces d'une vie* (Paris, 1989)

Bowes, A. M., *Kibbutz Goshen: An Israeli Commune* (Prospect Heights, IL, 1989)

Boyle, T. C., *Drop City* (London, 2003)

Butler, J., *Gender Trouble: Feminism and the Subversion of Identity* (New York, 1990)

Butt, G., *Between You and Me: Queer Disclosures in the New York Art World, 1948–1963* (Durham, NC, and London, 2005)

Campbell-Lange, B. A., *John Lautner: Disappearing Space* (Cologne, 2005)

Carr-Gomm, P., *A Brief History of Nakedness* (London, 2010)

Carveth, R., and J. B. South, eds, *'Mad Men' and Philosophy: Nothing is as it Seems* (Hoboken, NJ, 2010)

Centre d'Art Nicolas de Staël, *Ricardo Bofill: Taller de Arquitectura* (Braine, 1989)

Chaplin, S., *Japanese Love Hotels: A Cultural History* (London, 2007)

Clark, T. J., *The Painting of Modern Life: Paris in the Art of Manet and His Followers* (New York and London, 1984)

Coates, N., *Guide to Ecstacity* (London, 2003)

Cohen, J.-L., *Ludwig Mies van der Rohe* (Basel, Boston and Berlin, 2007)

Cohn, L., *The Door to a Secret Room: A Portrait of Wells Coates* (Aldershot, 1999)

Colomina, B., ed., *Sexuality and Space* (Princeton, NJ, 1992)

Crumb, R., 'The Many Faces of R. Crumb', in *The Complete Crumb Comics*, vol. IX: *R. Crumb versus the Sisterhood* (Seattle, 2009)

Curl, J., *Memories of Drop City: The First Hippie Commune of the 1960s and the Summer of Love* (Lincoln, NE, 2007)

Deleuze, G., and F. Guattari, *Anti-Oedipus: Capitalism and Schizophrenia*, trans. R. Hurley, M. Seem and H. R. Lane (London, 1984)

Dillon, B., J. Rendell and R. Rugoff, *Psycho Buildings: Artists Take On Architecture*, exh. cat., Hayward Gallery, London (2008)

Douglas, M., *Purity and Danger: An Analysis of the Concept of Pollution and Taboo* (London, 2004)

Durning, L. and R. Wrigley, *Gender and Architecture* (Chichester, 2000)

Duvert, T., *Good Sex Illustrated* (Los Angeles, 2007)

Dworkin, A., *Pornography: Men Possessing Women* (London, 1981)

—, *Intercourse* (New York, 1987)

Edgren, G., *Inside the Playboy Mansion* (London, 1998)

Engel, J., *American Therapy: The Rise of Psychotherapy in the United States* (New York, 2008)

Evans, D. T., *Sexual Citizenship: The Material Construction of Sexualities* (London, 1993)

Figes, O., *A People's Tragedy: The Russian Revolution, 1891–1924* (London, 1996)

Flynt, L., *An Unseemly Man: My Life as a Pornographer, Pundit and Social Outcast* (London, 1996)

Forty, A., *Words and Buildings: A Vocabulary of Modern Architecture* (London, 2000)

Foucault, M., *The History of Sexuality*, vol. I, trans. R. Hurley (New York, 1990)

Frampton, K., *Modern Architecture: A Critical History* (London and New York, 1992)

Fraterrigo, E., *Playboy and the Making of the Good Life in Modern America* (New York, 2009)

Freeman, D., *Margaret Mead and Samoa: The Making and Unmaking of an Anthropological Myth* (Cambridge, MA, and London, 1983)

Freud, S., *Totem and Taboo: Resemblances Between the Psychic Lives of Savages and Neurotics*, trans. A. A. Brill (New York, 1946)

—, *The Penguin Freud Library*, vol. VII: *On Sexuality*, trans. J. Strachey (London, 1991)

—, *The Penguin Freud Library*, vol. XII: *Civilization, Society and Religion*, trans. J. Strachey (London, 1991)

Fullbrook, E., and K. Fullbrook, *Sex and Philosophy: Rethinking de Beauvoir and Sartre* (London, 2008)

Gathorne-Hardy, J., *Alfred Kinsey: Sex, The Measure of All Things* (London, 1999)

Giddens, A., *The Transformation of Intimacy: Sexuality, Love and Eroticism in Modern Societies* (Cambridge, 1992)

Gimaraens, D., and L. Cavalcanti, *Arquitetura de motéis Cariocas: Espaço e organização social* (Rio de Janeiro, 1982)

Gray, J., *Mars and Venus in the Bedroom: A Guide to Lasting Romance and Passion* (New York, 1995)

Gurley Brown, H., *Sex and the Single Girl* (New York, 1962)

—, *Sex and the Office* (London, 1965)

Hall, P., *Cities of Tomorrow* (Oxford, 1996)

Harris, J., and R. J. Williams, eds, *Regenerating Culture and Society* (Liverpool, 2011)

Hatherley, O., *Militant Modernism* (Winchester, 2008)

Hines, T. S., *Richard Neutra and the Search for Modern Architecture* (New York and Oxford, 1982)

Hitchcock, H.-R., and P. Johnson, *The International Style: Architecture since 1922* (New York, 1932)

Hopkins, D., *Dada's Boys: Masculinity After Duchamp* (New Haven, CT, 2007)

Hurewitz, D., *Bohemian Los Angeles and the Making of Modern Politics* (Berkeley, Los Angeles and London, 2007)

Irigaray, L., *The Sex Which is Not One* (Ithaca, NY, 1977)

Jacobs, J., *The Death and Life of Great American Cities* (New York, 1961)

Jencks, C., *Modern Movements in Architecture* (London, 1973)

Keim, K. P., *An Architectural Life: Memoirs and Memories of Charles W. Moore* (Boston, 1996)

Kinkade, K., *A Walden Two Experiment: The First Five Years of Twin Oaks Community* (New York, 1974)

Kinsey, A. C., *Sexual Behavior in the Human Male* (Philadelphia, 1948)

Kipnis, L., *Bound and Gagged: Pornography and the Politics of Fantasy in America* (New York, 1996)

Koolhaas, R., *Delirious New York: A Retroactive Manifesto for Manhattan* (New York, 1994)

Krakauer, J., *Under the Banner of Heaven* (London, 2004)

Krausz, E., and D. Glanz, eds, *The Sociology of the Kibbutz: Studies of Israeli Society*, vol. II (New Brunswick, NJ, and London, 1983)

Lacan, J., *The Four Fundamental Concepts of Psycho-Analysis*, trans. A. Sheridan (New York, 1978)

Laing, A., *R. D. Laing: A Life* (Stroud, 2006)

Laing, R. D., *The Politics of the Family and Other Essays* (London, 1971)

—, and A. Esterson, *Sanity, Madness and the Family: Families of Schizophrenics* (London, 1970)

Lamprecht, B. M., *Neutra: Complete Works* (Cologne and London, 2000)

—, *Richard Neutra, 1982–1970: Survival Through Design* (Cologne and London, 2004)

Lavin, S., *Form Follows Libido: Architecture and Richard Neutra in a Psychoanalytical Culture* (Cambridge, MA, and London, 2004)

Leach, N., ed., *Rethinking Architecture* (London, 1997)

Leader, D., and J. Groves, *Introducing Lacan* (Cambridge, 2000)

Lorenz, C., *Women in Architecture: A Contemporary Perspective* (London, 1990)

Lovell, P. M., *The Health of the Child* (Los Angeles, 1926)

McCorquodale, D., K. Rüedi and S. Wigglesworth, eds, *Desiring Practices: Architecture, Gender and the Interdisciplinary* (London, 1996)

McCoy, E., *Vienna to Los Angeles, Two Journeys: Letters Between R. M. Schindler and Richard Neutra* (Santa Monica, CA, 1979)

MacDougall, J., *The Many Faces of Eros: A Psychoanalytical Exploration of Human Sexuality* (London and New York, 1995)

Macey, D., *The Lives of Michel Foucault* (London, 1994)

McNally, D., *A Long Strange Trip: The Inside History of the Grateful Dead and the Making of Modern America* (London, 2002)

Marcuse, H., *One-Dimensional Man* (London, 1972)

—, *Eros and Civilization: A Philosophical Inquiry into Freud* (London, 1998)

Marinelli, L., *Die Couch: Vom Denken im Liegen* (Munich, 2006)

Marks, L. V., *Sexual Chemistry: A History of the Contraceptive Pill* (New Haven, CT, and London, 2001)

Matt, G., T. Edlinger and F. Waldvogel, *The Porn Identity: Expeditions into the Dark Zone*, exh. cat., Kunsthalle Wien, Vienna (2009)

Matthews, M., *Droppers: America's First Hippie Commune, Drop City* (Norman, OH, 2010)

Mead, M., *Coming of Age in Samoa: A Study of Adolescence and Sex in Primitive Societies* (London, 1977)

Mertens, D., ed., *The Presence of Mies* (Princeton, NJ, 1994)

Mitchell, J., *Psychoanalysis and Feminism* (London, 1974)

Moore, C., G. Allen and D. Lyndon, *The Place of Houses: Three Architects Suggest Ways to Build and Inhabit Houses* (New York, 1974)

Mumford, E., *The CIAM Conversation on Urbanism, 1928–1960* (Cambridge, MA, and London, 2000)

Neutra, R., *Life and Human Habitat* (Stuttgart, 1956)

Olsberg, N., ed., *Between Earth and Heaven: The Architecture of John Lautner* (New York, 2008)

Orbach, S., *The Impossibility of Sex* (New York, 2000)

Otero-Pailos, J., *Architecture's Historical Turn: Phenomenology and the Rise of the Postmodern* (Minneapolis and London, 2010)

Paglia, C., *Sexual Personae* (New York, 1992)

—, *Sex and Violence or Nature and Art* (London, 1995)

—, *The Birds* (London, 1998)

Perel, E., *Mating in Captivity: Sex, Lies and Domestic Bliss* (London, 2007)

Petit, E., ed., *Philip Johnson: The Constancy of Change* (New Haven, CT, 2009)

Phillips, A., *Monogamy* (New York, 1996)

Pomeroy, W. A., *Dr. Kinsey and the Institute for Sex Research* (New York, 1972)

Portman, J., and J. Barnett, *The Architect as Developer* (New York, 1976)

Potts, A., *The Science/Fiction of Sex: Feminist Deconstruction and the Vocabularies of Heterosex* (London, 2002)

Powell, K., *New London Architecture* (London and New York, 2005)

Rand, A., *The Fountainhead* (London, 1994)

Reich, P., *A Book of Dreams* (London, 1974)

Reich, W., *The Sexual Revolution* (New York, 1969)

—, *The Function of the Orgasm* (London, 1970)

—, *The Invasion of Compulsory Sex-Morality* (New York, 1971)

—, *Listen, Little Man!* (New York, 1974)

—, *The Mass Psychology of Fascism* (London, 1975)

—, and A. S. Neill, *Record of a Friendship: The Correspondence Between Wilhelm Reich and A. S. Neill, 1936–1957*, ed. Beverley R. Placzek (London, 1982)

Rendell, J., *The Pursuit of Pleasure: Gender, Space and Architecture in Regency London* (London, 2002)

—, B. Penner and I. Borden, *Gender Space Architecture: An Interdisciplinary Introduction* (London, 2000)

Riani, P., P. Goldberger and J. Portman, *John Portman* (Milan, 1990)

Richards, S., *Le Corbusier and the Concept of Self* (London and New Haven, CT, 2003)

Roberts, M., *Living in a Man-made World: Gender Assumptions in Modern Housing Design* (London, 1991)

Russell, F., ed., *Mies van der Rohe: European Works* (London, 1986)

Sanders, J., ed., *Stud: Architectures of Masculinity* (Princeton, NJ, 1996)

Schulz, F., *Mies van der Rohe: A Critical Biography* (Chicago, 1985)

—, ed., *Mies van der Rohe: Critical Essays* (New York, 1989)

Scott, F. D., *Architecture or Techno-Utopia: Politics After Modernism* (Cambridge, MA, and London, 2007)

Scruton, R., *Sexual Desire, A Philosophical Investigation* (London, 1994)

Sennett, R., *Flesh and Stone: The Body and the City in Western Civilization* (New York, 1994)

Serraino, P., and J. Shulman, *Modernism Rediscovered* (Cologne, 2000)

Sharaf, M., *Fury on Earth: A Biography of Wilhelm Reich* (New York, 1994)

Skinner, B. F., *Walden Two* (Englewood Cliffs, NJ, 1976)

Spain, D., *Gendered Spaces* (Chapel Hill, NC, and London, 1992)

Spiro, M., *Kibbutz: Venture in Utopia* (Cambridge, MA, 1956)

Stallybrass, P., and A. White, *The Poetics and Politics of Transgression* (Ithaca, NY, 1986)

Steele, J., *R. M. Schindler, 1887–1953: An Exploration of Space* (Cologne, 2005)

Stern, A. M., *Eugenic Nation: Faults and Frontiers of Better Breeding in Modern America* (Berkeley, Los Angeles and London, 2005).

Stern, R.A.M., T. Mellins and D. Fishman, *New York, 1960: Architecture and Urbanism Between the Second World War and the Bicentennial* (Cologne, 1997)

Taylor, J. R., *Hitch: The Life and Times of Alfred Hitchcock* (New York, 1976)

Therborn, G., *Between Sex and Power: Family in the World, 1900–2000* (London, 2004)

Tschumi, B., *Architecture and Disjunction* (Cambridge, MA, and London, 1996)

Turner, C., *Adventures in the Orgasmatron: How the Sexual Revolution Came to America* (New York, 2011)

Vidler, A., *The Architectural Uncanny: Essays in the Modern Unhomely* (Cambridge, MA, and London, 1992)

—, *Warped Space: Art, Architecture and Anxiety in Modern Culture* (Cambridge, MA, and London, 2000)

Weeks, J., *Sex, Politics and Society: The Regulation of Sexuality since 1800* (London, 1981)

—, *Sexuality and Its Discontents: Meanings, Myths and Modern Sexualities* (London, 1985)

White, E., *City Boy: My Life in New York during the 1960s and 1970s* (London, 2009)

Whitney, D., and J. Kipnis, eds, *Philip Johnson: The Glass House* (New York, 1993)

Wigley, M., *White Walls, Designer Dresses: The Fashioning of Modern Architecture* (Cambridge, MA, and London, 1995)

Wilhelm Reich: Sex! Pol! Energy!, exh. cat., Jewish Museum, Vienna (2008)

Williams, R. J., *The Anxious City* (London, 2004)

—, *Brazil: Modern Architectures in History* (London, 2009)

Wolfe, T., *From Bauhaus to Our House* (London, 1982)

Zimmerman, C., *Mies van der Rohe, 1886–1969: The Structure of Space* (Cologne, 2006)

Zweig, S., *The World of Yesterday* (London, 1943)

Articles and Reviews

'A Playboy Pad: Pleasure on the Rocks', *Playboy*, XVIII/11 (November 1971),
    pp. 151–5, 208

Allen, I., 'Modernism's Pioneering Housing Has Not Quite Left the Legacy Planned',
    Architect's Journal (30 March 2006), p. 3

'Art: Less is More', at www.time.com, 14 June 1954

Bersani, L., 'Is the Rectum a Grave?', *October*, 43 (Winter 1987), pp. 197–222

Blasberg, D., 'Who the Hell is James Goldstein?', www.interviewmagazine.com,
    22 January 2010

Brady, M. E., 'The New Cult of Sex and Anarchy', *Harper's Magazine* (April 1947),
    pp. 312–22

—, 'The Strange Case of Wilhelm Reich', *New Republic* (26 May 1947), p. 20

Chave, A., 'Minimalism and the Rhetoric of Power', *Arts*, 64 (January 1990), pp. 44–63,
    reprinted in *Art in Modern Culture*, ed. Frascina and Harris (London, 1992),
    pp. 264–81

'Concrete House for Rocky Ridge in Palm Springs, California', *Architectural Record*,
    11 (November 1970), pp. 116–17

Croft, C., 'A Pioneering Modern Masterpiece with Very Well-connected Friends',
    Architect's Journal (30 March 2006), pp. 26–37

Crowther, B., 'The Screen in Review: Gary Cooper Plays an Idealistic Architect in Film
    Version of *The Fountainhead*', http://movies.nytimes.com, 9 July 1949

Cumming, L., 'Alex Hartley, The World is Still Big', www.guardian.co.uk,
    27 November 2011

Darling, E., 'Wells Coates: Maker of a Modern British Architecture', *Architectural
    Review*, CCXXIV/1339 (September 2008), pp. 882–7

Dwan, L., 'Roundabout: I Have Dined in the Future and it is Somewhere at the
    Bonaventure', *Los Angeles Times* (31 July 1977), p. 90

Freeman, N., 'Sexless and the City', www.observer.com, 15 March 2011

Glancey, J., 'Space Odyssey', *Guardian* (8 December 2003)

Goldberger, P., 'Two Hotels in Los Angeles: Contrast in Fresh Attempts', *New York
    Times* (7 March 1977), p. 6

Grief, M., 'You'll Love the Way it Makes you Feel', *London Review of Books*, XXX/20
    (23 October 2008), pp. 15–16

Hayden, D., 'What Would a Non-Sexist City Be Like?', *Signs: Journal of Women in
    Culture and Society*, V/3 (1980), pp. S170–87

'The Hippies: Philosophy of a Subculture', *Time*, XC/1 (7 July 1967), p. 22

Hobsbawm, E., 'Retreat of the Male', *London Review of Books*, XXVII/5 (4 August 2005),
    pp. 8–9

Hood, B., 'Everyone's Bored of Sex', www.theatlanticwire.com, 17 April 2011

'House in the Colorado Desert Designed by Richard Neutra', *Architect's Journal*
    (7 August 1947), pp. 119–23

Jameson, F., 'Progress Versus Utopia; or, Can We Imagine the Future?', *Science Fiction
    Studies*, IX/2 (July 1982), pp. 147–58

—, 'The Cultural Logic of Late Capitalism', in *Rethinking Architecture: A Reader in
    Cultural Theory*, ed. N. Leach (London, 1996), pp. 238–46

'John C. Portman', *L'Architecture d'Aujourd'hui*, 193 (October 1977), pp. 48–61

Kates, J. G., 'Artist Helen Taylor Sheats, 89', www.chicagotribune.com, 8 May 1999

Kendrick, W., 'The Analyst as Outsider', *New York Times* (3 April 1983)

McKay, D., 'Monumental Mass Housing', *Building Design* (24 March 1978), pp. 10–11

McNamara, M., 'Back When Men Were "Mad Men"', *Los Angeles Times* (19 July 2007)

Malcolm, D., 'Dusan Makavejev: *WR: Mysteries of the Organism*', *Guardian* (3 June 1999)

'The Many Different Lives of an Office Building', *Life*, 42 (11 February 1957), pp. 89–96

Marcus, G., 'Still Lifes' (review of T. S. Hines, *Richard Neutra and the Search for Modern Architecture*), *California Magazine* (February 1983), pp. 110–12

Marmostein, G., 'Steel and Slurry: Dr Philip M. Lovell, Architectural Patron', *Southern California Quarterly*, LXXXIV/3–4 (Fall/Winter 2002), pp. 241–70

Marzá, F., and N. Moyano, 'Walden 7; Taller de Arquitectura', *Quaderns*, 244 (December 2004), pp. 18–53

May, J., 'Sid Rawle Obituary', www.guardian.co.uk, 15 September 2010

Melton, M., 'Julius Shulman', www.lamag.com, 17 January 2009

Miró i Rufà, J-M., 'Walden 7', *Cuadernos*, CXI/6 (November 1975), pp. 13–21

'Modern Flats at Hampstead', *Architectural Review*, 76 (August 1934), pp. 77–82

Ouroussoff, N., 'Keeping Houses, Not Building Them', www.nytimes.com, 31 October 2007

'Peachtree Hotel; Architects: John Portman & Associates', *Architectural Review*, CLXI/963 (May 1977), pp. 265–7

'People Who Live in Flying Saucers . . .', *New York Times* (29 April 1961)

Peres, J., 'In 50 Years the Kibbutz Movement Has Undergone Many Changes', *Chicago Tribune* (9 May 1998)

'The Playboy Bed', *Playboy* (November 1959), pp. 66–8

Portman, J., 'An Architecture for People and not for Things', *Architectural Record*, CLXI/1 (January 1977), pp. 133–40

Reese, J., 'Dream House or Nightmare?', *Saturday Evening Post* (20 August 1960), pp. 30, 62–4

Richards, J. M., 'Wells Coates', *Architectural Review*, CXXIV/743 (December 1958), pp. 357–60

Ross, M. F., 'A Star for Tinseltown', *Progressive Architecture*, CIX/2 (February 1978), pp. 52–6

Sadler, S., 'Drop City Revisited', *Journal of Architectural Education*, LVIII/1 (2006), pp. 5–14

Seidenbaum, A., 'The Portman Prescription', *Los Angeles Times* (18 June 1976), p. OC B15

Singmaster, D., 'A Room With a Loo', *Architect's Journal*, CCVIII/5 (July 1998), pp. 23–36

Smith, J., 'A Bonny Adventure', *Los Angeles Times* (16 February 1977), p. OC A1

'Snazzy Four-story Home for Gold Coast', *Chicago Daily News* (23 September 1959), p. 42

'Spectacular Home that Grows Out of a Desert Ridge', *Los Angeles Times* (3 November 1968), pp. 19–28

Stead, N., 'Interview with Beatriz Colomina', *Architecture Australia*, XCIII/5 (September–October 2004), p. 102.

Sudjic, D., 'Power Oozes from Each Piece of steel', www.guardian.co.uk, 17 October 2004

Unique, VI/2 (Summer 1978)

'Walden 7 by Taller de Arquitectura, Ricardo Bofill', *GA Houses*, 1 (1976), pp. 18–35

Walker, P., 'Occupy Finsbury Square Camp Removed', www.guardian.co.uk, 14 June 2012

Whitman, A., 'Obituary: Mies van der Rohe Dies at 83; Leader of Modern Architecture',
    New York Times (19 August 1969)
Williams, R. J., 'Rethinking Architecture?', *Art History*, XXII/1 (March 1999), pp. 131–6
Winters, B., 'LA's new Superhotel', *Baltimore Sun* (27 December 1976), p. B1
Wolfe, B., 'Swimming in Red Ink', *Playboy*, 11 (July 1964), pp. 93, 98

Acknowledgements

To all those who gave me access to houses, archives and libraries, and all those others who talked with me about this project, many thanks. Vivian Constantinopoulos of Reaktion took it on, and proved again to be a marvellous editor. The Carnegie Trust and the University of Edinburgh generously provided funds and time to do most of the work. The following people also need particular mention for help, advice and ideas at various times: Tim Abrahams, Frances Anderton, Nick Barley, Liz Bondi, Iain Borden, Jill Burke, Stephen Cairns, Nigel Coates, Richard Coyne, Ruth Cruickshank, Robert Crumb, Angela Dimitrakaki, Frank Escher, Russell Ferguson, the staff of the Getty Research Institute, Jocelyn Gibb, Jim Goldstein, Murray Grigor, Jonathan Harris, Alex Hartley, David Hopkins, Jane Jacobs, Moira Jeffrey, Paul Jenkins, Tiffany Jenkins, Adrianne Jones, Shirley Jordan, Kevin Keim, Mike Kilroy, Roberta Leighton, Penny Lewis, the staff of the Library of Congress, Washington, DC, Christoph Lindner, Kirsten Lloyd, Christopher Long, Sarah Lorenzen, the staff of Los Angeles Public Library, Dennis McNally, Dorothy Miell, Suzanne Moore, Katherine Papineau, the staff of the Wilhelm Reich Museum, Karl Sharro, Jo Shaw, Mark Stahl and Mrs Stahl, Igor Stiks, UCLA Library Special Collections, Madelon Vriesendorp, Volker Welter, Jennifer Whitlock, Iain Boyd Whyte, Wim de Wit, Jon Wood, Ruth Verde Zein, Laura diZerega, and Sharon Zukin. Mark Crinson was again a splendid intellectual mentor, and the source of some of the best ideas in here (of course, anything the reader doesn't like was his idea too). Stacy Boldrick, Abigail Williams and Alex Williams kept the home fires burning, and me sane during the writing. Finally, very special thanks are due to Robin Sellar and the staff of the Department of Clinical Neurosciences at the Western General Hospital, Edinburgh. Without their timely intervention in early March 2011, there probably would not have been a book at all. The book is dedicated to them.

Photo Acknowledgements

The author and the publishers wish to express their thanks to the below sources of illustrative material and/or permission to reproduce it:

Copyright © Werner Blaser: p. 92; image courtesy Nigel Coates: p. 177; Corbis: p. 106 (Arne Dedert/EPA); image courtesy Robert Crumb/Lora Fountain and Associates: p. 23; Getty Images: p. 96 (Time Life/Walter Sanders); image courtesy Getty Research Institute: pp. 24, 110 (photo Julius Shulman); courtesy Alex Hartley: p. 82; © David Hockney/Collection Walker Art Gallery: p. 168 (photo Richard Schmidt); image courtesy John Portman & Associates Archive: p. 136; image courtesy Gary Lovell: p. 30; courtesy Norman McGrath: p. 184 (photo Norman McGrath); courtesy Morley Baer Photography Trust: p. 183 (photo Morley Baer); courtesy Maggie Murray: p. 163 (photo Raissa Page); Neutra Papers, UCLA Special Collections: p. 36 (photo Jean Murray Bangs Harris); image courtesy New Line Cinema: p. 108; Noroton: p. 91; Rex Features: pp. 102 (Everett Collection), 105 (Moviestore Collection); Tom of Finland Foundation Permanent Collection #64.22, © 1964 Tom of Finland Foundation: p. 175; courtesy UCLA Special Collections: pp. 39, 40 (photo Luckhaus); image courtesy Madelon Vriesendorp: p. 84; photo Thomas Weir: p. 75; Richard J. Williams: pp. 6, 20, 28, 32, 34, 44, 46, 50, 56, 57, 59, 62, 63, 86, 94, 116, 117, 120, 121, 122, 123, 125, 138, 139, 140, 141, 142, 170, 171, 189, 191.

Index